COUNTERFEIT KIDS

COUNTERFEIT KIDS

WHY THEY CAN'T THINK
AND HOW TO SAVE THEM

ROD BAIRD

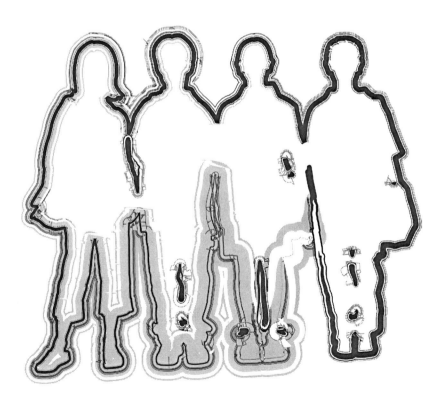

ELDER ROAD BOOKS
BELLEVUE WA

Published by Elder Road Books

Elder Road LLC

15600 NE 8th St. · Suite B1-PMB#392

Bellevue WA 98008

ISBN 978-0-9856606-7-3

Cover design by Lynn Bell

Monroe Street Studios

http://www.MonroeSt.com

Book design by Nathan Everett

Elder Road Books

http://www.ElderRoad.com

To the Coach of All Things
My wife, Nancy…

TABLE OF CONTENTS

PREFACE

"ANY QUESTIONS?" BEGAN THE class led by the young professor at the Yale Law School in the 1920s. If there were none, he would walk out of the lecture hall, immediately dismissing his audience, and leaving the students upside down in their expectations. This pattern would continue until the class understood its responsibilities to inquire. Robert Maynard Hutchins later served the University of Chicago as its president and chancellor for 22 years. There he dropped intercollegiate football and introduced the Socratic dialogue into the undergraduate course of study. It made him renowned but also, down to the present, it left a legacy that remains controversial. Today, when pressed to imagine any college or high school in America allowing the widespread equivalent of the Hutchins theory in class or program, we would plausibly see teachers destined for professional oblivion.

And yet, there are exceptional instances, maybe saving remnants, of dedicated individual teachers, brave schools, and exciting colleges that are seriously reexamining the insufficiency of an American education. They worry about a poisonous passivity in the contemplation of broad liberal learning. Instead, the more common school agenda is driven and dominated by specific results and "measurable outcomes," rather than the inculcation of lifelong values, the kind that ask, even by the sciences, what matters and why? The irony, of course, is that "teaching the test," which is now a coined cliché, has generally had the unplanned effect of poorer test results.

Students increasingly seem underprepared for higher learning, often incapable of abstract thought, so that eventually they become detached from ever knowing the deep pleasures of reflection whether about virtue, beauty, or human mortality. If asked about the ends of an education, they and their parents frequently respond, and do so in very public ways, that being competitive and employable are all that matter.

After more than a decade in his second career as a high school English teacher, Rod Baird cogently, soberly, and courageously writes about a problematic educational transaction, or the deal (to get into college, to get out, better done without savings or sacrifice, and to get a high-salaried job), as if our society is literally printing counterfeit money while calling it the "full faith and credit" currency of learning. His warnings are forensic in nature. And his critique is at times a devastating commentary on diplomas that will spend like wooden nickels in years to come. He has had recent and direct frontline experience, particularly in a community that possesses ample affluence and financial security to invest long. Baird's school serves as a microcosm of a much larger phenomenon that is recognizably similar at many other school districts in town or city; they have sold short.

Baird returned in midlife to his youthful passion for literature and the desire to share that passion with young people. He himself was first inspired by a high school teacher, one who made an immense difference and an unforgettable impression. He may have already been inclined toward a Socratic approach owing to a rigorous liberal arts education, but he somehow surprised himself as he entered the first years of his teaching career because he was actually a radical traditionalist or maybe even ahead of his moment as a post-post-modernist. The master teachers I have observed over many years were never conformists, though what each represents is an enduring wisdom that transcends the course material, something that ties them back to the immortal magic of great teaching.

Counterfeit Kids is a memoir that disturbs and entertains, but it is also much like a particular kind of work found in ancient literature called an *enchiridion*. Its discourse and anecdotes form a handbook in parenting, teacher preparation, the development of classrooms alive in conversation, and, most importantly, it is a manual about young people first examining their lives and priorities. Baird is tough-minded, especially about the material drift of parental concerns, but he is also, in the end, very protective of his students, mindful that we owe them a quality, really a touchstone of ideals, mentioned in a phrase from Lampadusa's masterwork, *The Leopard*, "the sense…of everlasting childhood." This is not the same as J. M. Barre's Peter Pan, the notion of sustaining childhood indefinitely, but rather, keeping alive child-like curiosity into the years of heavy responsibility. Baird fights for this first principle as if his own life and its meaning depended absolutely on getting it right in thought, word, and deed. His syllabus is a marvel, more than he knows.

This work will be misunderstood if read as only another jeremiad from an academy insider. It has plenty of wallop as a prophetic warning, but its main point is a matter of belief. Theologians have said that religion is an ultimate optimism founded on provisional pessimism. Perhaps our schools and colleges have been chronically wanting in an honest, provisional pessimism. The glib optimism, however, that money really is life's report card, has the potential to become the coin of the realm. But that, too, is merely provisional and temporary, arguably counterfeit; that narrow perspective fails to grasp the full meaning of the ultimate optimism that rests on the ability of a student to speak up when asked, "Any questions?"

Ultimately an optimist, Rod Baird puts a silver coin in the pocket of his readers and suggests we spend it wisely.

William L. Fox, President
St. Lawrence University
Canton, New York.

ACKNOWLEDGMENTS

No MAN IS AN ISLAND, certainly when it comes to producing a book, and *Counterfeit Kids* would not exist without the support of many talented and caring people to whom I will be forever indebted:

Thanks to my dear friend, Igor, who encouraged and helped me to become a teacher.

Thanks to my school district for allowing me to teach "out of the box."

Thank you, Jay Simone, courageous colleague, for the hundreds of conversations we shared trying to figure out how to better educate kids.

Much thanks to the two best editors a writer could ever hope for, Elizabeth Lyon and Lisa Dale Norton, whose expert eyes guided the manuscript to where it needed to be.

Thank you Nathan Everett, my enthusiastic publisher, for your urgent commitment to this project.

A very warm thank you to my wife, Nancy, my daughters, Tara, Lesley and Megan, my sons-in-law, John and Paul, brothers Bill and John and sister Andrea, and my mother for the close reading you gave my drafts.

A huge thanks to April Eberhardt, the best agent a writer could have—selfless, dedicated, brilliant, thorough, but most importantly loyal, a true friend.

Finally, I want to thank my students who listened and worked harder than they needed to so they could find their minds and learn how to think.

PART ONE
THEIR PARENTS

I
THE AGE OF UNREASON

IT WAS MY FIRST day as a teacher, my first class. Those who have never taught simply cannot imagine the anticipation. I was about to stand solo before twenty-three 10th graders for forty-four minutes and attempt to teach them something. My lesson plan was carefully prepared. I was anxious but eager, excited and confident. I decided to greet the students at the door to my room. The bell rang. The first few filed through, smiling distractedly. I was all set. Then, surprisingly, a mother arrived.

"You have my son this period. That's him there. We need to talk," she said forcefully. "His name is Adam. There are a few things you will need to know—"

"Excuse me, Mrs.?"

She told me her name then went right on explaining how her son needed extra attention. She wanted to be contacted immediately if there were any indications he was not succeeding, that it was my job to keep her informed. I glanced over at her son, who I assumed would be mortally embarrassed by all this attention but instead he looked fine, taking it all stride as if this had happened many times before. I was astonished. Had that been me, at his age, and this woman my mother, I would have crawled under my desk and hoped to die. The bell rang signaling the beginning of the period, but she went right on talking.

I had to interrupt her. "Please call and we'll set up an appointment so we can discuss this at an appropriate time."

She let her jaw fall as if she'd never been spoken to like this before, spun back and walked away.

I took a breath and stepped in the front of the swarming heads. Stragglers shuffled in, a gaggle of toothy awkward grins. Then, like a special operations commando on a mission, Sam appeared. Wearing heavy combat boots and camouflage fatigues, her fingernails and lips painted black, she clomped to the back of room. I quieted the class and began by asking why writing should be important to our lives. Eager hands waved. I called on a few. To communicate, one young thing said, through a mouth full of braces. To express ourselves, to share our feelings, the others called out.

"To keep the fucking creepy things away," Sam said from her seat in the last row, more to herself than the rest of us, scanning the room with penetrating eyes.

The kids gasped. In a high achieving school like ours inappropriate language wasn't tolerated. I thought of all the different classroom management techniques I'd learned in the graduate education courses I'd been mandated to take. None seemed to apply. The kids waited for my response, but all I could do was nod in approval, because Sam was right, of course. Writing is often a desperate attempt to gain control over the terrifyingly uncontrollable, and she had articulated it in a profound way.

"You are a writer?" I asked, nodding to her.

"A poet."

"I would like to read some."

"I'm a painter, too."

I liked her immediately.

All year she wrote brilliant impassioned essays about the texts we read: *Antigone, Jane Eyre, Huck Finn.* She found a way to live in each of those worlds, especially *Catcher in the Rye.* She inhabited them, resided there. She became those characters, or they became her. But while my other students marched along obediently, she stubbornly refused to do the standard homework assignments because she genuinely felt they were boring and unnecessary. She wouldn't compromise. She loved to read and write and think but she could do without the rest. She was so real. Her grades were a unique mixture of A+s and Fs. It would take me a few years to learn what she appeared to know instinctively, that most schoolwork was "phony," as Holden liked to say, assigned mainly to create GPAs.

One time I was waiting to speak to our principal when I overheard a conversation he was having with a mother. She kept insisting, loudly, that a teacher be fired because her son's Bs were proof she wasn't teaching properly. He'd always been an A student. The principal replied that he'd observed this teacher many times and had only seen solid teaching.

"Have you talked to the teacher about this?" he asked.

"I don't intend to. I am talking to you, her boss."

"Well, you should speak to the teacher who is much closer to the situation. All I can say, since I don't know the facts, is that she is a fine teacher and there are many reasons why your son could be getting these grades. One is that this is an Honors course and the material is more difficult. You'll recall that you insisted he be in this class."

"That is impossible," the mother insisted. "My son will have the brass ring and no one will get in his way. If I have to go to the next level I will. You should know I was in Whole Foods and ran into a board member and we had this same conversation."

Another time a 12th grader lost his parking privileges when the surveillance cameras caught him driving backward at high speed across the parking lot. When his parents were informed, they insisted on watching the videotape and afterward claimed that their son was not driving backward as alleged, but merely backing up.

"At that speed? The entire length of the parking lot?" the principal asked. "And then in circles?"

He was not going fast, the parents argued. We'll show you, they said. Then they went out, got into their car and backed around the parking lot themselves, returning to exclaim there was nothing dangerous about it. And besides, the parents concluded, if their son lost his parking privileges, he would have to park down the block. It wouldn't be as safe. He would get cold walking back up the hill to the school. The principal reduced the punishment to two weeks.

Then there was the time when an 11th grade boy turned in the exact same project his older sister had done the previous year for another class. He was caught and received a failing grade, but the father refused to believe his son's complicity. He first berated the teacher. He actually burst into her classroom while she was teaching and began screaming so loudly at her I heard it from my classroom way down the hall, and fearing something very serious was happening, I ran to help, but the principal had arrived and the father began screaming at him for supporting the teacher. The father was escorted from the building. He then made a plea to the school board that both the teacher and the principal be fired, and when that didn't work, he filed a lawsuit to the state's governing board in Albany.

When students turn in papers, after too many incidents of plagiarism, they are first required to submit a report from an online originality checking service called Turn-it-in.com. Most high schools use it. Many colleges must use it now too, because with the advent of the Internet, plagiarism has become so rampant. Our district pays for the service. Once a student finishes his paper he emails it to the service and it compares the paper's phrases, sentences, paragraphs, and direct quotes to every other document that can be found online, millions of them, scholarly journals, books, web sites, other students' papers. An originality report is issued revealing what percentage of the student's paper also appeared in some other source. Because of the random sharing of common language, most papers earn a score below 10 percent. Anything more signals a red flag to the student that he has "borrowed" too much from another source, and if the material is not cited accurately he is in danger of plagiarism. Students can then revise. Our intent is not so much to catch students as it is to teach them.

One year as I graded my seniors' *Hamlet* research papers our librarian called me to say she had discovered something odd. She oversees our Turn-it-in program. When I went down to see her she was sitting at her computer screen.

"I hope you don't mind that I went into your students' files," she said.

"Not at all. You know me and technology."

She laughed. My dinosaur status in the school was well established. "Look what I found," she said, pointing to her screen.

It showed what I had already seen, that one of my student's reports reflected that zero percent of her paper crossed over with any other source, a perfect originality score, not at all uncommon.

"Yeah," I said. "She turned it in with her paper."

"Now look at this," the librarian said.

She hit a key and a second originality report appeared, revealing that the paper had taken 66 percent of its content directly from two online sources.

"What?" I was confused.

"Yeah, it popped up when I doubled checked. You have not seen this?"

"No, I saw only the report with zero percent."

"This student figured out how to get by the checking system and I have no idea how she did it. She not only plagiarized her paper, she was able to falsify the Turn-it-in report."

"I would not have caught this," I said. "And if she had gotten away with it…"

"The entire student body would have known about it."

"I'm sure they already do."

"And how to get around the system," she said. "We will need to change the whole thing now."

I re-read her paper and cross-referenced it to the report. I found paragraphs, pages, whole sections, nearly her entire paper, had been copied word for word from a web site. Even the supporting research and citations the website had used she had copied verbatim. Yet her receipt said it was clean.

Plagiarizing is a serious academic offense in our school and requires from us an equally serious response, but first we teachers must be absolutely certain that plagiarism has occurred before any accusation can be made. We need to be able to prove it. I knew what I was about to embark upon would be a lengthy, ugly process. The reason for this is that in today's schools it is the student's word against the teacher's. There no longer is any distinction given to the teacher's professional status, the teacher's inherent objectivity. A teacher rarely carries a grudge, has no vendetta, no agenda, no skin in the game, whereas a student might. Teachers' instincts and experience and judgment have been rendered irrelevant. Any student's word is as good as mine, and so, like a court of law, each student is presumed innocent, given due process, and the allegation must be proved beyond a reasonable doubt. In fact, the scales of justice inevitably lean in the students' behalf. And they, and their parents, know it. We teachers are all well aware of this, reconciled to it, and too often allow suspected cheaters to go unchecked because we cannot provide undeniable proof. The word spreads, of course. Cheating proliferates. The cafeteria during lunchtime is a sea of students' copying each other's homework, but there is little we can do about it.

"No," a student says when you ask if he has cheated.

The onus then becomes ours to prove it.

But this seemed like a pretty clear-cut case. I had hard evidence, not only of her plagiarizing, but also of her falsifying her receipt. I still felt badly. No teacher wants this to happen. She was an ordinary student, mostly disinterested, but popular and at least willing to go through the motions, although chatty enough so that I'd had to move her seat. It was the end of the second quarter. Report cards would be issued the following week. Midyear grades would then be sent to the colleges.

This had happened to me a few times before and I knew the protocols: write the referral to the assistant principal who would discipline the student with detentions, and contact the parents and guidance counselors. What grade the student finally receives remained the teacher's decision. Most teachers automatically give a zero, which horribly affects the student's average. I am reluctant to. Instead I prefer to interview carefully any student I catch cheating, hoping he or she will give me some good reason to be lenient, that a lesson can be learned. Usually I can get them to admit it and understand its seriousness. We make a deal. They have to write the paper over, provide extra quotes and citations. For all the extra work I'll give them a D but not fail them. My job is to teach, not punish, and I hope the second chance I give them will accomplish that.

After class the next day I asked this student to stay behind. It was her lunch period.

"I'm in kind of a hurry," she said as her friends beckoned.

"And this is kind of important, so tell them to go on without you."

She rolled her eyes and shrugged, gesturing them away.

"Take a seat."

Another eye roll.

"I've read your research paper," I began, spreading it out before her. "I've also read the Turn-it-in report you submitted with it." I took it out of my folder.

"Yeah?"

"I also found and read this Turn-it-in report that says 66 percent of your paper is plagiarized."

Now she was interested.

"Can you explain this?" I asked.

"No."

"Let me ask you again, very slowly, so pay attention. I'm giving you a chance here. Can you explain this?"

"I said, no."

"Why didn't you turn this report in?"

"I've never seen that report before. I saw this one, printed it, and turned it in."

"What the real report reveals is that almost your entire paper was taken from this online source, copied, with no citations, without you even including the source in your bibliography. The report you turned in shows zero percent plagiarism receipt. Can you explain how it came out to zero percent when you can plainly see all these words, phrases, whole paragraphs and pages have been directly copied from this source."

"No."

"Did you plagiarize?"

"No."

"Then why are the words in your paper exactly the same as the words from this source?"

"I don't know. Because it's wrong. You're wrong."

"Okay, then. You will receive a zero for this paper. This zero will bring your quarterly average down to an F. You will fail the second marking period and that grade will be reported to the colleges you are applying to. Do you understand that?"

"What do you mean an F? What about the B I got on that big project—"

I took out my grade book, wrote down all her marks for the quarter, then averaged them. "As you can see, F. This paper is the most heavily weighted grade of the quarter and this is what a zero does."

"This can't happen," she said.

"But it will."

"No, you need to change this."

"Listen, you are guilty of something very serious. In addition to the F, I will be referring you to the assistant principal who will contact your parents."

"You don't understand. This can't be."

"Once again, for the last time. You are a kid. Kids screw up. Can you explain to me what happened?" I asked. "Any circumstances I should know about?"

"There's nothing to explain. I didn't do it. That's all you need to know. This cannot happen. I didn't do anything. You need to change that grade right now or else!"

Then she stormed out of my room.

Later that afternoon I called the student's home. The mother answered.

"Hello. This is—" I began.

"I know who it is," she interrupted. Her tone told me everything I needed to know about how the conversation would proceed.

"Then I can assume that your daughter told you what happened."

"She told me that you would not allow her to explain herself, that you shut her off, and that you refused to listen to her. We'll see about that!"

"Well, that is your daughter's account. Are you interested in hearing mine?"

"No. I am backing my daughter on this."

"Well, I will tell you anyway. First, and this is the issue here, so I suggest you stay focused on it. Your daughter plagiarized her very important senior research paper. Now, what your daughter told you is not the truth, but again, that is not the issue here anyway. The issue is that your daughter has plagiarized and the evidence is clear. I asked her to stay after class so we could discuss it. I asked her to explain what happened and all she kept saying was that she didn't do it and this cannot be allowed to happen. I asked her again and again to explain her actions, but all she did was deny them, in spite of the evidence."

"If she said she didn't do it, then she didn't do it. I find your attitude appalling."

"My attitude is not the issue here. You're free to take this to a higher level."

"Oh, I intend to!" she yelled. "You are not going to get away with this!"

And with that she hung up.

As we consider the plight of today's students, especially the seniors soon to go off to college and then enter the workplace, keep this in mind: every teacher I know has had multiple conversations with parents just like this. Imagine the message these parents are sending to their children. Now imagine these same children taking that message along with them as they go through their lives. Now imagine the consequences. Is it too much to say that there is a lot at stake here?

The mother's inquiry moved up the chain of command. First the assistant principal called me in to her office:

"I have spoken with the student who denies everything," she told me. "I showed her the evidence and she denied falsifying it. I spoke with the mother on the phone and told her I would be supporting your decision to fail her. She intends now to go to the principal with it."

A day later the principal called me in.

"I really am sorry for having to ask you this, but I have to," he began. "The mother is accusing you of being mean to her daughter, of calling her out by name in your other classes and saying cruel things about her, that you have it in for her. I have to ask you, is this true?"

I was not surprised. "Aren't we a little off topic here?"

He laughed. We were both all too familiar with how parents went on the attack to protect their children.

"Legally, I have to ask you. Are you picking on this student?"

"No," I said. "I suppose it isn't worth asking how someone who is caught lying can then make another claim and have it taken seriously."

"No, it is not worth asking. It is irrelevant, even though you are absolutely right. Okay, back to the real issue: I had the student in here. She denied knowing anything about copying from this site. I had the parent in here and walked her through all the documentation."

"What could she have possibly said?"

"She said that her daughter didn't do it."

"But look. Here is the evidence. Irrefutable." I laid out her paper and the Turn-it-in reports. "How can she deny facts?"

"I pointed all this out to her and she refused to listen. Her daughter did not commit plagiarism, she insisted. Now, back to their allegation. The student did produce one student who corroborated her story, who said that you criticized this student in front of your 4th period class."

"So she recruited a friend. You know how this works."

"Yes, so I then brought in six other students from that class and all of them said they had never heard you mention anything about the student."

"What a minute." Now I was furious. "You conducted some kind of kangaroo court here? Trying me?"

"I have to do this."

"Without telling me first?"

"They completely exonerated you.

"They exonerated me," I added sarcastically.

"I told this to the mother, but she insisted that six other students testifying on your behalf were not enough proof and insisted I bring everyone from all your classes in to testify. I told her I wouldn't be doing that, that it was obvious her daughter was caught in yet another lie and I would be removing her from your class because she could no longer be trusted. The zero and the F for the quarter would stand."

"What did she say?"

"She said she would be taking it over my head to the superintendent, then to the school board if necessary."

For a long time I couldn't get my mind around all of this. Of course, it took me a while to calm down after the personal attacks and insults and accusations and inquisitions and violations, but all of that goes with the territory of being a teacher these days. We know what too many of these children and their parents are capable of. No, it was something else, and it bothered me a lot, until I figured it out.

You see, logic, rationality, reasoning, these are precious to me. For example, I enjoy debating my young colleagues in the social studies department because they are smart and precise and they present cohesive arguments, which I sometimes disagree with, such as why Keynesian economics works better in a recession than supply side tax cuts. They challenge me with proofs and facts, and I argue back with my own evidence, and somewhere in between resides this beaming, bright, astounding place where we become enlightened because reason is more appealing, better, than our own opinions. We have fun. This pursuit of this empirical truth is what makes us human. The Age of Reason replaced the ignorant superstitions of the Middle Ages, freeing us, allowing us to pursue true knowledge. Fear receded. Scientific thought reigned. The German philosopher, Immanuel Kant, once said that enlightenment is the liberation of man from his self-caused state of minority, the incapacity of using one's understanding without the direction of another.

What occurred to me, thinking this through after this incident with the student's mother, was that perhaps our progress as humans has shifted. Three hundred years after Descartes said "I think, therefore I am," 250 years after Thomas Paine wrote his *Age of Reason* and Thomas Jefferson employed deductive reasoning in our Declaration of Independence providing an Enlightenment platform for our unique nation, we seem to be slipping into a new Dark Age, an age of unreason. Too many of today's parents appear to be driven more by medieval-like fear, superstition, and an almost mystical approach to raising their children, a belief in the impossible instead of the reasonable.

What I realized, and it caused me to feel sorry for her rather than remain angry, is that the mother of the student who plagiarized was not simply following her daughter's lead, denying, conniving, knowing full well the truth but hoping for a better outcome. Assuming that, reasonably, I was hung up trying to figure out her obfuscation. But there was no obfuscation at all, no carefully planned Machiavellian strategy. She, like so many parents, simply could not *see*. She was blind. She was simply unable to understand, unable to deduce reasonably. Her urgent state had trapped her inside the minority of herself to such an extent that when the undeniable evidence, the perfection of the pure tautological argument lay before her in no uncertain terms—if A = B, and if B = C, then therefore it must be that A = C—she couldn't comprehend it. She couldn't see that if those words appeared on a website source, and if those exact same words, hundreds of them, then appeared in her daughter's paper, then her daughter must have copied them illegitimately. Instead this mother saw only what she wanted to believe in. Why? A disturbing answer swelled in my mind. "I will get my kid into a good college even if it destroys her in the process!"

2
WHY GOD EVER CREATED YOU

IT HAPPENED DURING MY third year teaching, my tenure year. I was sitting at my desk staring at a stack of essays. But instead of grading them, I picked up Sam's poetry collection and turned to the one entitled *Why God Ever Created You,* seemingly about a fourteen-year-old whose prostitute mother sells her to men who feed on kids. The child tells herself that she refuses to suffer like this anymore so tomorrow she will tell her teacher, but then fears her teacher would never understand.

I had read it before, a few times, concerned. I didn't know what to do with it. As if on cue she barged in dragging her black art portfolio carrying something wrapped in brown paper.

"You need wheels for that thing," I teased.

She smiled, lowering herself onto the chair beside my desk. Now that she was a senior, her costume had changed. Instead of army fatigues she wore high top black Keds, white ankle socks, long baggy black shorts, a smock and a purple beret. Her hands were filthy with paint. She'd become a very good artist. She was also taking my creative writing course where she held court like a dark high priestess.

She noticed I was reading her poem.

"What do you think?" she asked.

"It's good," I said.

"Are you going to tell the school psychologist?" she teased back.

Teachers are trained to be vigilant to any student who appears troubled emotionally and are required to report it immediately. But by then the staff was familiar with Sam's situation. There was no father to speak of. Her erratic behavior was well documented. She was bi-polar with psychotic features. She also suffered post-traumatic stress from a confidential case many of us feared had been childhood abuse. But she seemed fine now on a regimen of strong medications.

"I think we should publish your poems in our literary magazine," I said.

She straightened in the chair.

"But this school has never seen anything this edgy," I warned. "I will need to get permission from the principal."

Sam checked for my sincerity. She was always probing, looking for authenticity, testing for impurities. She hated being pandered to. She was pure, as if her illness had purged her.

"You can show them to him," she finally said, satisfied I meant what I said. "And I finished my novel. Do you want to read it? It's three hundred pages."

She dropped the package on my desk.

Two of her friends poked their heads through the doorway. They would be late for track practice, they said. I liked seeing Sam with friends. As a sophomore she had always seemed so alone. Her friends saw the package then glanced at each other.

"Have you guys read it?" I asked, sensing something.

"I didn't know things like that could happen to people," one of them said.

"If you read it you will have to report it," the other said flatly.

They left in a flurry of giggles. I put her novel in my drawer feeling guilty I couldn't get to it, then waded through some of the essays.

Later as I walked to my car in the yellow gloom, Sam ran laps way out on the track with her team. I yelled and waved, but the distance was too great. She hadn't heard me.

That night I told my wife, a veteran teacher, I was thinking about quitting.

"Do you know that half of all new teachers don't make it through their third year?" I asked, remembering the statistic from one of the education courses I'd been required to take.

"Yes, but for you it's too late," she said.

"I can always get back into business."

"That's not what I mean. Whether you know it or not, you've changed. Your students are all you talk about. You spent thirty years in business and never talked about it once."

"There was nothing to talk about. Teaching is like having a front row seat to the end of civilization. It's hard to watch. I had to tell my seniors again today to take out their books. I finally asked them why they were never ready and you know what they said? That they were waiting for me to tell them to. And these kids are going to college in the fall. When did all this start?"

"I don't know. Maybe this generation of parents." She looked away for a moment, thinking. "I passed a big SUV today with not one, but two of those TVs in the back, one for each kid," she said. "They can't look out the window for ten minutes and use their imagination? They can't even learn how to share a movie? When I gave my fifth graders a drawing assignment today, they all looked around to see what their neighbor was doing."

"They're not TVs. They're RSES's," I said. "Pronounced like recess. Rear Seat Entertainment Systems. My students corrected me. Did you know they use their learning disabilities as verbs? 'I can't do the assignment, Mr. B. I'm ADDing.' Their designations are like all those trophies they've won for losing. OCD, ADHD, ESP."

"Don't forget PPD," she added. "Pervasive Development Disorders."

"What's that?"

"Essentially it's what they call anything they can't come up with another label for. I'm surprised they don't have Picking Nose Disorder."

I laughed. "But they've got ODD. Oppositional Defiance Disorder. It means you can't disagree with them because they get all upset. When they don't do as they're told, it's okay, because they can't help it. I'm too old for this. I know what these kids will have to face someday. It hurts too much to see what's happening to them, how unprepared they will be."

"Or prepared."

She was right, which was even sadder. One of the reasons I had sold my company was because I could no longer do business in a way I felt proud of. The rules had changed. Few of my customers seemed interested in doing a good job. They merely did their jobs long enough to trade up to a better one, avoiding accountability, like skipping from one melting ice flow to the next, always a step ahead of being caught. No one spoke on the phone anymore or held meetings. I couldn't sell anybody anything because it seemed there were no flesh and blood human beings left. Everything had to be done invisibly, online.

"There's nothing left of the world we came up in," I said. "Not that it was perfect before, but now everything's a con game, and that's the skill the kids are learning, how to copy and cheat. Maybe they will be better suited. This past fall a senior turned in her personal essay, the one she is sending to colleges. It was all boilerplate. I asked her who wrote it because it wasn't her voice. She squirmed a bit and then admitted a consultant her parents had hired had written the essay. I told her I hoped she hadn't already submitted it, because the admissions people would laugh at it. But then you know what she did? She laughed at me. She said that the same consultant had used the exact same essay for her older brother, and he had gotten into every college he applied to."

"I'll bet the consultant charged the parents twice."

I laughed again. One of the best things about my wife is how she makes me laugh.

"Hey, you're getting tenure," she said, "In a district other teachers would give anything to work in. You've reinvented yourself. That is an accomplishment."

"Tenure is all new teachers talk about, as if once they get it, they'll be protected for life. Is that what I've done, run away?"

"No. You've run right into it. You're up close now. That's why you feel the way you do. Remember that a few of them are watching, listening," she continued. "Maybe only one kid, usually the quiet one, way off your radar screen and you will probably never know about it."

"Some rate of success."

"Teaching isn't a job that gives out bonus checks."

3
TENURE

THE NEXT DAY THE 12th graders were unteachable again. Tomorrow they would all cut school and fly to the Bahamas for Spring Break, paid for by their parents. Michael wore his Yankee cap sideways, a wife-beater shirt, gold chains. His biceps newly buffed, he spoke glowingly of how much he would enjoy the cocktails as soon as their jet reached international air space. Amanda was on a "special diet" for weeks so she could win the bikini and wet t-shirt contests. Shari, a tall, raven-haired athlete with a diamond pierced navel said she intended to have all her drinks bought for her by strange men. I warned her about Rohypnol.

"You mean roofies?" someone corrected.

I was trying to get them through Kafka's *The Metamorphosis* and I took their boredom personally. I valued the story, the notion that if we don't recognize the beauty of the small things in life, that if we allow our dreams to die and live according to other people's expectations we will lose ourselves and deteriorate into something hideous. I knew people like that, and they were miserable, and I wanted to spare my students.

"He turns into a cockroach? How big? Who thinks up this crap?" one of my students asked.

Who could blame them? Why contemplate surreal night-mares when you can reside safely inside a comfortable delusion? The pull of their postmodern culture was far more powerful than Kafka could ever be. Collectively they formed a norm I no longer recognized. Everything I deeply believed in they quickly discarded. I felt like the Traveler in H.G. Wells' novel *The Time Machine*. I'd been transported to the future, to some decaying world where I was an alien on my own planet. I didn't comprehend any of it. Through some twisted irony I was the one who had become estranged.

In an effort to provoke a discussion, I related Gregor's predica-ment to *The Matrix*, knowing they had all seen the movie. "Which would you choose, the red or the blue pill?"

The blue pill would allow them to remain prisoners in the Ma-trix, contented by a contrived reality, an artificial intelligence, while farmed by machines for electricity. The red pill would awaken them to the stark need of survival.

"The blue one," they all agreed.

After class I headed down for a meeting with the principal to discuss Sam's poems.

"I think what you are trying to do with our literary magazine is important, shaking things up a bit, and I support it and am tempted to let these poems go as they are," he said. "But I still need to check school board policy on obscenity and see if it applies."

"We couldn't edit them. It would ruin the poems. It would hurt her."

"I don't think it will come to that. But you need to tell me, since I'm not an English teacher. Is it obscene, this poem about the abuse of children, a fourteen-year-old girl being raped by this man, or is it art? Are you sure this is not real, that this is not happening to her and she is crying out for help?"

I thought about the question, the searing awful responsibility it implied.

"Her case workers know all this," I said. "I worry it happened to her, but she has all kinds of support. I have to treat it as art. I have to treat her like an artist. This is what she wants."

"Then I'll stand by it. I'll take the heat if it comes."

On the way back to my classroom I stopped at the copying machine where a colleague threw me the thumbs-up sign. I looked at her quizzically.

"Only fifty-four days to go," she explained.

"Oh, right," I remembered.

The countdown had begun. Tomorrow another teacher would beam how the number was down to fifty-three. By the last week of school the countdown would be conducted in hours.

It had worried me at first. It reminded me of the answer I'd received when I began considering switching careers and asked teachers why they did it. Because we get our summers off, most of them had said, and it made me wonder if the stereotype was true: that those who can do; the others teach. But I was beginning to understand how by April some welcome home stretch had been reached, and I realized that not only did teachers' eagerness to get the year over with have nothing to do with being lazy or disliking the job, it had everything to do with caring so much about it, the staggering energy it required, the exhausting personal punishment of giving so much. They needed rest and repair.

Suddenly the school librarian charged around the corner out of breath, her face stretched with fear. "Oh, God! Someone please help before she jumps!" She whirred past me toward the principal's office.

I ran down the hallway as fast as I could and barged through the library's glass doors. A few students had gathered, their heads lifted upward. I followed their gaze and found Sam. She had pulled a chair over to the edge of the balcony and raised herself over the railing, balancing dangerously, lost in a deep psychotic gaze. A soundless delay hung over the gleaming modern space.

Then she began screaming. "Fuck all of you! I was doing so well! I was doing so well!"

She was just high enough that if she were to slip or let herself fall she would be seriously hurt or even killed. I positioned myself directly below her so if she jumped I would break her fall. John, a beefy young math teacher, joined me.

"Samantha!" I called up, careful to appear calm but firm. "Look. It's me, Mr. Baird. Look at me!"

For an instant her eyes met mine and I was jolted by their fear. It was as if in that brief exchange she sent me a telepathic message. She was lost and she meant it. She'd had enough. Her red face twisted with pain and rage. Something had snapped and dropped her back into the same dark and terrible place her poetry came from. She would jump if we didn't stop her.

"If she comes down we're not moving," I said to John.

"I got no other plans," he said.

"I hate all of you! Do you hear me! I hate all of you so much!" she exploded.

Dawn, the school psychologist, burst into the library.

"Get that bitch away from me! You're all whores!" Sam's body convulsed. Saliva sprayed from her mouth. Damp hair draped her face. Her eyes raced.

"I'm going up," I told John.

"I got her if she comes down."

I took the stairs in three bounds. Dawn and I reached her at the same time. We pulled her from the railing and wrestled her onto the carpet.

"No! I want to die!"

Sam fought on for a moment, then weakened and furled into our arms. I held her hands, cold and splattered with paint from her art projects. Her body steamed with heat. Her face flowed with tears and spit. Dawn stroked her head, removed the matted hair from her eyes and assured her that everything would be fine, that she was just having a bad day. A bead of sweat had gathered over Dawn's lip. She looked at me and her eyes welled with tears. It will be okay, she kept repeating, swaying with Sam like a mother rocking a sick infant. Dawn rolled back her head and scanned the vaulted library ceiling and tightened her jaw as if to scold God.

After a while Sam began to calm down, sobbing weakly. Dawn asked her if she would come with us to her office where there was more privacy. School had ended and the word had spread. Kids had gathered to gawk. The police and an ambulance had arrived.

We led Sam down the hallway to the guidance wing where she sat on Dawn's couch as two police officers asked her questions and took notes. An EMT wanted to know what medications Sam was taking.

"Zoloft, Clozaril," she answered.

"Any others?"

"Mysoline."

"Who is your psychiatrist?"

Sam answered as if she'd been asked the questions too many times. The principal came in to say her mother had been called and was on her way. I got Sam to laugh when I made a joke about how I guessed this meant I would have to give her an extension on the work she owed me, since the marking period ended today. Dawn leaned over her desk busy on the phone making hospital arrangements.

Sam began chatting quietly with one of the police officers. They appeared to know each. I was impressed with how gently they treated her. One of the officers had a shaved head. The other kept adjusting the squawking volume of his radio. They showed an interest in the buttons Sam had attached to her bag.

"They are band buttons," she said, carefully describing each one, seeming completely lucid now. "I'm not into grunge anymore."

"They can take her at County," I overheard Dawn telling one of the EMTs.

They were anxious to get going. "An incident like this requires immediate admittance to a psychiatric facility," he confided to me.

More arrangements were made. Sam's mother arrived. She would drive Sam's car, because Sam needed to ride in the ambulance, even though she didn't want to. The police officer explained that it was the rules.

"Then can Mr. Baird go with me?"

She looked at me. Her pleading eyes erased all the restrictive protocols.

"Of course I'm going with you," I said.

I was worried that I was in the way, so I got up.

"Where are you going?" Sam asked.

"To look for your portfolio," I said.

"Where is it?" She was becoming nervous again. She never went anywhere without it, like a child attached to her blanket.

"Don't worry. I'll hunt it down."

"Come right back."

"I will. I promise."

I went upstairs to the classroom where Sam took Advanced Placement (AP) literature. Her portfolio leaned against the blackboard. Her teacher sat at her desk.

"She walked out and didn't come back," she said. "Is anything wrong?"

"Yes," I said, but didn't have time to explain.

The principal stopped me on my way out to the ambulance.

"You don't have to do this," he said. "One of our students just tried to commit suicide, in a public school building. This is a very big deal, and not your responsibility. You are not trained for this. If you go with her and something happens—"

"I'm going with her," I said.

He smiled knowingly. "Call me if you need a ride back. I'll come get you."

I yanked open the heavy back door of the ambulance. Sam was already belted inside.

"See," the EMT said to her. "I told you."

I climbed in and sat next to her. "What?"

"Sam was worried we'd leave without you," she added.

I threw her a fake hurt look and she laughed. The tech wrapped a cuff around Sam's arm and took her blood pressure. The ambulance lurched forward.

Except for its sealed entranceway the psychiatric wing was an unremarkable building adjacent to the main hospital. We waited, then we were carefully identified and let in, directed to stop before a series of metal detectors. Sam was asked to empty her pockets and bag. When I asked why, an attendant said they were searching for drugs and weapons. Sam warned them of the silver studs in her black rock band pants. Another aide led us through a locked door into a cluttered, unpainted office space that served as an admitting area. Sam sat down and answered more questions. The aide took her vital signs again. I stepped outside into the corridor to give her some privacy and watch for her mother. When she arrived I let her inside. She thanked me and joined her daughter. I tapped on the window glass and waved good-bye and flashed the thumbs-up sign. I got a lift back to the school in the ambulance.

The next day her mother called me to say Sam would be okay. They believed she hadn't taken all her medications. They'd also been trying different doses and might have decreased the levels too much. She would need to be in the hospital for at least a week to see how she would respond. Then Sam called. It was a relief to hear her voice the way I remembered it, rapid-fire, full of observations and reflections on her ordeal, alive with sensibility. She rambled on about this and that, the other patients in the ward, how she'd stayed up all night thinking. "And I've written more poems," she said.

The administrators put Sam and her mother through a lot of red tape before she was allowed to return, but she was lugging her art portfolio through the hallway soon after school resumed. The seniors came back bronzed and giddy from their vacation in the Bahamas. The principal warned the teachers to be careful when they wanted to show us their pictures, because some of girls had posed topless. A mother found out about the warning and called the principal to say how appalled she was, not that her daughter had posed that way, but that the principal had stigmatized it. Her daughter had a beautiful body and should be made to feel proud of it, not ashamed, and she only wished she had a body like hers.

"Here they are," Sam said, handing me her new poems.

"This one," I said, after reading a few. "About you finally realizing you don't like who you are without the aid of medicine."

"I tried to stop taking them, to see if I could find the real me."

"Samantha, you are the real you when you take them. You aren't the real you when you don't," I said. I thought for a moment. "I have a similar deal."

"You do?"

"I'll tell you a secret. I had a heart attack last year. It was a close call."

Her eyes widened.

"I'm fine, as long as I take my medicine," I reassured her. "With me, it's my liver. It makes too much cholesterol. If I don't take my pills it could kill me. With you, it's your brain. Your illness is much more glamorous than mine," I teased.

She smiled. "Then you have to promise me you will take your medicine."

"Only if you promise me you will always take yours."

"I promise," she said.

"Forever?"

"Forever."

"And Sam?"

"What?"

"Thanks."

"Why? You saved me."

"No. You saved me."

One morning a few days later her AP English teacher stopped me in the hallway and handed me a wrinkled sheet of unlined paper. "We are reading *The Things They Carried*," she said. "It's Sam's assignment. She wrote it in the hospital."

I went back to my room and read:

I came into this place—separated from myself—from what was real—from anything that made sense... Weight-

less... the feeling the soldiers try to achieve. Like them I don't want to replay the day but I don't ever want to forget it either, because "the bad stuff never stops happening: it lives in its own dimension, replaying itself over and over." When O'Brien thinks he's a coward for separating himself from his beliefs, I kept wondering if that was me... I intended to jump. The last thing I saw was Mr. Baird's face filled with what seemed to be wonder. I was so alive and so dead inside, separate-but-together. I didn't feel the fall off the chair, didn't feel them tackle me, but I felt their arms hold me safe after my war was over.

In June I went to their prom, held in one of those pre-fab fantasy palaces with fake chandeliers, bubbling water fountains, and crystal mirrors. Sam wore a chiffon gown, her hair done in little braids and tied with flowers. Her date was the quiet computer geek who had designed the layout for our literary magazine in which three of her poems appeared. She tipped awkwardly on her high-heeled slippers as they danced.

The last day of school I found in my mail slot an official letter from the school board granting me tenure. I also found a piece of notepad paper.

Thank you for recognizing a talent that no one ever really noticed. Thank you for riding in the ambulance with me. You're the father I never really had. —Sam

I stopped thinking about quitting after that.

4
The Fungus of Fear

ONE LATE AFTERNOON I was driving along a quiet tree-lined street in the small town I have lived in for the past thirty years, a community of stately, hundred-year-old homes occupied increasingly by lawyers and investment bankers and media executives. After days of rain the sun finally shown warmly. A small caravan of Volvos, big SUVs, and BMWs was parked along one of the baseball fields where a gaggle of eight- or nine-year-olds played what appeared to be a practice game. I pulled over to watch. Fit blond pony-tailed moms clapped and cheered and aimed digital video cameras. Dads arrived in their business suits. One mother had assumed the role of umpire. What immediately struck me was that the kids all wore immaculate uniforms, even though it wasn't an official game. I watched for a while, the mother calling balls and strikes.

When the practice broke up, the kids scurried over to the ubiquitous jingling ice cream truck. After buying her son a cone that looked like a rocket ship one mom then took him by the hand to the cross walk. She carried his mitt, hat and bat. While her son studied his ice cream, attacking it at odd angles, she looked first in the one direction then the other, determining when it would be okay for them to cross. There I saw it, in her eyes. Fear. This mom's eyes darted and blazed with a penetrating need to protect her son, to do everything possible to save him from something. She saw danger everywhere. Even though there were no cars coming she seemed to sense an opening in the nonexistent threat and seized it, yanking her son's arm, causing him to miss his mouth with his cone. She stabbed her remote at a Lexus. The lights flashed. She pushed the boy urgently into the back, fastened his seat belt, and adjusted the bill of his cap as he gummed his ice cream. When she climbed behind the wheel a small TV popped up in the back. A cartoon came on. The baseball player's attention shifted from the cone to the screen. Before the Lexus lurched away, she scanned the scene one more time, like a secret service agent, making sure everything was clear for their escape.

I felt sorry for her. What was she so afraid of? Why such over-involvement? Her son's safety? Sure, that concern stays with parents a lifetime. But why this excess? If her son's well being was so important to her, why hadn't she considered this simple fact: her fear was preventing her son from thinking. During this entire activity, he didn't have to think about a thing, not getting to the field, not picking teams and keeping score and settling disputes, not buying his own ice-cream and crossing the street. Riding home in the back seat he didn't even have to look out the window and think about what to think about. He simply watched TV. And this is pretty much how he will spend his days, in one form or another, until I get to see him as a 12th grader.

I wished I could wash her clean with the quiet, perhaps naive confidence my mother had. When I was eight or nine years old, I was allowed to ride my bike (without a helmet because bike helmets hadn't been invented yet) to a lot we had cleared in the woods because it was flat and seemed like the right size for a baseball field. We took off our shirts and used them as bases and played and played until we no longer needed to use our shirts anymore because we played so often the grass wore away. There weren't any grown-ups around. In the fall, we played tackle football without pads. In the winter it was hockey on a frozen pond in the woods. One time a loose stick slashed my chin to the bone. My friend's father was a dentist, so we went to his house where he stitched the gash with a needle and thread from his mother's sewing kit. I still have the scar. Today that father would be sued. We skied down a nearby hill. We built jumps by burying logs in the snow. I knocked out my front tooth this way. This is how we invented ourselves, by creating our own fun. Sometimes we got hurt but we always survived. "Don't come home unless you are bleeding," my mother used to say only half-jokingly.

When I tell my students this, trying to get them to think about their lives in the context of all the lives that have preceded theirs, they seem strangely annoyed. "Your mother must not have cared for you very much," they say, defensively.

Of course she cared, but in an uncomplicated way, intuitively. Although she probably wasn't conscious of it her ancient role was to teach us by allowing us to learn for ourselves, the hard way, if necessary. She did it by instinct, common sense. If we weren't bleeding, then how serious could it be? She was simply saying go play, with all of play's profound implications. I'm not going to bother you unless you get in over your heads. And if something does go wrong, I'm here for you, but not until then, so go figure things out for yourself.

Her approach wasn't acquired from "how to" books or Dr. Phil. She didn't need to be told what to do. She just somehow *knew*. Her knowing had been passed along for eons by preceding generations and as a result she had become a bona fide grown-up. Yeah, my parents smoked cigarettes because they didn't know any better and we would be fools to do that now, although I do wonder why all those adorable three- and four-year-olds clinging to their tiny pink tricycles, hands held by wary dads, need those oversized helmets. How far could they fall? How badly, really, could they get hurt? I guess they are being taught a *lesson*.

But it might be time to ask ourselves what our exaggerated caution is costing our kids. Why are parents so worried all the time? Sure, many times I would come home from playing war in the woods with my head split open. In fact, my brothers and I kept track as we grew up who had accumulated the most stitches. My mother would calmly take us to emergency room where she chain-smoked Lucky Strikes while watching the doctor sew up our wounds. There was never any panic or despair or hand wringing. The TV had three channels, computers hadn't been invented yet, phones were black and you had to spin the wheel to dial. But unlike too many of today's children we were never bored, because we had two wonderfully non-technological tools to entertain and teach us, our freedom and our imagination.

It would be easy to dismiss these as tales from the good old days, irrelevant and nostalgic, even sentimental, but it would be unwise not to heed the value of learning a *lesson* this way. Parents now negotiate with corporate Human Resources departments the salaries and benefits packages their grown children will receive for their jobs. There are consequences to this, far worse than a bleeding forehead.

"I told a third grader the other day to tie his sneakers and he said he didn't know how," my wife told me once.

"Every morning the mothers and the fathers line up in the hall-ways, holding their coffee cups in one hand and their kids' back-packs in the other. They not only walk their kids to school, they walk their kids *into* the school, then to their cubbies where they take off their kids' coats and hang them up for them. Then when the kids finally go into the classrooms they linger around trying to listen."

But after all, these parents are merely doing what they think is right for their children, and isn't that something to be admired, when we consider all the parents who don't?

And there's the metaphorical answer. His shoes have always been tied for him.

One day, my colleague, our school's football coach, knowing I was studying this problem, forwarded to me an email he got from the mother of one of his players:

I've been asking around, and it seems that every one I have spoken with, their District REQUIRES supportive cups for their players. I took my son to Modell's where one of the employees assisted. He put on a men's medium and the cup was way too large and yet the 220lbs boxer briefs were way too tight on his 130 lb body. Why is that? He doesn't think he needs a supportive cup and I feel he does. Since I am his only advocate and his father is not involved in his daily life (other than visits, when applicable) I feel that if you, as his coach and male role model, speak to him about wearing a supportive cup and let him know how important it is, then maybe he will.

I feel badly for this single mom too, although to her credit, at least she is allowing her son to play football. She is trying to do things she has no business doing. I want to sit her down, too, and tell her that it will be okay, but not if she continues to embarrass her son and herself like this, no matter how desperate she is in her need to protect him. I am sorry that another father is not around to do his job. But let her son get hit in the balls a few times and he will figure it out. I'm sure I was as valuable to my parents, in some unstated way, but what was clearly more valuable to them, more precious perhaps than even I was, or my brothers and sister, and certainly prized by their parents, my grandparents, which now seem lost, were ancient truths:

If you fall down, get up.
Don't complain.
Work hard.
Don't lie.
Actions have consequences.
Respect your elders.
Play fair.
Say please and thank you.

Clean up your mess.
Giving is better than getting.
Life is not about you.
Figure it out for yourself.

These were important. My parents didn't love us any less than today's parents love their children. They weren't afraid of not pampering us, of making a mistake, of doing the parenting thing wrong. We children were not the center of their universe. They and their truths were the center of ours. We hovered around them, much to their occasional dismay. We wanted to be like them, not vice versa. They certainly didn't want to be like us. They didn't envy us or our youth, as many of today's parents seem to do. We were just dumb kids who did goofy things and needed discipline and had everything to learn.

Today, kids seem to be an extension of their parents' self-esteem, so they need to be guarded continuously all day, then tucked into the vault at night. In other words, maybe parents value their children so much because they value themselves too much. It could even be argued that today's parents actually don't really love their children as much as covet them. If they did love them, why would they be doing their children so much harm? Of course, they don't see it that way. Instead, they feel they are helping them. Or is it themselves they are helping, so that they can get an A+ on the parenting report card: my kid got into a good college. They are doing what's right for themselves. Ironically, by lavishing so much praise and pampering on their children, they are putting themselves first. That's one thing my parents and their parents never did.

And there are curious inconsistencies.

The other day one of my seniors revealed that she had been offered a full scholarship to play volleyball for a "good" college in upstate New York. She knew nothing about the school and showed no interest in learning about it. I told her that my brother had attended that college, and not only was it one of the most beautiful campuses but it also ranked in the top ten colleges in America. I encouraged her to consider it.

"How far away is it?" she asked indifferently.

"About a four hour drive."

"Too far. My parents want me close to home."

The same thing happened a few years ago to another one of my students, who was offered a full scholarship to play football for my alma mater.

"Too far. I want to be close to home."

I knew his mother so I called to encourage her to take a look.

"Too far. We want him close to home."

So he attended a local college instead, and his parents paid full price. Every day I hear about students transferring from college. High schools like mine may do a good job training students to get into college, but are they doing a good job teaching students enough about themselves so that they can pick the right college, are parents and schools preparing students to be socially and intellectually adaptable so they feel fulfilled and successful at the college they attend? The statistics say no. Sixty percent of American students go to more than one college. The transfer rate has been going up for years, but recently it's exploded. The reasons cited? Homesickness, the kids say, and a vague unhappiness with their social lives. There are consequences for parents' needing their children so much and for making them feel so safe. "We've made them too comfortable," a retired assistant principal told me. "We've given them their own rooms stocked with computers, TVs, surround sound systems, and video games. Why would they want to leave that?"

I brought this up in class one day with my 12th graders.

"How many of your looking forward to leaving home in the fall?" I asked.

About half raised their hands, and they did so hesitatingly.

I mentioned the trend in transfer rates. "This means that many of you won't be happy by this time next year."

"If it wasn't for the parties, I wouldn't want to go," one boy said. "Why would I? I've got everything I want right here."

I pressed. "Come on, it's college. It's what you've been trying to achieve since before you can remember."

"Because we have to."

"So a lot of you aren't looking forward to it?"

"No, we are, Mr. B. I want to go. I want to try something new. I want to meet new friends. It's just that I don't want all the other stuff."

"What other stuff?"

"Sharing a room. The work."

Shouldn't young people have learned by this time to want to leave the nest, regardless of how comfortable it is? By the time they turn eighteen they should want to be challenged, they should be curious, they should be desperate to test their wings, to enjoy the dignity and self-respect that comes from independence and adulthood and hard work, regardless of the inconveniences. Yet too many of my seniors are not interested in any of this.

"I was reading this article," I continued, "about this guy who is transferring after his first semester. They interviewed him because so many kids like him are transferring. He said something to the effect that he wasn't surprised that so many college students choose to transfer. He says when you are in high school, you do not always know what you like, or what you are good at and you're forced to make a decision about college before you really understand who you are. He said the way high school is set up now, you can't really make a good decision as far as college goes, that high school didn't really motivate him to pick any direction at all. What do you think about that?"

They looked around at each other and nodded.

"Yeah," one boy said, as if this was obvious.

At their age we wanted to explore. We experimented, with courses and subjects and professors, with everything, until we found ourselves. And our parents let us. Now kids don't have that.

They are supposed to know, or worse, they have been led to believe that they are supposed to know, what they want to become as adults, which, of course, is impossible. Some luck out, but it is no wonder they go off to college and become unhappy. It's absurd to think that an eighteen-year-old can decide what she wants to become, let's say an investment banker or civil engineer, then go to a college to pursue it, and end up happy. They have all the wrong expectations. The probable reason for this is the parents' relentless rush for their children to establish as soon as possible a path toward a lucrative career, even if the child has little or no interest in it.

Our youngest daughter majored in classical voice performance. She wants to be an opera singer.

"Why would you ever allow her to do that?" my wife and I are constantly asked. "What will she ever be able to do?"

"Why did your parents let you major in that?" she is constantly asked. "Didn't they pressure you to study something practical?"

To us, a more *practical* question would be, Why would we not allow her to follow her dream and develop her talents and interests, regardless of how impractical they may seem? Of course it will be difficult if not impossible for her to ever make a living singing, but one thing is certain: she will spend the rest of her adult life educated in a subject she loves. Because of that education she will know history, she will have traveled, she will have heard applause directed solely at her, she will have sung in her own lovely voice the heavenly music of Mozart and Verdi. It has been said that to have done music is to have lived life. We are not afraid.

Every year a dozen or so of my seniors tell me they would like to study art or writing or photography, but their parents tell them they won't pay their tuition unless they study something that will earn them a lot of money. There is evidence that fearful strategy is backfiring.

One day I put a slide up on my Smart Board showing that, according to a collegegrad.com poll, 80 percent of 2009 college graduates move back home with their parents after graduation, up from

77 percent in 2008, and 67 percent in 2006. I asked my students if they can explain the trend.

"The economy is so bad," most said.

"That's part of it," I replied, putting another slide up. "But what about many recent graduates turning down good job offers, holding out for better jobs and salaries believing that a college degree entitles them to more than entry level?"

"I wouldn't take just any job," one girl said. "Why should I? After all this crap?"

I clicked one last slide revealing how Gen Y students, born in the late 1980s and 1990s, tend to have unusually close ties with their parents, depend on them for support and guidance, and feel no stigma at moving back home after graduation. "Is this true?"

"I would love it if I could move back in with them after college," one student laughed.

Generation Y, the children of Gen Xers, seems to be resisting the hard work of growing up. Born in 1951, my wife and I are Boomers. What's remarkable about being a high school teacher at my age is that I have this odd perspective. I can actually see our society changing. Normally, trends, demographic shifts, generational swings, emerging attitudinal patterns happen too slowly to perceive. But I can really see them! I can remember clearly that when I was a teenager, my goal was to become an adult, in spite of what my parents and their friends told me about it, that I would have to start at the bottom and be poor until years later after I had worked my way to the top. It would be a challenge. And adulthood seemed cool, unlike childhood. Adults got to make decisions, boss people around, drink fancy cocktails, drive big cars, make money and buy things, and best of all they seemed a lot smarter than I was.

Yet when I polled another class of my seniors the other day, nearly all of them admitted they had no interest at all in joining the grown-up world full of its high costs and the heavy responsibilities of work and raising a family. In fact, they feared the prospect. Like my other classes, most certainly wanted to go away to college as soon as possible, not so much as a process of becoming an adult, but really more to extend their childhood. "I can't wait to be left alone!" To them college is a place to play unsupervised, a kind of postmodern Never-Never Land. Sociologists are saying that adolescence has now extended well into our young people's late twenties.

Perhaps these children were not allowed enough freedom to discover themselves when they were growing up. Instead of letting them play, their Gen X parents busied them preparing for lives they now don't seem to want. All over America school recess is giving way to additional instructional hours. Among policy makers and educators the debate rages over the value in pre- and elementary schools of make-believe and other games. Is this stuff just a waste of precious time in a globally competitive world, or is the development of imagination and social skills essential to a child becoming a functioning adult?

My wife supervises what is left of recess at her school (most of the kids now stay inside for "extra help") and tells me that without a teacher organizing their games they don't know what to do with themselves. Is it any wonder so many of them are unhappy when they go away to college?

In a *Washington Post* article entitled "The Playtime's The Thing" Emma Brown writes that kindergartners are playing fewer than 30 minutes a day. They spend four to six times more on literacy, math and test taking. When children are forced to attend to the business of academics almost from time they are first conscious of being human, is it any wonder that they are burned out and hate hard work by the time they become seniors in high school? Capable coaches are very careful not to over-train their athletes, making sure they peak at just the right time, say before an important competition. That can't be said of our students. Just as they are about to go off to college, too many seem to have lost all interest in learning, if they ever had any in the first place.

When our daughters were 12, 9 and 3 we decided to rent a condo at Stratton Mountain in Vermont and become season-long skiers. My wife and I had grown up skiing, she in the White Mountains of New Hampshire and I the Adirondacks, and we loved winter and we wanted to give our children the same experience, to play in the snow and be free. It meant making a four-hour drive each way, up Friday night, in all kinds of weather, then back late on Sunday. And it was expensive. Fortunately we were good enough skiers to be hired as coaches for one of the seasonal programs, which helped defray some of the costs, and we also shared the rent of the condo with our neighbors. But after a season or two, they decided they didn't want to ski anymore, preferring to stay home on weekends instead.

"We need to be sure the kids are prepared for the next school week," they said. "We can read to them and do math and vocabulary flash cards. They can practice their musical instruments. Weekends are when the tutors come. Vermont is just too time-consuming. It is interfering with their education."

They were afraid of doing the parenting thing wrong. We were afraid they might be right. Being away every weekend our kids would miss out on all kinds of school activities. We'd already seen that getting done the mounds of homework teachers felt they needed to pile on was a big problem.

"But being free to play on a mountain all by themselves in the snow is their education," I said, but our neighbors' minds were made up.

My wife and I took a chance and continued going to Vermont with our kids each winter. I'm sure their grades suffered, tests not studied for, papers turned in late, SATs ignored. We pulled into our driveway late every Sunday night exhausted. We rented for a few more years, then, realizing we loved the whole experience as much for ourselves as for children, we bought a small place. Eventually our kids trained to become coaches themselves, and by the time they were seniors in high school they were employees of the resort, decked out in cool ski instructor uniforms, earning a paycheck, responsible for their own gaggle of young skiers.

Even though they have grown up and moved away my wife and I still go, still coach, still yak and cackle laughing to each other in the glow of the dashboard lamps under the eternal winter sky, no radio or IPods. Today one daughter lives in Salt Lake City where she volunteers for avalanche duty in the Wasatch backcountry. Another daughter and her husband drive each winter weekend from their home in Chicago to a "mountain" in Wisconsin that claims all of eight-hundred vertical feet searching for somewhere they can share snow with their own children. In college for an English composition assignment on the most influential place in her life, my youngest daughter wrote:

> "I am who I am because of the hundreds of rides I took to Vermont with my family in the back seat of our trusty truck. Granted I sometimes felt like an outsider at school because I never went to any of the parties and missed out on all the drama. But now I realize, who cares? I got something else more valuable, a second world. In some ways it may be why my parents have been together for so long. Those rides gave them the opportunity to get know each other even better and to talk and talk. And my sisters and I would listen and listen.
>
> So many rides I can't count them, but I remember all the conversations and silly jokes. Those road trips were a chance to unwind and take in what's around you and communicate with the person sitting right beside you. Each trip was a chance to hear another story, ask advice about a problem or take a nice long nap and wake up somewhere new. We all go to school and are taught by teachers and professors, but I learned more valuable lessons from my private teachers, my parents and two sisters. The most influential place in my life has been the back seat of our truck."

When I was a senior in high school I asked my parents if I could hitchhike all by myself from where I lived in upstate New York to Florida to visit my grandmother.

"That's a long ways," they said, their way of saying be careful.

It wasn't that my parents were reckless, allowing me to take a chance like this. It was more that they somehow knew interfering might be worse. Sure, they were worried, but they weren't afraid, and that's the important difference with today's parents. They simply trusted that things would work out all right in the end, and usually they did.

And because of them, I wasn't afraid. I wasn't afraid to go alone. Most of my students today say that being alone, even for the shortest time, terrifies them. Along the way I found myself deep in South Carolina. The superhighways hadn't been constructed yet, and I was between rides on a remote country road. As the sun drooped below the tobacco fields, the red soil seemed to broil. Rows of ramshackle buildings leaned against the low hills. A couple of curious Black kids scurried over.

"Where you walking to, mister?" one asked.

"Florida."

"Isn't that a long ways off?"

"Yup."

They walked with me a few yards.

"You hungry?" the littlest one asked.

"I'm starved."

"Mama's cooking. You want some?"

That night I shared a meal with a migrant farm family, entertained the boys with stories of my adventures and slept on the floor of their two-room shack. I remember it like it was yesterday. The pot the mama had used. The dad's thick hands. I remember it so vividly because like all my stories it was all mine. You can't forget what you create yourself.

Later in the trip I was between rides again, this time stuck in a Mississippi bayou. It must have been four o'clock in the morning, pitch-dark, not a sign of a car anywhere. I was seventeen, and cell phones wouldn't be invented for another twenty-five years. The otherworldly sounds seeping up from the swamp were certainly unlike any I had ever encountered. I was in a bit of a mess, but whatever happened was up to me. Consequence was how I would learn.

Suddenly out of nowhere, as if by magic, a pair of headlights flashed into sight. I stuck out my thumb. A sports car buzzed by then braked a little ways ahead along the dusty shoulder. It was a Royal Green Triumph convertible, my dream car.

I caught up to it.

"Can you drive a shift?" the hippie driver asked.

"Yup."

"Take over. I need to get some sleep."

I climbed into the leather cockpit, gripped the teak-wood wheel, toyed with the glowing toggle switches, looked up once to thank the unfamiliar stars, then eased the smooth shift into gear. While the hippie slept, I drove, impossibly happy. A few hours later as the sun rose and the new day settled like scented dust over the orange groves I knew I had crossed over into Florida.

My freedom was like that ride. Thanks to my parents' quiet confidence in me to fend for myself I was acquiring a fearlessness to fail or succeed on my own terms that would shape my entire life.

When I tell this story to my students they are envious, because in their world they know freedoms like hitchhiking don't exist.

"It is a different now," they say. "Our world is much more dangerous."

Perhaps, but not in the way the kids and their parents perceive it. Is that metaphorical highway I hitchhiked on any more dangerous than the walls of their Facebook pages or YouTube videos, adorned with our children's provocative poses, or the homes of parents who have gone away for the weekend leaving their children and their friends to play drinking and oral sex games? Or do parents only think the world is unsafe for their children because of the enormous proliferation of media and the twenty-four hour cable news cycle that make such good use of the journalistic anachronism: if it bleeds it leads? We certainly feel the world is much more threatening, but there is little data to suggest that more horrible crimes befall us per capita now than in the 60s when I came of age. In fact, if you check out the statistics they say otherwise. Violent crime rates declined in the 80s and 90s and have been stable for the last ten years. Incidents of rape, robbery, murder and assault have been reduced by more than half since 1980. Crime statistics specific to children and abduction seem even less threatening. The US Department of Justice reports that out of a total population of over 100 million only 58,200 children were victims of non-family abductions, and of these, only 115 children were the victims of the kind of stereotypical kidnapping that most terrifies parents, when the child is abducted by a stranger who intends to kills the child, demand ransom, or keep the child. The odds of this happening to your child are incalculably small.

In a *Time* magazine cover story called "The Case Against Over-Parenting," Nancy Gibbs writes:

> *...in the 1990s something dramatic happened.... From peace and prosperity arose fear and anxiety; crime went down, yet parents stopped letting kids out of their sight.*

Fewer and fewer kids were allowed to walk or bike to school, or even ride the bus. Instead anxious moms and dads drove them. Even though fatal injuries among children had dropped more than 50 percent since the late 1980s parents lobbied to take jungle gyms out of playground.

> *Fear is a kind of parenting fungus: invisible, insidious, perfectly designed to decompose your peace of mind. Fear of physical danger is at least subject to rational argument; fear of failure is harder to hose down.... It is this fear that inspires parents to demand homework in preschool, produces the snazzy bilingual campaign video for the third grader's race for class rep, continues to provide the morning wake-up call long after he's headed off to college.*

Yet parents don't seem to mind when their children are in danger as long as they are inside their own bedrooms. Parents don't seem as afraid of the Internet, even though more than a third of older children, 10- through 17-year-olds, have had an unwanted exposure online to pictures of naked people or people having sex. One in seven received a sexual solicitation and one in twenty-five directly asked the child to meet the predator somewhere. There is a paradox here, a revealing one, which raises the question: how well-intended are parents, really?

I think one sad reason too many parents don't mind it when they sequester kids behind closed doors in their command and control centers with their camera-equipped cell phones and computers instantly linked to all sorts of potential predators is because while their kids are networking the social sites and posting provocative photos of themselves for the whole World-wide Web to see, they aren't interfering with their parents' pursuits, whatever they may be. And their kids' tech-laden lives somehow allow the parents to feel good about themselves. They have been able to provide all this expensive gadgetry. They are keeping up with their neighbors. Therefore, they are being good parents. This is also part of the problem. They are desperate to be good parents, but they have little idea how to go about it, when, actually, it is quite simple: don't try so hard, think, and know how to say no.

"Good" parenting is a relatively new phenomenon. My grandparents, for sure, never thought once about being good parents. My own parents may have considered it from time to time, but it was much more important to have rules. Yet with Gen Xers it seems an obsession, simply because, as with so much else about this generation, thanks to us Boomers, it is about them. After all, their child hides out upstairs in her own room, not forced to share it with a sibling, as we had to. She has the latest iPhone with unlimited text messaging, the newest laptop, and lots of friends on her Facebook, all pointing to what good providers her parents are.

Another self-centered reason for their fear might be that Gen X parents actually *want* to be afraid. Their fearfulness aggrandizes them. If there is something to fear, then they must be necessary, indispensable. Do today's parents, always self-serving, harbor a deep-seated need to be constantly needed?

I like to tell my seniors the following story:

One day in my tenth grade biology class the bell had just rung signaling the beginning of the period, and our teacher, Mrs. Beals, began to lecture. She was an older woman with a bun of silver hair stacked on her head, held in place by elaborate pins that changed daily. I kept on talking loudly to one of my friends. Mrs. Beals glared at me over her half glasses.

"Mr. Baird, exactly what do you think you are doing?"

"I'm talking. What does it look like?"

"You are being fresh and rude, that is what you are doing. Stop," she scolded and began teaching again.

I made the big mistake of defying her.

It is important to add that at the time I weighed about a hundred and ninety five pounds and started on both the varsity hockey and football teams. Also, this was a public high school, not parochial. Continuing my conversation with my friend, I looked up to find Mrs. Beals wading through the desks toward me. With a round-house punch to the chin she launched me sprawling out of my chair onto the floor. I looked up at where she stood over me, hands on her hips.

This is when I stop the story and ask my students to guess what was running through my mind at the time.

"Hitting her back," one boy says.

"How much money you are going to get when your parents sued the school," another offers.

What I was doing, I tell them, was praying.

"Praying?" they ask.

"Praying," I say.

"For what?"

"For my mother and father to never find out, because if they ever did, they would kill me."

My students have never been able to guess this answer. When I tell them this, they don't believe me, although it is true. It is simply unimaginable to them. They all agree the first thing they would do is call their parents, on their cell phones.

My parents weren't afraid. We were. Somehow that got reversed.

After all these years I still remember her name. And that's what happened when my parents punished us, sometimes even hitting us. We remembered. It never hurt. It taught. My brothers and I didn't hate my parents for the discipline they doled out. In fact, we never even got mad at them. It was their duty and we actually respected them for it, although we never would have admitted it at the time. We were wrong. Period. We knew it when we were committing the crime, we knew it immediately afterward, and we knew if we got caught we would pay.

One time after I told this story to a class, one senior boy sitting in the front row lowered his head and mumbled: "I wish, just once, my parents would hit me." The kid was desperate for an adult, an authority figure more powerful and important than he was, to show him in no uncertain terms the difference between right and wrong. But then even that distinction has been clouded by rationalizations.

"It depends," is my students' favorite response to moral or ethical questions.

I asked my wife to help me understand it.

"There is no longer a moral compass, only moral relevance," she offered as possible answer. "People now do whatever they want whenever they want to and to them that's perfectly okay."

Too many parents today seem to be hunkered down in a sort of bunker mentality, in survival mode, so to speak, suspicious, cynical, and distrusting. Nothing or no one can do right by their children other than themselves. For example, a teacher friend from another district told me about what happened to one of her colleagues, the school psychologist. The psychologist had noticed a third grader who seemed to be having trouble making friends. She was always left out, sat alone at lunch. So he began attending her classes making sure that when there were group activities she had someone to partner with. He also invited her to his office during recess where she could talk and play and he told her to bring a friend. She did, a few times, with the same girl, and the strategy appeared to be working, but then one day the friend's mother stormed into school demanding to know why her daughter was spending so much time with this male staff member in his office. She accused him of stalking her daughter and having the classic profile of a child molester. Even though the principal carefully explained that he had been a trusted and valuable member of the faculty for over twenty years, without incident, and that his methods were clinically acceptable, the mother went over the principal's head to the superintendent. To calm her down, the administrators agreed to include in the psychologist's permanent file an official warning letter.

What has caused many parents today to lose their moral footing, to eschew virtuousness, to misbehave like children themselves, rash, anxious, while treating their children like babies, insisting they too get whatever they want whenever they want it, throwing fits if they don't, threatening teachers, defying thousands of years of philosophical, even religious teaching? And worse, to do so right in front of their children, setting such poor examples that their children quickly learn to behave badly too. How did they depart so completely from what natural "goodness" and "good parenting" used to be, resulting in the consequence of their children being conscious only of their own narcissistic needs? The reason my mother and father would have knocked my head off if they ever found out what happened in that biology class was because things were so clear to them. For one, the teacher was always right, period. Even when she was wrong! The terms of life were so simple then that they had confidence. The parents of my generation had unfailing trust in and respect for their institutions, perhaps naively so, but it was unwavering trust, and it made parenting much easier for them.

What parent can say that now? Their confidence is gone, replaced by aggressiveness, almost as if they are shell-shocked, because the terms of their lives are too complicated for them. So they hover over their children, afraid and dispirited, risking ruining them in the process, obsessed with the only escape route they seem to know, which is to get their children into good colleges. Yet they remain seemingly unconcerned with how well their children will adjust once they get there and what kind of citizens they will eventually become. Where did this fungus come from? To answer this fairly I needed to review some history, especially my own.

5
GENERATION ME

GENERATION X, THE PARENTS of most school age children today, were born sometime around the mid-1960s. Many become known as the "latch key" kids, whose moms and dads both worked. Many were products of divorce. Many saw their parents downsized or outsourced when the workplace started changing in the 80s. The result was many Gen Xers became disillusioned and learned to be distrustful. They came of age during the late 1970s, the decade Tom Wolfe, in his famous 1976 essay for *New York Magazine*, dubbed "The Me Decade," asserting that this generation really wasn't so much ennobled by the massive political and social upheaval of the sixties that preceded them as it was defined by a new, virulent strain of self-centeredness which sprang, ironically, from the prosperity and optimism of the Boomers and the 1950s: the big-finned cars, the burgeoning suburbs, the sleek new schools. Color TV! And those family shows: "Ozzie and Harriet," "Donna Reed," "Father Knows Best." Finally in human history a real middle class had emerged. As Wolfe put it, the relatively new "combination of money, free time and personal freedom" that defines a society's middle class allowed the "common man" to begin "realizing his potential as a human being."

Of course, typical of the Boomer generation, we took our new found personal freedom to excess. Remember encounter groups?

The appeal was simply enough. It is summed up in the notion: Let's talk about Me. No matter whether you managed to renovate your personality through the encounter session or not, you had finally focused your attention and your energies on the most fascinating subject on earth: Me.

What we Boomers did was pass along to Generation X the attitude that they could do their own thing too. And, importantly, we also passed along the prosperity to afford it. One indication of this was that during the 70s women began leaving their homes and families in record numbers to pursue careers. There was even a magazine for them: *Working Woman*. As women pursued "self-fulfilling" careers, their family's income often doubled, which caused greater and greater consumer demand. With greater and greater demand and limited supply, prices rose. My wife and I bought our house in 1978 for $79,000. Three years later its value had doubled. That had never happened to real estate before. Three years later it doubled again. Then it doubled again and again so that my successful daughters cannot afford to live in the town they grew up in. This absurd incongruity takes a toll. The more expensive life becomes the greater the pressure to make more and more money, and the vicious gut-wrenching degrading cycle continues.

On a seamier side, men, in the 70s, apparently seeking their own form of self-fulfillment, started sleeping in record numbers with women who weren't their wives.

Until the 1970s, wife-shucking made it impossible for an astronaut to be chosen to go into space. In the Me Decade, it becomes normal behavior, one of the factors that have pushed the divorce rate to 50 percent.

Wolfe's essay charted how the 70s saw a paradigm shift in which the new generation learned quite well how to pursue something new, not service to their country or community or church, but *self-service*, the ever upwardly mobile march, even if it meant leaving their children behind with a nanny or whichever spouse the divorce court decided should have custody. And if Mommy and Daddy both worked all day and often well into the night to pay for their new status, unable to attend Junior's little league games, if Daddy decided to run off with his secretary or some other woman who finally "understood" him, someone he could finally "communicate" with, the byproduct was not only familial upheaval but massive guilt.

Mommy and Daddy felt so badly about what they were doing they began showering Junior not only with endless material goods but something far more insidious—too much attention, too much self-esteem. Even worse than that, they felt the need to become their children's friends! What parent, coming home exhausted from a business trip or an illicit affair, wants to play the bad cop when he or she so rarely sees his or her children? "It's not the quantity of time you spend with them, it's the quality," these young parents would say to my stay-at-home wife, assuaging their guilt, ever rationalizing their chronic busyness. What Gen X parents ceased to be—incapable of the stern discipline that required them to use that nasty NO word because they were so wracked by fear, pressure, guilt and fatigue—were parents.

> *Most people, historically, have not lived their lives as if thinking, 'I have only one life to live.' Instead they lived as if they are living their ancestors' lives and their offspring's lives and perhaps their neighbors' lives as well. They have seen themselves as inseparable from the great tide of chromosomes of which they are created and which they pass on. The mere fact that you were only going to be here a short time and would be dead soon enough did not give you the license to try to climb out of the stream and change the natural order of things. But once the dreary little bastards*

started getting money, they did an astonishing thing—they took the money and ran. They created the greatest age of individualism in American history! All rules are broken! The prophets are out of business!

Gen X's offspring are the seventy million Gen Yers born in late 1980s and 1990s, sometimes called Trophy Kids, not so much because of how much they are valued but for all the meaningless awards that are bestowed upon them, usually for merely participating. Because their Gen X parents have such high expectations of them, they over-scheduled them, ever hopeful they will "earn" more trophies, no matter how underserved, but Jean Twenge, Ph.D., a GenMe'er herself and a professor of psychology, author of *Generation Me: How Today's Young American's Are More Confident, Assertive, Entitled—and More Miserable Than Ever Before*, sees a problem:

Television, movies, and school programs have told us we were special from toddlerhood to high school, and we believe it with a self-confidence that approaches boredom. Our childhoods of constant praise, self-esteem boosting, and unrealistic expectations did not prepare us for an increasingly competitive workplace and the economic squeeze created by sky-high housing prices and rapidly accelerating health care costs. After a childhood of buoyancy, GenMe is working harder to get less.

Elementary school kids color in a workbook titled "We Are All Special." Later these same kids, choking on their inflated esteem will tell me with unabashed conviction Shakespeare and Kafka and Beckett are bullshit. They resent the way these authors challenge their perceptions, suggest they live unexamined lives. How could that possibly be true, they contend, after all the ribbons and trophies and Honor Roll certificates they have received? A psychiatrist friend of mine tells me: "The attention today's parents lavish upon their children is much more than narcissism. These parents' limitless urge to celebrate themselves has led to the ultimate extension of their own egos." Is it too much to say, then, that in a way these parents are like forgers, that they are producing counterfeit kids, who, like fake currency, will ultimately be found out and proved valueless?

6
EDDY

MY 12TH GRADE ENGLISH teacher's name was Miss Shupp. She had crooked teeth, was thin and serious and unflappable and we loved her, even though our class consisted mostly of the starters for the football team. (We even got her to come to one of our games once!) We all sat in the first few rows, big upstate boys, sons of farmers, traveling salesmen, tavern owners, and auto shop mechanics. It was large central school near Utica. It was 1969. Less than half of our graduating class would go on to some kind of higher education. The rest went to work or were shipped to Vietnam.

Even though most of the class wasn't "college material," Miss Shupp taught what she referred to as idea books, mainly modern European literature. This is what we read: *Crime and Punishment, The Metamorphosis, The Stranger, Waiting for Godot*, Turgenev's *Fathers and Sons*, Ibsen's *Master Builder, Hedda Gabler*, and *A Doll's House*, Chekhov's *Uncle Vanya, The Sea Gull* and *The Cherry Orchard*, and Schopenhauer's *World of Will and Ideas*. This is what we wrote: ten 3-page analytical essays and two research papers, one 5 pages and the other 10. I know, because I kept them.

Today you would be hard pressed to find a curriculum this rigorous in an upper level English course at a prestigious university.

We weren't Honors or AP students. Those tracking mechanisms hadn't been invented yet. We were just ordinary kids in an ordinary high school far removed from the affluence and privilege and opportunity of areas like Westchester County. To demonstrate how much we've changed it should be enough to say that a course like this would be impossible to teach to seniors today, even though virtually all of them are college-bound. They simply would not stand for it. The students would refuse to do that much work, for many reasons, such as the relentless stream of technological distractions that floods their postmodern lives, but mainly because they would feel no need to. They would find the books useless and boring, so they wouldn't read them. A few might lie and say they had. They might flip through a few pages, then go online and download any summary they needed to get by the next day's quiz or discussion, but there would be no sustained and engaged intellectual conversation. And most teachers wouldn't put up with it: too much effort for too little return. Why, then, had the petite Miss Shupp been able to pull it off, correcting each paper so tirelessly and carefully with her perfect little handwriting?

First of all, there was no such thing as senioritis back then, probably because the ignobility it suggests didn't exist yet, but even if it had reared its ugly head it would have been immediately beaten (literally) down by the parents, unlike today. Second, Miss Shupp didn't have the demands put on her time that teachers today have. She and her students weren't slowed by the requirements imposed by well-intended administrators demanding differentiated learning, technology implementation, Bloom's Taxonomy, CSE meetings, ESP meetings, multiple progress reports. Nor was she ever interrupted by parents' emails and phone calls. The only standardized test was the New York State Regents exams, which were so easy to pass that teachers paid no attention to them. But the student/teacher ratio then was twice what it is now. And the cost of educating a student was ¼ what it is now, in inflation-adjusted dollars. The teaching wheel is constantly being reinvented, ostensibly to serve the children, but ever changing pedagogy also bloats the already swollen educational bureaucracy. The SATs have been "normed" at least three times, in other words, defined downward. What would have scored an 800 then now earns a 1000. Ranking of high schools, published test results, these wouldn't have been allowed because privacy was important back then, and back then who would have cared anyway? No one thought twice about the value of real estate, mainly because it never went up much. A house wasn't an investment; it was a home.

Of course the two eras are unequal, with too many variables to render any comparison. But because I became a teacher at such a late stage in my life, I find myself every day, unlike most adults my age, in a world of teenagers, the epicenter of the current brave new world. As a result I am a man of two radically different times. One is ancient history. But it is also who I am, where I come from. To dismiss it is to dismiss me. And I am also, because of my proximity to these kids, very much a man of this 21st century era, too. And a teacher in it, no less. How do I square the experiences of my past with what I am experiencing now? Isn't character still character, bitter irony still bitter?

Perhaps most telling is this: while those texts were difficult and took us a long time of squirming to read, it never would have occurred to us to call them boring, or worse, not read them at all, as today's seniors would do. The other day I asked some of them about the progress they were making on an independent reading assignment I had given them. I had recommended a half dozen non-fiction books on topics I felt might interest them. One was a slim book I loved called *Against Happiness*, by Emory University English professor Eric Wilson. One student said, "I didn't finish the book. The author repeats himself too much. And he uses all these big words to show off."

"Yeah," another student imitated. "I stopped reading it."

"Me too. It was too boring," a third offered.

Somehow it was the author's fault that these students hadn't completed their assigned reading. Even though they later admitted only reading the first few pages, and probably skimmed those, they could confidently conclude that the author, a distinguished professor at one of those "good colleges" they were willing to kill each other to attend, repeated himself too much and therefore didn't know what he was doing. Worse he had used vocabulary they didn't understand, "big words" my seventeen-year-old students asserted were inserted merely to inflate and show off. My students, supercharged with false self-esteem, felt they could somehow position themselves squarely as Wilson's intellectual equivalent, maybe even his superior, and so they were entitled and qualified to blow off the assignment. Who or what did this to these students, empowering them way beyond their means, causing them to appear foolish in front of those of us who know?

"That book sucks," the others agreed.

"The other books you recommended suck too," one added.

"How do you know? Did you read them?" I asked.

"No. I can just tell."

Was it my authority they were resisting, resenting? Wilson's?

After school the other day I sat in on a meeting called by one of my 9th grader's parents. His other teachers had to be there as well. One by one they reported on the student's progress.

"But there is one issue I do need to bring up," the student's social studies teacher said after a generally favorable review. "He can be very inappropriate. For example, the other day when I introduced our lesson for the day, he said loud enough for everyone to hear, 'this sounds really dumb.' I had to reprimand him."

The father and mother showed no interest.

When it was my turn, I had a few stories of my own to tell:

"I have seen some inappropriate behavior as well. He is still young, so I'm not getting all over him for it just yet, but if it keeps up, he is going to find himself in trouble. For example, I will introduce a lesson and he will sigh and roll his eyes and make sure he lets his classmates know that whatever it is I'm trying to teach is way below him. I had to move his friend to the front row because the two of them were constantly talking. But then when your son went right on talking to someone else and I threatened to move his seat to the front row, he laughed and said snidely there were no more seats. I like to draw a picture of a doghouse on the board and when the kids don't do their homework I write their names in it. It is fun, and it works. But your son has made it clear that he thinks it is a waste of his time. If fact, the other day he asked if the principal knew I was doing this. 'Do you have tenure?' he asked. It was a threat. You need to tell him that I am the boss, not him."

The mother and father looked at each other, then shrugged indifferently. "My son would beg to differ with your assertion about being the boss," the father then said. "We are the boss. We pay your salary. We have taught our son to be his own advocate. Now let's get back to his academics."

What this means is the fourteen-year-old gets to treat his teachers, and their ideas, as if they were his servants.

But in 1969 the consensus among us that kept us plodding along was this: We all shared the deeply held conviction that we were dumb. We were dumb mainly because we lived in this forgettable town impossible to find on a map located just south of a run-down rusting city, but our dumbness was also reinforced by our society. We were *young*. That implies an age-appropriate lack of sophistication and an inability on every level. In every sense, we were unimportant. And that was okay. It was part of being a kid. It was our job, our role. The books weren't dumb and boring; we were. Unlike students today, we just somehow knew how much we didn't matter and how much we didn't know, and according to Miss Shupp these were the books that only truly educated people read and understood and let drive their lives and that was good enough for us. We had something unambiguous to aspire to. We decided early on that if we did exactly what someone "smart" like Miss Shupp asked of us, then maybe, just maybe someday we wouldn't be dumb anymore, and that was our only academic goal. The one thing we knew for sure was that not only were we *not* the center of the universe, we were barely discernible in it, at best cold distant planets like icy Pluto. Certainly we were not the big bright hot Sun, as today's students feel.

After her class we would sit at the football table in the cafeteria and debate Bazarov's and Raskolnikov's nihilism, Gregor's alienation, and Vladimir and Estragon's absurdity. We began to identify with the philosophies these books presented. Of course while we were busy being enlightened by Miss Shupp, the world swirled around us nearly apocalyptically, and because we'd somehow become philosophers, thinkers, in other words, we were able to take an interest in it and discuss it. After school we would drop by Miss Schupp's room before practice to test our ideas. Beneath our yearbook pictures we included quotes that proudly proclaimed our new found learning: "God is Dead," "I think, therefore I am," "The Unexamined Life is Not Worth Living."

Yet as I write this, President Obama has just delivered a speech at the United Nations, followed by Ahmadinejad from Iran, then Israel's Netanyahu. The implications and potential ramifications of the three disparate speeches are as profound and potentially apocalyptic as anything from the 60s. Yet when I asked my seniors what they thought of the speeches, none knew what I was talking about. What speeches? Not only hadn't they listened to them, they weren't even aware they had taken place. Later in the day during her personal essay presentation a Muslim student described her parents' life in Pakistan before they immigrated to America. When I opened up the presentation to discussion and questions, only a few hands rose, all with the same eager question. After a fascinating presentation rich with cultural differences, all the students wanted to know about was the drinking age in Pakistan. They don't drink there, the Muslim student responded shyly. She then went on to talk about Sharia law, which my colleagues in the social studies department make a point of emphasizing during their 9th and 10th grade Global Studies classes, but none of my seniors could recall what it was. They had no idea or had forgotten that the young woman standing before them, their classmate, would have her marriage arranged for her, even here in America. Worse, they seemed not to care, and this while we are at war on two fronts with fundamentalist Islamic terrorism.

When I got around to applying to college I hand wrote my essay, filed in the information and mailed it away. My parents never saw it. They had no interest. Why should they? I applied to three schools. I was an average student. If I didn't get into any of them, I probably would have been drafted, but my parents showed no urgency, and my father was a Marine. He knew what could happen to me, something far worse than what could happen to a senior today, if I somehow didn't get into a good college. But my parents simply had *faith*. Unlike parents today they held a kind of quiet belief in the natural order of things and certainly they didn't have the ego to try and interfere with it.

There was another beloved English teacher, Mr. Forest. Students raved about him. While we were glad we had Miss Shupp some of my buddies and I regretted not having ever had Mr. Forest, so when we found out he was teaching a summer school class that year, we signed up and took it, even though we had already graduated. He taught us *Hamlet*.

"You went to summer school and you didn't have to?" my students ask incredulously.

That fall inspired by his new interest in learning, my friend Ted went to the local community college to get his grades up. After that, he went on to Albany State. He didn't do it to get a good job. He did it because he really enjoyed the feeling of getting smarter. And of course because he got much smarter he ended up with a good job.

My other friend Eddy didn't go to college. Instead he went to Vietnam. What good philosophy was to him in the jungle near Bong Son I'll never know because he never came home. He was killed, along with 58,209 other young soldiers, and as a result of this and those tumultuous times, I and other Boomers began to learn something that Gen Xers would pick up on, that things don't always work out, that the natural order includes distortions and lies and manipulations and that maybe Nietzsche was right after all: God had died, so you'd better fend for yourself.

7
THE PO-MO KIDS

MODERNISM GAVE WAY TO Postmodernism sometime in the late 60s or early 70s. The grotesque nightmare of Vietnam probably caused it, somehow surpassing even the absurd horrors of the first half of the 20th century. After reading Modernist works like *The Sun Also Rises*, *The Metamorphosis* and *Waiting for Godot*, I then have my students read *The Things They Carried* because it's considered a Postmodern text. O'Brien's book blends facts with fiction, distorting both to provide a whole new view, and it is as much about the vagaries of truth and love and all of life, the impossibility of certainly, as it is about the tragic ridiculousness of war. It's why Sam loved it, of course.

During their senior year in my class I try to teach them how these artistic movements, from Romanticism to Realism to Modernism, including Surrealism and Absurdity, and finally to Postmodernism have affected them, that they exist not in a vacuum, detached, but that they arrived here, part of a continuum, participants in the long parade, products of the great sweep of human history. I explain the Postmodern movement's characteristics: that there are no answers, so unlike the Modernists, why even contemplate trying to find them. Yes, life is meaningless, so instead of worrying about it, like the Modernists did, let's just play. They seem to like the designation. It validates their behavior. It gives them a new way to identify themselves. They also like it when I describe to them that because I was born when I was, and came of age only when the cultural movement shifted, I am more of the Modernist tradition, doomed to forever wonder, hoping to figure it all it. I am Vladmir, hoping Godot will show up tomorrow. I would take the red pill. They laugh. We battle and debate from our two radically different eras.

After high school I was lucky to go off to a small liberal arts college in the very northern most part of New York State, saved from the draft because they offered me a football scholarship that paid my tuition. My new Selective Service status was 2-S, a deferment for being a full-time student. In November of my freshman year Nixon signed an amendment to The Military Selective Service Act that established conscription based on random selection. The first "draft lottery" was held in December. In 1971, with the end of the war still four years away, student deferments ended.

I drew a low number. In spite of this, other than feeling guilty because I was reading Victorian novels under leafy Elm trees while my friend Eddy was dying, I really didn't think too much about my future. I certainly never once thought about how what I was studying might help me get a "good job." What I did think about, a lot, was how what I was studying might help me get a good life, maybe as a kind of contrition, and I wasn't alone in this. I would say most students, at least the ones I knew, felt the same way. Our liberal educations were important. We majored in subjects like English, philosophy, history, theology, modern languages, art history, chemistry, and mathematics. We chose them because we liked them. We were interested. The college didn't offer a single course in any subject that could be considered vocational such as business, communications, even education. The closest might have been economics. We all were required to take two courses in mathematics, four courses of history and literature, two of science, one in philosophy and religion, four of a modern language, and one monster course called humanities which spanned all Western thought from the time of the pre-Socratic philosophers to modern existentialism. I chose to major in English, simply because I loved literature. After studying in Vienna during my junior year, I added German as a second major, then a minor in writing. My girlfriend majored in French. Most of my buddies studied history. None of us ever thought, not even for a minute, how these subjects might or might not land us high-paying jobs.

Madeline Levine, Ph.D. writes in her book *The Price of Privilege: How Parental Pressure and Material Advantage Are Creating a Generation of Disconnected and Unhappy Kids* about how researchers at UCLA and the American Council on Education have studied hundreds of thousands of students over the last forty years and found they are increasingly superficial. When those who went to college in the 60s and 70s were asked their reasons for going, most said they wanted to become an educated person or find a philosophy of life. Only a few said to make a lot of money. But beginning in the 90s that few turned into the vast majority. Making a lot of money has become the main reason for a college education. What is even sadder is that at the same time, this shift in values has led to increased rates of depression, suicide and other psychological problems, not the least of which is that vague unhappiness that leads so many to transfer in often futile attempts to find themselves in some other places rather than within their minds. This is what happens, Levine writes, when pursing money is more important than personal, moral and intellectual development.

I would go even further. I would argue that the recent inordinate shift in values to the materialistic is unnatural; it defies our human nature, which has always been more inquisitive, inventive, and curious, than acquisitive. It is dangerous to our civilization, counter-productive. We've turned and are headed backward. The creation of new ideas that lead to advancements, progress, in other words, is what got us up here, at the top of the food chain. Bill Gates and Steve Jobs and Mark Zuckerberg didn't start out wanting to be the richest men in the world. They started out interested in something, very interested.

I saw a lot of hippies at college. Many were the real deal, genuine in their hatred of the war and the establishment. They really wanted a revolution and were willing to sacrifice everything to achieve it and I admired them for it. But many more were simply looking for the easy way out, a good excuse—opposing the war—to get high or have sex. They were only superficially defiant. What struck me most about them was their childishness. They skipped around the quad at our university holding hands the way kindergartners do. It was as if they were looking for a good reason to be babies again. When Kent State happened their main concern was closing the college so they wouldn't have to take final exams and could play Frisbee instead, and it occurred to me that they weren't so much protesting the war as protesting the draft, so they wouldn't have to go.

I think this childishness and selfishness is what many of the hippies carried with them as they aged. Then passed it along to the next generation. I remember that in the 60s our culture began to emulate the young in such a way that it made becoming an adult, and assuming the behavior associated with being a grown-up, almost undesirable, but it takes grown-ups to run a civilization.

Was this when the "self" first began to assert itself? Never before in American history had our citizenry behaved like this when asked to serve its country. I think when Lyndon Johnson resigned and the draft and eventually the war ended, future parents began to believe that in spite of the Rolling Stones lyrics, you *can* always get what you want.

Surely it is part of it, for the childlike and selfish behavior of so many of today's parents, transferred to their children, cannot be denied. But I think there is more to it. These parents are not bad people. I think that my students' apathy and indifference is also born from the cynicism Gen Xers developed when so many guys like Eddy didn't come home, while we Boomers stubbornly held on to some kind of blind conviction. Something profound happened to them. Yes, the 60s, the counter-culture movement and its indignation weren't really all that righteous. Yes, those of us who were draft-age in the 60s were mainly worried about having to fight in a war and acted mainly out of self-interest, not morality. And yes, the realization that we could get away with these things gave rise to the Me Decade and an epoch of self-indulgence. Because of this, I think, along with God and Eddy, Gen Xers' sense of duty died, along with any commitment to causes larger than themselves, because there wasn't anything larger than themselves left. They had learned that they couldn't trust their institutions. The truth, the distinctions between right and wrong, good and bad, blurred, then faded away to the point where they no longer wanted to do the right thing instead of the wrong, no longer wanted to be good instead of bad, because there seemed to be no difference. Ironically, as their self-centeredness grew, their souls seemed to fade away as they concluded that no one was looking out for them. There was nothing left to *believe* in, except their own endurance. After all, couldn't it be claimed that anyone born after 1973 was an abortion survivor? From what they saw all around them, they learned the dangerous lesson that they didn't have to do what authority and tradition and morals had dictated for centuries, because too often they could not be believed. Their government, they had discovered, had lied to them. So had their mothers and fathers and professors, then their employers, even their husbands and wives. As a result, everything became *relative*. Not only could they do whatever they wanted to and get away with it, they should. *Have it your way*, one fast food burger joint proclaimed. And why not? Living in America was like trying to play a game in which everyone else was cheating: Watergate, Cambodia, the hostages in Iran, gas lines, stagflation, Chrysler's bail out, Lennon's murder. Instead of an optimism that things would always turn out right, Gen Xers inherited an updated version of T. S. Eliot's wasteland: their children, my students—Gen Y, GenMe, the Millennials—are the *Po-Mo* kids.

8
THIS BOTTOM LINE THING

IT IS NOW BEING written that the Crash of 2008 and the economic devastation that followed in its wake will have significant long-term implications for consumers, investors and our collective psychology. If that is true, then certainly our collective psychology was affected by the nasty stagflation that occupied the last years of the Carter presidency, the recession of first few years of Reagan's, then the unprecedented rise in the stock market.

In 1980 I was twenty-nine years old. I had been married for five years. My wife had resigned her art teacher's job at a nearby parish elementary school to take care of our first child. As young parents we, along with many like us, were trying to get a toehold, but our hopes and expectations seemed pitted against forces much bigger than ourselves. The Dow had been locked in a narrow trading range for over 18 years. My salary and commissions amounted to about $30,000 a year. I was selling advertising space for *The New Yorker* magazine. Unemployment was at 10.8 percent and the prime rate was 17 percent. New York City was a filthy bankrupt jungle. Hungry for more, I approached my boss and asked when I might be promoted.

"How long have you had this job?" he asked

"Five years."

"Is that all? Our customers are just getting to know you. How do you think they would feel if all of a sudden some new guy came in?"

And with that, the meeting was over. I didn't question him. I wondered if he was merely putting me off but ruled it out. My boss really believed in this. And, for those times, he was right. I had been calling not only the same companies, but the same individual people, in the same positions, all those years and we had a good relationship, and business decisions were based on relationships, and relationships could be counted on.

That, too, was about to change.

My largest account, and one of the most important to the magazine, was a company called Heublein, now extinct, along with so many venerable companies, which made and imported such wide selling liquor brands as Smirnoff Vodka and Harvey's Bristol Cream. At least once a week I made the two hour drive to their headquarters in Hartford to call on the various managers.

One day arranging my appointments I was told the company had hired a new director to oversee the marketing division, and he and his new team would now make all advertising decisions. He had a degree most of us had never heard of, something called an MBA. I made an appointment and went to see him.

After I made my sales pitch and presented him with a proposal for an advertising schedule for his company's next fiscal year, I told him that our two companies had been doing business together since the Repeal of the Volstead Act, over fifty years, and it was customary for my magazine to host each year a golf outing at the nearby Farmington Country Club for Heublein's employees as a token of our appreciation. This was how *The New Yorker* and most companies then conducted business. Personal, courteous, respectful. We valued our relationship.

"What would that cost?" he asked curtly.

I told him I had no idea. No one had ever asked that before.

"Find out," he said. "And get back to me."

I went back to the office and asked our support people. The number came in at around thirty thousand dollars, a lot of money in 1980. I called him back.

"Thirty thousand," he said. "Good. Now regarding your proposal, take that thirty thousand you would have spent for this party no one needs and apply it to our total cost."

I was shocked. In those days, the price was the price. There was no negotiating.

"I don't think we can do that," I said.

"Fine. Then no deal."

I tried to explain to him again that a golf outing was our way of saying thanks for the many years of doing business together. His people and ours could get to know each other better. The guest speaker would be our legendary golf writer Herbert Warren Wind.

"I don't care about Warren whatever his name is. I care about the bottom line. Take the cost off our advertising bill and we have a deal. If you don't you lose the account."

He hung up. I immediately went in to see my boss.

"Something big just happened," I said. "I don't know exactly what, but somehow I think everything just changed," I explained.

"What if this bottom line thing spreads?" he asked.

It did, like an untreated infection. To me, it was almost as if at that moment American capitalism morphed into something different from what it had always been. My grandfather's way of doing business suddenly seemed quaint, remote, and naive. He had borrowed money—capital—from a bank to start his business, a small wholesale drug company. It grew large enough so that he could employ his son who inherited it when he died. Selling the company and cashing in was never an option. The priority was sustaining what he had built and passing it on, but sometime around the middle part of the 1980s it seemed everyone's new goal was to get rich quickly. Even those who ran the venerable *The New Yorker*.

I learned about it at a stockholders meeting. A year before, I had been given 800 shares of preferred stock as part of a key employee incentive program, initiated by the company's president. The program quickly became contentious because only a very few of the company's employees were chosen for it. I was approached by a group of disgruntled colleagues who were also close friends and asked that I stand with them to insist the program be more inclusive. I did, which was easy because it came naturally to me, and eventually some of them were granted stock too, but I also remember being torn. There was a lot of money at stake. It was the first time in my life I felt greedy and I didn't like it. Doing the right thing had suddenly become complicated. Then at the stockholders meeting I learned why the key employee preferred stock plan had been conceived in the first place, and it had nothing to do with retaining key employees. After 60 years as a closely held family company, *The New Yorker* was being sold for $200 a share to S. I. Newhouse's Conde Nast, the media giant that publishes *Vogue, Glamour, Vanity Fair, Brides* and other slick magazines. The president had devised the plan with a few of the top executives to fill their own pockets with free stock, and a lot of it. When the transaction went public we found out that the number of shares granted to employees paled in comparison to theirs, but somehow their lawyers and accountants had conspired to make it all legal through the guise of an employee incentive plan.

Suddenly I found myself immersed in the madness of Wall Street intrigue. Even though the value of my stock was a fraction of what these top executives were taking, I was still numb, never having imagined I would ever own so much money. Soon I was invited to secret meetings with more accountants and lawyers and portfolio managers who advised us on how to avoid capital gains taxes. The huge Reagan cuts had not happened yet. It was sickening, and I was a part of it: here we had been given all this free money, yet we were all scrambling to retain as much of it as we could.

Inevitably state and federal taxes took over 60 percent of the value of my stock, but so what? What wealth remained was still beyond my wildest dreams, mainly because I hadn't done anything to earn it! Earning to me meant working hard. Of course, I told my wife the good news that our children's educations had just been paid for and then some, but I also felt somewhat dirty, as if a trust or tradition had been violated. The money had come too easily and at considerable expense to others. Within weeks of the take-over nearly the entire staff, including many of my friends who had no stock, was fired. Not only did I keep my job, I was even promoted a few times. But the damage had been done. If this is how the new system worked I'd better play along. The choice was simple: be on the inside or the outside. It was survival of the fittest and by then I had two young children. I would have been quite content if *The New Yorker* had never been sold, with me continuing to do my small part and earning a respectable living, having a career like my father had, working his entire life for one company that was like a family to him. But that wasn't to be, the same way it wasn't to be for employees all over America who were becoming hardened or losing their jobs to mergers and acquisitions and down-sizing and out-sourcing which fattened the bottom line and attracted more mergers and acquisitions. What resulted was a retreat into one's self. From then on, like the millions of the Gen Xers right behind me, I would look out only for me. I became my own bottom line.

A short time later the top tax rate was cut from 70 percent to 39.6 percent on individual income, from 50 percent to 35 percent on corporate income, and from 35 percent to 20 percent on capital gains. When I considered how much more money I would have kept if the new tax rates had been in effect when I cashed in my stock, I experienced a new emotion, a new kind of self-centered anger, a combination of greed and resentfulness, even though I had been so fortunate. The race to creating and hoarding wealth was on and I was a willing participant. I invested my money in the stock market and watched it grow. Of course, there were risks. On October 19, 1987, my business lunch appointment cancelled, so I jumped a cab and headed uptown to the New York Athletic Club on Central Park South where I am a member. I played a game of squash with a friend, showered, then went into the lounge to grab a quick sandwich. The lounge, unusually, was packed. Members in towels, half dressed, huddled around the small TV screen. It was Black Monday. All around the world the stock markets had crashed. The DJIA dropped by 508 points to 1738.74, a 22.61 percent decline, the largest one-day decline in stock market history. I watched as a big chunk of my new wealth disappeared.

This was all so new to me: getting money quickly, losing it as quickly. I had come from a time and place where money was not that important, and if you had any it meant you had saved it. All of my values were based on that old notion. This was stunningly different.

Of course the crash of '87 was nothing but a speed bump in the Dow's inexorable tear to 14,000, creating enormous wealth in its wake, but also displacing the old America. What caused it? Reagan's Supply Side Economics? The advent of mergers and acquisitions when parts of companies become more valuable than the whole? I'll leave it to economists to argue and assess. All I know is that the downsizing and the outsourcing forced most of us to work harder and longer, all under the guise of productivity, a kinder, gentle term for the bottom line, while a few others closer to the top, who didn't seem to work at all, did "very well." The incessant hurrying caused stress, left us no time to contemplate. All over America companies became obsessed with short term results. If they were good, executives could impress Wall Street and get rich quick. Even my grandfather's small business, passed along to his son after his death, was eventually taken over by a larger company, putting my cousin and a third generation, out of jobs. Our collective insecurity deepened. Our priorities changed.

In the 80s Gen Xers and even we Boomers unwittingly had entered into the new age of high-stakes volatility, with huge risks and rewards, which has only become more volatile since then. The beneficent corporate sugar daddy—a formidable presence that for generations had guaranteed its employees a decent wage, health care and a livable pension for life—had ceased to exist. Now it was up to us to take care of ourselves. The invention of the 401(k) made us players in the stock market, whether we wanted to be or not. Before that, employees didn't worry about crashes. But when we started to take care of our own investments, even indirectly, we needed to add to our increasingly demanding lives the necessity of learning about growth stocks vs. value stocks, bonds vs. equities, asset allocations and dollar cost averaging. If we lost our retirement it would be our fault. Stocks became part of the American mainstream. What needs to be understood, in order to appreciate what has happened to our students, is that before all of this, accumulating quick wealth was never the priority. Living a decent and contented life was. And having a stable predictable career with one company was a component. In other words, slowly, loyally and faithfully climbing the corporate ladder was the path to success, not only on the job, but in life, because you were applying timeless values that enriched you spiritually as well as financially. You *worked* your way up. The rules were simple. Come in early, leave late. Be well liked and eventually you would be promoted. And then promoted again, until one day thirty years after you started, you might be President or CEO or at least a VP. It was a metaphor for life. But that path was yanked away. Those golden rules were nullified, and with them a large degree of honesty and self-respect. The old values were just too slow. The mantra became *don't work hard; work smart*. Come in late and leave early. But there was nothing ambiguous about working hard, while working smart can have many undesirable connotations: short-cuts, deceptions, cynical transgressions. For long time Bernie Madoff worked smart. So did all the hedge fund guys and the Goldman and Morgan analysts who are now being arrested for insider trading.

9
Maul Mentality

IN 1985 MY SEVEN-YEAR-OLD daughter fell out of a tree in our neighbor's yard and broke her arm. I was doing some yard work out in front of my house talking to my wife when we heard her scream. I immediately ran toward the sound and she appeared from behind their house, strangely calm, holding her dangling left arm.

"Daddy, I think I hurt it."

The pain hadn't hit yet. Her left arm distended at the elbow, snapped back and contorted in an impossible angle. Hurt it? She had mutilated it. I tried to act as calmly as she.

By this time, my wife had backed the car out of the driveway, knowing from the sound of the shriek we would be going to the hospital. The neighbor appeared, looking shaken.

"She climbed the tree," he said. "It has an old ladder on it. Coming down the ladder broke and she fell. I know I should have checked the ladder. The kids are always playing on it. I am so sorry."

"Don't worry about it," I told him.

"I just want you to know that you do what you have to do. I have insurance."

At first I didn't know what he meant. I looked at him, puzzled.

"I mean when you sue me," he said.

"Sue you?" I asked. It hadn't occurred to me.

"Yes."

"I wouldn't do that," I told him. "You are my neighbor. Shit happens."

In the emergency room, the attending orthopedist appeared visibly nervous when he reviewed her x-rays with us.

"I will do everything I can, and there is a chance she will be able to recover at least some motion of her elbow, but it is a very bad fracture, through the growth plates."

He was scared. I had never seen a doctor scared before, and it wasn't just because of the severity of my daughter's injury. It was that he had been the unlucky one on call when a difficult case came in.

"Do what you can," we said.

"I just want you to know up front there are no guarantees."

"What are you trying to say?"

"That this is very bad and I will do all I can."

He wasn't a young doctor, wasn't new, we found out later. In fact he was quite well respected. He performed a closed reduction, which means manipulating the bone back into place without surgery, then casting it. But there was something about his fear and hesitation that really troubled me.

"This poor guy thinks we're going to sue him," I told my wife. "He can't function."

"What are you going to do?"

"I'm going to get her x-rays and take them to Hospital for Special Surgery and find a doctor who still has a pair of balls."

I drove into Manhattan, went to the pediatric wing, stopped some young top-gun surgeon in the hallway, showed him the pictures, and told him the story. He told me to get my daughter in to see him as soon as possible, and when we did he operated on her arm, pinned her bones together, and all she has to show for her very bad injury is a really cool scar.

A few years later a woman sued McDonald's for millions of dollars alleging that she burned herself because their coffee was too hot and came without any warning.

"If you do, I'll sue you," my students say when I threaten them with the humiliating horror of having to stand out in the hallway because they won't stop interrupting the class.

A recent CBS Sunday Morning episode reported that school playgrounds all over America are being stripped of every conceivable danger. Swing sets are being modified, sliding boards are being made so safe they no longer provide the childish thrill they were originally designed for, all to avoid lawsuits.

The Litigious Age had a dance partner, the Age of Conspicuous Consumption, and as the greedy race toward accumulating wealth gained speed, the accelerator pad seemed to be the equity people held in their homes. Except for a brief letdown around 1987, the price of real estate kept rising. My wife and I watched the house across the street turn over two times in less than four years. One of its occupants, an outgoing young Gen Xer who always seemed to have a cocktail in his hand, teased me when he heard we had been in the same house for almost ten years.

"Don't be so old-school," he teased. "Flip it for something bigger. You'll do nothing but make money."

"I like my house," I told him.

He laughed, and within a year he was gone too, off to a fancier neighborhood, chasing higher and higher capital gains.

What I did, instead of moving to a bigger better house, was obtain a home equity loan and build a large wing to make more room for our growing family, which made sense, because my home's value had increased so much, and by comparison, what I owed on it was so little. All across America homeowners were doing the same thing, leveraging their homes to buy things. Another age had begun, the age of conspicuous consumption. George Will, whose columns I enjoy, wrote in *Newsweek* that for thirty or more years after World War II, private consumption as a percentage of Gross

Domestic Product (GDP) held between 61 and 63 percent but in the 80s it began to rise and was over 70 percent by 2007, fueled in part by home-equity loans. That's a trillion extra consumer dollars spent, not to mention the charges to credit cards. Instead of having to save enough money to buy something, which takes time and discipline, Americans began using their homes, whose value they believed would continue rising forever, to bankroll their lifestyles.

During the last twenty-five years people, feeling wealthy because of their leverage, bought bigger and bigger homes and bigger and bigger SUVs, watched bigger and better commercials on ever bigger flat screen TVs, convinced they needed to go to bigger stores, load their SUVs and fill their homes with more stuff they didn't need. Thrift, common sense had become uncommon. The result, I believe, was an unprecedented kind of anxiety, caused by a nonsensical view that people could have whatever they wanted because somehow they felt they deserved it, even though deep down they knew it was wrong, that it was unsustainable, that this was not how the world was supposed to work, and in a backward attempt to inoculate their children from their mistakes, instead of teaching them not to do what they had done, they began pressuring them to keep up, to get better and better grades so they could get into better and better colleges, so they too could get bigger and better jobs so they could buy even bigger and better homes, cars, and TVs than even their parents had, as if that would be a solution to the high anxiety brought on by the vicious cycle of the age of conspicuous consumption. It has become not so much a matter of maintaining a standard of living as maintaining a standard of consumption. Is it any wonder our students are having so much trouble learning how to think? Why would they want to, when their role is so clearly defined? Acquire.

In *Against Happiness*, Wilson calls this a "mall mentality," a "love of bland comfort" that will one day "ironically get us exactly what we think we want, an utterly undifferentiated landscape where everything is exactly the same as everything else. This is a high price to pay for superficial bliss. The happy types want to boil the world down to quick contentment." The world becomes all the same and in it "one loses an immediate experience of what's most alive. In the name of American happiness, one comes to love ghostly ideas and wispy notions, moribund haunts and filmy grids." I think it is more insidious than that, more like a *maul* mentality. Ravage thy neighbor. Wilson's words can be read metaphorically though. They speak of my students, who favor the bland easiness of getting good grades over the jostling wilderness of their minds. They speak of how lost my students are in their ghostly ideas and wispy notions, such as "if I go to a good college I will get a good job and then I will make a lot of money which will make me happy." Their moribund haunts and filmy grids are their video games and cell phones and Facebook pages.

The fear which people felt at the beginning of the 80s—from the oil shortage, the hostage crisis, the deep recession, which bordered on hopelessness and even panic among those we trusted to lead us— turned into a single-minded relentlessness in the late 80s, an almost savage competitiveness that continues today. The traditional virtues of loyalty, respect, discipline, honesty, and perseverance crashed and burned into charred remains like the C-130 transport plane and the A-C Stallion helicopter in the Iranian desert during Carter's feeble, ill-fated rescue attempt, another setback, another humiliation: three Marines and eight airmen dead, the Ayatollah's henchmen taunting us that we had failed and would fail again. America's proud might, as in Vietnam, had once again revealed itself to be vulnerable and sus- pect. These events shaped the Gen Xers, the parents of my students. Along with their souls and sense of duty their dignity also died. Contemptuous, myopic self-interest filled the void. Greed became the only good (god?) they could believe in. They desperately sought to keep up with or surpass their fellow citizens by owning better and more things than they did. "Demoralize thy neighbor" became a war cry from a popular car commercial then and is every bit as applicable now. What they learned was that "the guy with the most toys wins," as a popular bumper sticker proclaimed. Disillusionment and rage set in, replacing temperance and civility. Many became not just cynical, sarcastic, and temporal, but downright mean. All the old bets were off. Those old adages of working hard and following your leaders and being patient and nice and you will succeed no longer were valid. Those myths had been debunked. From then on it was me first. The consequences are their kids.

The go-go nineties only heightened the frenzy. Ever increasing productivity—cost cutting, streamlining, tightening, the rise of the Internet—led like a crushing wave to more and more depersonalization. Robotic voices replaced receptionists. *Office Space*-like drones descended into their cave-like cubicles each morning to stare at wavering computer screens all day. People literally disappeared. They no longer called or wrote, they emailed.

By the early part of the decade I had started a business that thrust me into this brave new world. My company provided magazine publishers with a freelance sales team. We would sell advertising space for them strictly on a straight commission basis. No salaries, no benefits, no offices to rent, no travel and entertainment expense. We were an *out-source*. Efficient. Lean. The company grew quickly. Articles appeared about us in national trade journals, dubbing us a new breed of brokers, praising us as trendsetters. While my employees and I profited nicely we also caused a lot of people to be laid off. How ironic that only a decade earlier I'd found corrupt and abhorrent the Heublein executive's demand for a rate cut. Even I, a Boomer, had changed. I was an eager participant in the money game, no matter what the moral cost. It seemed I had no choice.

The economy sizzled, fueled by the tech boom. Many got rich. But as good as the times were companies didn't build for the future, focusing on long term or even yearly performance. It was quarterly and even weekly results they were after. Day to day performance was what counted. And here is why: many managers stopped caring about what was real, what was tangible, what was true. All that mattered was the illusion, the appearance, the perception. The venture capital guys, the investment bankers who primed the pump, wanted quick returns. Wall Street valued the stock of start-up Dot Com companies in the billions even though they had enormous costs and no revenue. To further their careers, all managers needed to do was be able to show that impressive growth was *projected*, so they could take credit, then they could jump for more money to the next job where the sleight of hand began all over again. It was akin to balancing on an ice flow until it began to melt, then leaping to the next one. Executives were amazingly successful at taking a job, staying at it just long enough—six months, nine months, at most a year—to accumulate enough "successes" to be able to pad their resumes. Then they would leave, and whoever replaced them knew the game so would blame the inherited mess on their predecessors, lie to garner a few new "successes,," then leave. Much of it was a charade. The employee turnover rate in companies we needed to call on in order to make our sales was so high that it seemed we were dealing with new people all the time. No one stuck around long enough for us to sell to. It was like hitting a moving target. The act of doing business had been rendered utterly undependable and unpredictable. What happened to a company in the long run didn't matter to many of its managers and executives because they wouldn't be there long. The company was something merely to use to further their own end. As a result the only way a company was valued depended on Wall Street. The model for a successful business changed. What the stock was worth, rather than where the company would be in five years, became the modus operandi. For generations we had been taught not to lie, cheat and steal, but about this time in business the exact opposite became the new rule: if you were quick enough on your feet you could make a lot of money flipping jobs or companies the way people had learned to flip real estate, regardless of the impact on the company or the consequences that would inevitably result or that what you were doing was morally and ethically questionable. Who cared about that stuff anymore? The bottom line was all that mattered. To put it another way, five hundred years after Machiavelli, we now seem to belong to a society where the ends justified the means.

10
"HAPPY AXE MURDERERS"

ALL THIS GREED, UNCERTAINTY, precariousness, fleetingness, false-ness, this get-ahead Darwinian competitiveness denuded parents of their confidence and reasonability to such an extent that they began an obsession with the one thing they had at a least some control over. No, it wasn't their moral, intellectual, or spiritual selves, often touted as inherited from the 60s, however pseudo righteous that time may have been. These inner selves were dead inside them, or stillborn. Their focus, strangely, became what they considered to be their greatest manifestation, the most obvious extension of their selfish selves, their *children*, and so they desperately wanted them not only to survive this mess they had created, but thrive in it, and the way to do that, they decided, was to push their kids headlong into an updated version of Wolfe's nightmare: "If I have one life, let me live it as a hedge fund manager." They were going to spare their children from the insanity, even if it meant adding to it. Parents of every generation generally want to provide more for their children than they had. That is human nature. But this time it was differ-ent. For Generation X, spawned during the Vietnam 60s, this would be an all-out different guerilla war, with soccer moms as first lieu-tenants. All those mothers who had gone off to work and suffered the dehumanizing pressures of postmodern productivity dragged themselves home at night to tackle yet another urgent project, the creation and marketing of another brand: Junior. Some, sensing something was missing, quit their high-power positions and came home for good, but brought with them and applied to their children the same results-oriented corporate urgency.

One February evening in 1996 when I got home after work my wife waved the current issue of *The New Yorker* at me.

"There is an article in here about Sera and Carol," she said.

"Who?"

"Two parents I know from school. You know them too."

She told me their last names. I vaguely recalled them. I sat down at the kitchen table and took the magazine from her.

She laughed and shook her head. "How many years have you been living here and you don't know your neighbors yet?"

I laughed back. She was right, and I wasn't exactly proud of it, my obliviousness. For the last twenty years it seemed all I had done at home was sleep; the rest of the time I was working. I saw that the article was by Mark Singer, the wonderful young writer whom I remembered and admired from my years working for *The New Yorker*. At least I knew he had moved to our town a few years ago. The article was entitled "Mom Overboard!"

"It makes sense now," my wife said.

"What does?"

"I was at Sera's house once when we were on the PTA together and there were vocabulary words pasted on colored index cards all over the walls, even on the back of the toilet seat."

"On the toilet seat?"

"She told me it was so that when her son was going to the bathroom he could study."

I laughed.

"The article describes the way they are raising their kids, like they are extensions of their careers, like they're projects that have to be completed on deadline," she said.

The subtitle was "What do power women who decide to quit the fast track do with themselves all day?"

I read the article, mainly because she seemed to want me to. But I was too preoccupied with my own concerns for it to mean much to me at the time, other than the obvious entertainment value of reading in a famous national magazine about people we knew. Okay, so they seemed a bit obsessive; I was excessively busy at my own work, probably even dangerously so, engaged in my own obsessive behaviors. The company I had started had grown nicely, but success can often spawn greed, and we were embroiled in a nasty partnership struggle over equity. Also, our clients were demanding more and more attention from us, insisting we not take on any more accounts, preventing us from growing any more, often expecting the impossible. They would insist, for example, that we sell a company an advertising program when the company had no marketing budget. No wasn't an option. Increasingly we were required to perform meaningless tasks, such as filing reports to show that a sale was imminent just so our clients could show the report to their bosses and hold them off long enough to jump ship for other jobs. It was almost as if we were involved in some sort of managerial Ponzi scheme. I had to travel relentlessly. It seemed all I did was put out fires. Fear ruled. A kind of absurd diminishing return had descended upon us.

Many years later, though, while writing this book, I recalled that treadmill I was running on, the nauseating spinning sensation, and I feel sorry for these parents of today who no doubt are caught up in the same swirling grind, which explains in large measure their own obsessive behavior. They too are scared; they too have little time to think these things through. I also recalled *The New Yorker* piece, found it online, reread it, and this is what I learned about our neighbors and their child-raising methods:

Less than a month after Sera's first child, also named Sera, was born, she was back at work as a high-powered architect, congratulated by her boss for her dedication. She had been the first woman in the firm's ninety-year history to be a project manager, which meant she supervised every phase of major construction projects. A little more than a year later little Sera's brother was born. A live-in nanny took care of the babies. Each day the nanny received explicit instructions meticulously listed by such categories as *Intake, Sleep, Alert*, with an hour-by-hour timeline. Even the babies' bowel movements were charted. Matisse prints hung on the bedroom walls and one of the nanny's duties was to direct the babies' attention to them for several minutes per day so their eyes would focus on the sharp edges. When the children weren't napping they were to be listening to classical music. As they grew older Sera would devise more complex charts and activities such as crayoning, stencils, Color-forms, Legos, puzzles, alphabet tapes, tools, all to stimulate visual, motor and auditory progress. Television wasn't allowed.

When her third child was born Sera quit her job, deciding that her training as an architect had given her the discipline to do "visual mapping inside my head." She could "see the path to her children's future engraved in her brain." So she got very busy in her new "job" building her children's lives.

She continued to draw lists because keeping pace with her instincts and impulses required plotting and budgeting. "I'm a designer," she said. "You have to design your children's future to a certain point. You have to create an environment for them to flourish. Sometimes I wake in the middle of the night and have an anxiety attack—that I've forgotten about this or that part of my child's brain."

Sera's master plan included swimming lessons for little Sera and William and competitions that resulted in trophies, dancing school at age three for Sera, who by four began to "specialize in jazz and tap," eurhythmics classes, and drawing and ceramics classes at the local arts center, although these had to be dropped because of "scheduling conflicts."

To compensate, big Sera made private arrangements with an instructor from the arts center who agreed to come to the house every couple of months to do projects with the children in an 'art room' that had been carved out of the basement play area. Little Sera was five and William was four when they learned to play chess—which they lost enthusiasm for after a few years. When William resumed playing, in second grade, Sera hired a private chess tutor, and he started winning tournaments. Skating lessons for William at three that led to hockey at six, then piano lessons: "The piano was in the kitchen, which enabled big Sera simultaneously to cook and observe little Sera as she practiced or worked with her teacher. "You have to be there with them to show your interest," she told me. "You have to make it pleasant."

The New Yorker article also followed Carol, another involved parent my wife knew from school who had quit practicing law, also to stay at home and see to the kids, even though she "missed the gamesmanship, the rituals of the Type A personalities meticulously sharpening their knives." But she was "conditioned to believe she could accomplish whatever she wanted."

> *The girls would learn to ride horses, she decided, so she arranged back-to-back half-hour lessons—with a particular teacher whose only available time slot was Wednesday from four o'clock to five. That her older daughter had a one-hour swim-team practice every Wednesday at four-thirty, as well as a Brownies meeting every other Wednesday at five-thirty, she regarded less as an inconvenience than an amusing challenge. That Carol herself was also the Brownie troop leader provided a bonus hurdle. The older girl wore her bathing suit under her riding clothes. "Pay attention, I might be micro-managing your lives now and turning you into little axe murderers," she told her daughters. "But trust me, you'll be happy axe murderers."*

I am curious about how these children turned out. Maybe I will call "big" Sera, ask her if I could contact "little" Sera who is now twenty-seven. After all this micro-managing has she become a cello player, a poet, a teacher or sculptor or painter or even a chef?

An inventor, an entrepreneur? An astronomer or philosopher? A surgeon? I somehow doubt it. The good news, I suppose, is that she probably isn't an axe murderer either. But whether I ever find out what became of little Sera or not, I see signs, glimpses, that things aren't quite right with so many other young people little Sera's age, who were similarly raised. They move back home, they have difficulty in relationships. Outside of work they have few interests. There's a tension, as if they are about to scream at any moment, a lack of imagination, an inability to converse. They have trouble trusting. Is it because thus far life has been all about them?

"In my next life, I'd like to be a man," Sera told Singer for his piece. "I wouldn't have any emotional attachment to anybody. I'd just have fun making money. And have a wife who takes care of everything."

I asked my own wife about that, wondering if this dilemma of our children not learning how to think has something to do with the evolving role of women.

"It's a part of it. You are a man," she said. "You can't understand what it is like for us, to be pulled like this. Even I can't understand what women must be going through these days. You and I were very lucky, the last of an era. I stayed home with the kids. I didn't want to work. I didn't have to go to work. Yes, women can pretty much do anything they want now, have anything they want, but the children still need to get raised. With everything women have achieved they still envy men, want what men have, want to do what men do. This has to affect the kids."

PART TWO
THEIR SCHOOLING

II
THE LIE

SOCRATES' MAIN TEACHING PRINCIPLE was that, while his students could voice their unexamined opinions, reason must rule in the end. He also believed that what is found within people is more fundamental than the facts of the external world. The inner life, Socrates said, in other words, *knowing*, is what leads to the practical activity of doing. It cannot be the other way around. For Aristotle the soul was the capacity for intelligence and character—"that within us in virtue of which we are pronounced wise or foolish, good or bad."

Socrates was Plato's teacher, Plato was Aristotle's teacher, and Aristotle's latter day disciple, Robert Hutchins, legendary University of Chicago President wrote in his *University of Utopia*: "The object of the educational system, taken as a whole, is not to produce hands for industry or to teach the young how to make a living. It is to produce responsible citizens." His perfect society centers on an educational system whose main purpose is "promoting the intellectual development of the people." He warns that education is becoming little more than a trade school, that it has shifted its focus from being educational to custodial. Hutchins' educational philosophy contends that good teaching leads to wisdom and reasoning on a universal scale. But education has veered toward something more relativistic than relevant and the results are inevitably disturbing: "The products of American high schools are illiterate; and a degree from a famous college or university is no guarantee that the graduate is in any better case. One of the most remarkable features of American society is that the difference between the 'uneducated' and the 'educated' is so slight."

In *Real Education: Four Simple Truths for Bringing America's Schools Back to Reality*, Charles Murray wrote, "The educational system is living a lie." Reflecting on Socrates, Plato and Aristotle, I fear he might be right. What becomes of most high school students by the time they graduate clearly reveals a wholesale absence of universality, wisdom and reasoning. Nothing about it resembles the "empirical good." At the start of any first period many of our senior classrooms are a third empty. One by one, the tardy seniors sleepily drift in, shuffle aimlessly to their desks carrying a coffee cup, cell phone, car keys, but no books. When asked to write, they need to borrow paper and a pen. The classroom door squeals open, another late senior straggles in. When the door opens again an administrator from the Assistant Principal's office appears, calling three or four seniors out into the hallway to hand out detention notices for cutting classes. After all the interruptions the teacher attempts to begin a discussion but the class lists indifferently. Few have done the homework. I have heard that during many of the final periods of the day, many seniors, deeply resenting having to be there, are more unruly, mean, and disrespectful than our worst 9th graders.

One of my colleagues, who teaches 12th grade Economics and Government, told me this the other day:

> *I had had these same kids as 9th graders in Global History. They all scored highly on the Regents. But today, in my lesson on economics I asked them to remember two philosophers representing different ideologies. Not one student could do it. I gave them hints. Socialism. He was German. First name Karl. Finally one kid yelled out Marx. The*

same thing happened with Adam Smith. How can they interact with history if they can't even remember basic facts?

They can't.

The same thing happens every year in my 12th grade English class. Only a few of my students can recall the titles, the authors, the characters and themes of the books they have read (or were supposed to have read) in 9th, 10th, and 11th grades, because the books meant nothing more to them than the grade they would earn on the test or paper, so they carry forward no lessons learned from Lady Macbeth or Holden Caulfield. What would the results be if those same state tests were administered just before these same kids graduated? They would fail. What does this imply about our system of teaching? Is this what educated eighteen-year-olds about to go off to college from an award-winning high school should look like: uninterested, uninteresting, bored and boring, brandishing stellar transcripts because they figured out how to do well on tests but essentially devoid of knowledge?

The word school derives from the ancient word Greek *schole*, which means leisure, but not the idleness too many of our students cherish. No. In fact *schole* means the opposite. It means the freedom to attend rigorously to "the business of being a man," of *working* at being human. This freedom comes from a true liberal education for its own sake and results in what Professor Wilson describes as a kind of melancholic joy, the opposite of our country's current "crass self-satisfaction, its wretched contentment. While the liberal arts education was once a studious course emphasizing the intrinsic value of education, it is now mostly a precursor to trade. American education is largely a preparation for American capitalism. The precise science of economics translates into sloppy personal supply and demand: I need a Beemer to be happy, and I shall provide the labor, whatever it is, to get it. That's finally it; happy types ultimately don't live their own lives at all. They follow some prefabricated script, some ten-step plan for bliss or some stairway to heaven. Doing so, they separate themselves from the present moment, immediate and unrepeatable and pressing. Driven by a desire for happiness at the expense of sadness, bolstered by capitalistic seeing and virtual reality, obsessed with abstraction and delusion, most of us are walking around half blind."

Deep heavenly melancholy, derived only from a true embrace of the learning of history, poetry, music, mathematics, philosophy, the natural sciences is our safeguard. It is what protects us from the political and commercial predators, because if one has really read and understood Aquinas and Melville one simply cannot become a corrupt inside trader because there will be things far more precious than money.

Schole is achieved through contemplation, through intellectual pursuits, by living a life of the mind, a mind free from material constraints. This is why Aristotle said, in his "Politics" that an education should never be vocational in nature, because "the meaner sort of artisan is a slave, not for all purposes but for a definite servile task." Yet it could be argued that the education we are providing our students is entirely vocational. It—the tests, the grades—serves only as the vocation of getting them into a "good" college so that they can then get a "good" job, therefore denying them the *schole* which would lead to their eventual joy and enslaving them to narrow minds.

Plato's cave allegory is about what it means to be educated. In the cave prisoners sit shackled so they must face forward, unable to turn around. Behind them a fire glows and before the fire lurk people who carry objects. The only reality the prisoners know is the shadows of these people and their objects as they pass before the fire. To be educated, the prisoners must be released from their blurred and distorted reality. They must first turn and face the fire. The light will hurt their eyes, but gradually they will adjust and realize the truth. Then they can ascend further, up and out of the cave to behold the sun. Have our students really come into the light by the time they graduate, or are they still chained in the cave believing the shadows are real? William Butler Yeats said that education is not the filling of a pail, but the lighting of a fire. I worry that we educators aren't even accomplishing the former, let alone the latter. Is it because we have capitulated to the obsessions of too many anxious parents who too often are unenlightened themselves, deluding ourselves that we are truly teaching when all we might really be doing is merely refereeing the game—the obstacle course our students are forced to navigate—keeping score so they can gather the necessary points to see who wins? Rather than produce young citizens who crave the light of learning our system seems more and more to result in young people who constantly turn away from learning toward ever new and improved ways of entertaining themselves. Has America become a land of bread and circuses, I ask them?

"What's that, Mr. B?" one student asks.

"It used to be a health food store in Boston," another replies. "I had to go there with my mom last summer when we were looking at colleges. She needed vitamins. It got taken over by Whole Foods."

Why don't they know? Is it because my allusion to the beginning of the end of the Roman Empire wasn't on their 9th grade Global Regents exam so they didn't have to know it? Or, worse, was it on the exam, and they studied it, but once the test was over, they forgot the importance?

So, bored, boring and indifferent, these seniors, like Vladimir and Estragon, wait for their Godot—the happy life—to materialize magically. What if this is how they spend their existence, forever pre-occupied with the destination, also deluded that the happiness they seek is but one or two stops away, perpetually asking "Daddy, are we there yet?" They don't know even by the time they are seniors that the end is never reached, that there is only the importance and beauty of the journey, and that joy comes from realizing this, and the reason is because they have only been taught to value the finished product, the results, instead of the importance of the process of accomplishing it.

"The seniors are worse than ever," I told my principal one spring. I've shared with him many times my feelings on the subject. "They just won't do a thing."

"They'll snap back into it next year when it counts," he said. Then he caught himself and looked at me knowingly. "But then that's your point, that they haven't learned the intrinsic value. Everything is extrinsic."

12
"A Spell They Cannot Resist"

In 1990, a year or so after starting my advertising sales company, about the same time many of my future students were being born, I was invited to a meeting with the editors of a famous glossy women's magazine after we'd been retained to develop new markets for it. The purpose of the meeting was for me to get a sense of their objectives and strategies and to introduce some preliminary ideas of my own. In their posh offices high above Madison Avenue I sat and watched the editor-in-chief review storyboards and photos for an upcoming issue. When she was finished she asked me to say a few words. I talked about the work our company did and said that with some supporting editorial material we believed we could position the magazine to appeal to other advertisers, such as financial and business-to-business advertising. One editor asked what kind of editorial support. I said that our targets, the big banks like Chase, the investment houses like Smith Barney, and the discount brokers like Schwab wanted to reach confident, successful decision makers who had money to invest. Editorial pointing to how independent and savvy the magazine's readers were on financial matters would demonstrate that the magazine reached this kind of discerning audience.

The editor-in-chief shook her head. "Have you read our magazine?" she asked.

I said I had.

"So you know its tone."

"It would need to be elevated," I said.

"Elevated," she repeated. "Mr. Baird, elevating is not what we do here. Look at this cover, these cover lines."

The cover typically featured a perfect looking woman, cleavage exposed. One of the cover blurbs invited readers to make their lovers' time in bed more satisfying.

"You are asking us to make our readers feel secure," she continued. "What we do here, quite successfully, is the exact opposite. We make our readers feel insecure, although they don't know it. They think we are empowering them, but we are really demeaning them. They will never look like this woman on the cover, dress like her, have sex like they imagine she does, so to console themselves they buy the products that are advertised here—the fashion, the cosmetics, the exercise machines, the shoes."

About the same time, Absolut Vodka's import rights were acquired by a marketing genius named Michel Roux who began playing on the word *absolute*, likening the brand to works of art through brilliant highbrow advertising. Once an obscure Swedish product selling only a few thousand cases in America, Absolut sales quickly soared to over a million cases. My company met with him many times as we pitched our magazines. He once told me that by law in America all vodka must be colorless, odorless, and tasteless, that essentially the liquor is just alcohol and water, so to distinguish it, he needed to trick consumers into paying twice as much for the product as it was worth. "So I cast a spell they cannot resist," he boasted.

Our children now buy vodkas that cost twice as much as Absolut.

In so many ways our 12th graders are the consequence of the enormous proliferation of the power of the media and the media's acumen in deception, distortion and lies, those shadows on the walls of Plato's cave. Our students not only don't resist the shadows, they embrace them, because they lack the critical thinking skills to question them. Instead of desiring the truth rather than distortions, instead of yearning for the light over the darkness, they scurry off to college with the sole purpose of getting a good job so they make enough money to join the consumer orgy.

"My dad is letting me drive the new Audi tomorrow!" one of my student's exclaims ecstatically. Another randomly asks me what kind of car I drive and when I tell him a Subaru he rolls his eyes disapprovingly.

It is not just the educational system that is living a lie. It is our entire culture, every bit as responsible for schooling our children as teachers are. And certainly more influential. Our dazed children reside in a dream world, a fantasy invented by marketing departments, yet not only don't parents guard them against it by teaching them to make informed decisions, they themselves eagerly participate in the con game and thereby encourage their children to join in. Lost in the maze of the media's advertising power, causing them to covet their neighbor's goods, our children then long only for a Mercedes of their own someday to justify their existence. "All the things my parents have," my students tell me when I ask them what they want most in life. This is the culture they bring to school with them, the culture that overrides all else. When pressed to identify the most important reason they are in school, if they could articulate it, they would have to say it is so someday they can buy the nice things the marketing sorcerers like Michel Roux sell them.

13
The College Cult

WHEN PEOPLE BELONG TO a cult it usually means they have a misguided or excessive admiration for a particular thing. Members of a cult eerily behave in the same way, are easily controlled, and often blindly recite faithful chants, again, like the Dark Ages.

Today, many parents and schools, because they are an extension of the parents, seem to belong to a college cult. And by default so do the kids.

What does a college cult look like? Instead of candle-lit chambers scented with incense and shadowy hooded figures, these anxious cult members assemble to gossip about teachers along soccer field side lines, crowd Kaplan SAT test prep centers, lurk behind closed doors in the guidance departments plotting on graphs children's likelihood acceptance. Like any cult, this one is obsessive, often dangerous, driven largely by fear, superstition, pressure to conform, a need to be "accepted," mindless devotion, and desperation to follow and not be left behind. Inevitably some smooth-talking guru (in this case, the elusive *good* college) lures his followers to some dubious Utopia. If your child does not get into a *good* college, his life will be a failure, goes the mantra. And as an added advantage, just look at all the magnificent resources these *good* colleges offer, such as this new ten million dollar fitness center featuring a state of the art climbing wall, all yours for a mere two hundred thousand dollars. Colleges today seem less like colleges and more like resorts, complete with course work that more resembles therapeutic, politically correct indoctrination than rigorous creative and scholarly pursuits. And so parents and schools, like all good cult members, are hard sold and willing to do whatever it takes to follow along, which often means sacrificing children's intellectual, ethical and moral well-being at the ceremonial altar, with students' apathy and inability to think critically as proof positive that in their fanatical zeal to get kids into *good* colleges, parents are willing to gut their kids' humanity.

I needed to be absent from school one day a few weeks ago to attend a conference. When I returned the next day, the teacher's assistant who had worked in my classroom for many years told me she had been my substitute teacher. She shook her head. I cringed. I had forgotten to warn my classes that I would be out and any misbehavior would not be tolerated. "How bad was it?" I asked.

"Bad."

What does this imply? What undeniable conclusion must be drawn from this? That what is inevitable, not just in an elementary school classroom but in 12th grade classrooms as well, is that as soon as the main authority figure leaves the classroom, replaced by a substitute teacher, the students will go wild, in this case, eighteen-year-olds who drive, who drink, who have sex, who go off to good colleges. The harsh undeniable implication is that they are not self-critical; they cannot reflect upon their actions and decipher them. Yes, they have been accepted into college, because for most of their lives this is all they have prepared for, at the expense of nearly every other human element, so that by the time they are "done," as they put it, they are still mere shells, heathens in many ways.

"What happened?" I asked.

She told me how they only reluctantly did the assignment I had left for them. When one young man finished, he waved it over his head and told her to come get it. Please bring it to me, she had asked. "No, sub. You come get it." This eighteen-year-old man will be attending Tulane University in the fall. Another boy got up and left the room, and when he returned and she asked him where he had been he said he had to go wee-wee, causing the class to laugh. Then he tipped his chair upside down and started to disassemble it. She asked him to stop and he told her she couldn't make him. He will be attending SUNY Binghamton.

For too many parents and high schools the colleges their students get into is like their own report card on how well they did parenting and teaching. But while they might get an A for these young men's acceptance into fine universities, they get an F for educating them with no scruples or character. Somewhere along the line, they messed up.

And it goes way back. Something as simple as play has a lot to do with forming character, yet unencumbered playtime has been rendered nearly obsolete in today's relentless push for good college acceptance. Think about the term *play date*. What it implies is that the play part—the act of inventing fun—gives way to an appointment, a scheduled, programmed predictable set of circumstances. It is a date. It is the exact opposite of what play is meant to be, free-form, spontaneous, creative, improvisational. Parents today are scheduling their children into submission, starving them of what they need to succeed in life in human terms. In a book called *Under Pressure: Rescuing Our Children from the Culture of Hyper-Parenting*, author Carl Honore suggests, "the brain in its relaxed state is more creative and makes more nuanced connections." He argues that children "need that space not to be entertained or distracted. What boredom does is take away the noise and leave them the space to think deeply, invent their own games, create their own distraction. It's a useful trampoline for children to learn how to get by." Denying children the opportunity to be free and instead cram their time with activities designed to package them for college acceptance also denies them the opportunity to encounter real-life situations that test and therefore develop character. The unsupervised backyard or playground can look a lot like what children will experience when they enter the grown-up world. Those Tulane and Binghamton-bound students might not have been so inclined to abuse the substitute teacher in my absence had they been exposed early in life to Jack London's natural law of club and fang, often present when kids are allowed to be off by themselves. What would they have become if, instead of being coddled all their lives, prepped for college, infused with false confidence, they had been left alone by their hovering parents and schools to fend for themselves? Probably they would have tried to bully someone, and like all bullies, they would have gotten beat up at some point, ending their abusive behavior forever, instilling in them the lessons that actions have consequences and you can't go around hurting people just because you feel like it.

Why then do parents and schools prevent children from growing socially and developing character, smothering them, which is so obviously detrimental to their long-term well-being, to their ability to think independently? Perhaps this cult-like behavior emanates not from their interest in the child's human success but from their own need for reassurance that they have done the best job possible of providing their children with the path to material success, from their craving for the prestige of acceptance letters from good colleges.

Sustainable material success—having a nice home in a nice town, maybe a second home, a club, nice cars, taking nice vacations, going out to dinner at nice restaurants, 64-inch flat screen TVs—are all things we want, and there is nothing wrong with that. But how do we acquire them? From my experience this kind of success is like a recipe. First you need the ingredients, then you mix them according to how much the recipe calls for. The ingredients list, from my experience, looks this:

Fortitude
Ingenuity

Integrity
Intelligence
Luck
Talent
Courage
Compassion
Discipline
Ambition
Competitiveness
Personality
Perseverance
Pedigree

While we may disagree on the proportions—what amounts of each ingredient should go into the mixing bowl to guarantee a savory result—we should agree that the least important ingredient is pedigree, and by pedigree I mean the name of the good college or university someone attends. This is America, after all. Yes, of course, pedigree (and nepotism and politics and favoritism) might help someone land a job, but it has nothing to do with someone doing the job well enough to succeed at it and then succeed again and again as a career unfolds.

If this is so obvious, then why do today's parents and schools insist that getting into a good college—pedigree—is the most important ingredient on the list, so important to them, in fact, that they are willing to omit so many of the other ingredients as they raise and educate children and propel them toward their futures? Because it is a form of winning, and in America today winning is all that matters, as everyone now wrongly believes. What people don't seem to know is that winning often becomes losing. Success does not come from knowing *what* you want to be—say an investment banker or sports agent—then becoming one; success does not come from knowing what things in life you want, then earning the money to buy them. Success comes from knowing *who* you want to be, brave or cowardly, kind or mean, honest or dishonest, then becoming that *good* person.

In another book I read called *Derailed,* Tim Erwin studies the catastrophic failures of six CEOs of major corporations, concluding that all leaders, whether of Fortune 500 companies, or middle managers or of families, fail for a similar reason, mainly because of a lack of character, humility in particular. Instead of humility, these failed CEOs exuded excessive confidence, which became reckless arrogance. Yet parents and schools eschew humility, instead they favor false self-esteem. No one would ever accuse my 12th graders of being too humble. On the other hand, no one would ever deny they are arrogant. The one character trait found in all long-term successful human beings is humility. Erwin "believes that these leaders suffer from failures of character that are common to each of us, even the most capable individuals. Deficits in authenticity, humility, self-management, and courage become more dangerous as we take on more leadership, and can cause us to ignore glaring signals that might otherwise save us from catastrophic demise." As I write this, the respected, charismatic CEO of Hewlett-Packard was just fired for filing false expense reports involving an alleged tryst with a young attractive consultant. News of his removal caused HP to lose $9 billion in stock market value.

The parents and schools of the college cult begin inculcating children at such an early age that by the time I first get to see them it is almost too late. Shortly after that first day teaching, when a mother cornered me about needing to give her son special attention, something else happened I won't forget. It was the same tenth grade class. I began introducing the first text we would be reading, "Romeo & Juliet." As I stood in front of them and talked, they listened intently. The lesson was on figurative language. This went on for a few minutes or so until I noticed that these 10th graders hadn't so much as opened their backpacks. Their desks were bare. They just sat there staring at me. I wondered what was going on, if I was doing something wrong. I had never taught before. I was fifty years old. It was as if I had been beamed into this world from another galaxy. Then it occurred to me.

Slowly, I reached for a piece of chalk. As I did this, as if by remote control, the students reached under their desks and began to pull out pens and paper. I put the chalk to the board. They put their pens to the paper. I wrote *Shakespeare's use of figurative language.* They copied the words verbatim.

Pun, I wrote

Pun, they wrote.

A play on words, I wrote.

A play on words, they copied.

Oxymoron, I wrote.

They started to copy the word.

"Okay, stop," I insisted. "What is going on here?"

They looked at other.

"You are all busy taking notes now that I am putting them on the board, but you weren't when I was talking. Why?"

From the puzzled looks on their faces, I could tell they didn't understand where I was going with this.

"Because there will be a quiz," a boy finally said.

"I didn't say anything about a quiz," I responded.

"But you wrote it on the board. That means there will be a quiz and this stuff will be on it."

"But you weren't taking notes when I was talking."

"When teachers only talk it means it won't be on the quiz."

"Were we supposed to?" another student asked nervously.

"The only thing you are supposed to do is learn," I said.

"But you didn't tell us to!"

"Does this mean there will be a quiz?" another boy called out frantically, suddenly lurching for his backpack.

"If there is no quiz and you don't write it on the board and we don't take notes, will that count as a grade?"

"What if we do take notes even though there is no quiz, can we get extra credit?"

"If there is no quiz then why would we take notes, if there is no extra credit?" someone else added.

I held up my arms to stop the whirr of panicked questions.

It was the same with the other two periods of 10th graders I taught that day.

The other course I taught that first year was 11th grade English, where things were very different. While the 10th graders were still innocent to a degree, having no idea why they were in high school other than to get good grades, which meant giving back to their teacher what they predicted he wanted, motivated primarily by pleasing their parents, the 11th graders had become complicit and cynical. A palpable contempt had set in, the way they slouched in their seats, the way they openly cheated. Instead of eager hands waving when I posed a question, they would sit there and smirk, even if they knew the answer or had an opinion. My biggest struggle was getting them to participate, mainly because they no longer cared. What they had learned in no uncertain terms was that a few of them would get into good colleges, but the rest wouldn't, and it was clear who was who. Those who had been placed into the 11th grade AP English class and other advanced courses had "won" the game while the "masses," the "middle" remained behind, resigned to take my regular English 11 course. What this meant to them was that they were not good enough. Success had passed them by. The race had already been run and won and they had lost. But they reacted to this perceived loss as only GenMe'ers could, by assuming there was something wrong with the system, not them. They had way too much self-esteem for that. Therefore, for the most part, by the time they had become 11th graders my students had learned to hate school. It was their defense. How could they like something that denied them? These were ordinary kids, nice kids, mainly, B and C students, essentially representing 80 percent of the student body, the real deal, so whatever they had become offered a look into what we were accomplishing as a school. I asked them why they hated English. Their responses were hard-boiled:

"The books are boring."

"I hate reading."

"We are forced to overanalyze everything."

"The teachers always tell me I am wrong."

I asked them about their other subjects

"At least with math or science you know exactly what is expected of you."

"It's either right or it's wrong."

"You get more credit for them."

I asked them what they meant.

"Your GPA. Those classes are weighted higher than social studies and English."

"Who cares?" one boy shrugged. "What's the point anyway? We're never going to use any of this again."

Something was rotten in the state of Education.

But during my free periods when I would walk through the halls and peek in the rooms of my colleagues who taught chemistry or biology or math, there they were, my students, eyes glued forward diligently scribbling the notes the teacher wrote on the board. They actually looked like they were trying to learn.

It took me a few years to realize that most were just pretending.

Our children are initiated into the college cult, introduced to the "make or break" importance of getting into a good college, almost from the time they are born, so that by the time they enter high school they are rigid faithful followers, but by the time they are upperclassmen they know the game, one way or the other. They are either insiders or outsiders. Those who have made it onto one of the accelerated tracks, such as AP, have mastered getting good grades and realize that "learning" is nothing but a means to an end. Those who haven't made it declare the educational system to be a scam and a waste of their time, so they go through the motions but have given up on learning. The cause? Parents begin plotting and planning their children's futures before their children have learned the alphabet. Schools track. When all a child hears on a daily basis is the consequentiality of getting into a good college, the child's sense of the rest of the world narrows. From age three these children see life through one lens, college acceptance, which necessarily blocks out or at least distorts any activity or interest, dream or passion, which is construed as extraneous. Worse, it makes a vocation of their interests. Worse, it destroys any desire for authentic learning.

My wife came home the other day to tell me about a Girl Scout meeting that was held in her art room. The district often uses her room for extracurricular activities and she had to stay late to work on a lesson, so she overheard the leader tell the girls they needed to do a better job accumulating more badges. They were falling behind their quotas. My wife said there was no discussion of the girls' interests in certain subjects or activities, only the number of badges they should be earning. A child's interest in clarinet becomes merely a way to impress admissions directors. These interests aren't interests at all, but means to an end rather than a rich and sublime end unto themselves. The love of music is no longer enough. In fact, it's impractical and discouraged. Don't even think of majoring in *that* in college? Where do you think *that* will lead you? What children learn, in no uncertain terms, is that they have been put on this earth for one reason: to accumulate enough merit badges to get into good college. This is their culture, the only culture they know.

The New York Athletic Club has a beach club located in our town. It has a wonderful 50-meter saltwater pool, tennis courts, a yacht club, and expansive lawns overlooking the Long Island Sound. Before she became a teacher my wife enjoyed being there, watching our kids play. It was how we spent our summers. I would catch the 5:45 out of Grand Central and meet them and we would sit out on the grass with a glass of wine and watch the sun set and the sails of the boats out on the sound turn pink while our daughters sat on the blanket, their skin puckered from being in the water all day. In those days, not many people from our town belonged. The club's members were mainly from the Bronx or Manhattan. When we moved there in the late 70s most of our neighbors were older, mainly Italian, their homes grand but in need of repair. It was why we could afford to live there. The school's playground up the street was always busy with moms and dads pushing their kids on the swings. But with the ascent of Wall Street, young corporate lawyers, traders, and investment bankers poured in. Home values soared along with the property taxes. They renovated the homes. The playground soon featured kids pushed on swings by Jamaican nannies. They joined the club. And my wife was their children's art teacher. Then I had to beg her to go over with me because she hated running into parents. But one beautiful early June evening I prevailed and she agreed. We took what had once been our favorite spot out on the lawn. Within a minute a mother spotted her, marched over and interrupted us.

"Stacy received only a *Satisfactory* on her Impressionism project," she said. "We expected an *Excellent*. Do you think we should get her a tutor this summer? And what more could you, as her teacher, be doing to make sure she is achieving at the highest possible level?"

My wife shielded her eyes and looked up at her, but before she could answer, the mother's cell phone blared. She scurried away answering it.

"Stacy's is only a first grader," my wife said sadly. "I need to leave, now, before she comes back."

Did this mom really want her daughter to know about Monet or was she already busy patrolling the locales of our town hoping to spot a teacher to browbeat, positioning Stacy to compete to win some later contest so she can pad her resume? Someday Stacy and her mom will wake at 4 a.m. to drive food to a homeless shelter, but would they, if their charity couldn't be added to Stacy's list of extracurricular activities, if she didn't "get credit" for it? The result will be that, like too many of my students, Stacy will grow up jaded, unable to enjoy the beauty of the Impressionists, perhaps even hating art, the same way she will learn to hate music, mathematics, history, and literature because they have been thrust at her as a forced means to the end of getting into a good college so she can get a good job. She will be one of the 98 percent who never visit a museum. And with all that money she will make she will walk the Earth, her one shot at existence, empty and unaware. I wanted to tell Stacy's mother to relax, to reassure her that everything would be okay, but she was still busy on her cell phone. We left, and my wife has not been back to the club since then.

In an eye-opening book called *Death of the Grown-Up: How America's Arrested Development is Bringing Down Western Civilization*, Diane West writes that "responsibility and restraint are not only bedrock virtues of liberal civilization, they are also hallmarks of the grown-up. Without them, civilization becomes anarchic, and the grown-up slips and regresses." Why then the urgency, the "irrational exuberance," causing parents like Stacy's mom to lose control over the basic codes of human decency? Yes, acceptance to a good college, but where is the evidence to support that acceptance to a good college is worth all the havoc, disruption, even destruction it can cause? What does *good* mean? Have parents thought this through? Are they even capable of thinking? While there is evidence that an undergraduate degree from Dartmouth, for example, can often provide a graduate an initially higher salary at his first job than a degree from, say, Hillsdale College, there is absolutely no data to suggest that "getting into" one of the most selective or highly selective colleges guarantees a successful *career*, whatever that means. Making lots of money, I suppose. It certainly doesn't guarantee happiness. Just because you might start any race with a slight lead doesn't mean you will win. Winners often come from behind. And what is a winner? One apt definition comes from my youngest daughter who likes to say that winners are people who don't cheat, and cheaters are people who don't win. Life, like a long race, unfolds slowly, with myriad detours, truly an obstacle course rich with possibility, unlike high school.

One of my students attended Duke University. He told me that in one of his economics classes he had a professor who had been in business many years and had started many companies. The professor told the class he would never hire a Duke graduate because its students came out of school thinking too highly of themselves, thinking they knew everything simply because they had attended a prestigious university.

When I ran a small company, each year I would hire two or three new college graduates, but I made a point of going to second, even third tier schools, avoiding the fancy ones altogether, because I wanted someone who was hungry and willing to learn.

I really enjoy reading the *Wall Street Journal,* not so much for the business reporting because I'm long gone from that world, but because of the little editorial gems and off-beat reviews I often find on books, opera, restaurants, all kinds of topics you won't find anywhere else. One day I happened upon a piece by one of my favorite columnists, Eric Felten, entitled "Those Little Lists: What College Rankings Tell Us," in which he took on *U.S. News & World Report's* annual ranking of universities and colleges: "I suspect that the abiding interest in school rankings reflects our conviction that college is less about getting an education than getting ahead...Perhaps most telling is an interview with a Princeton undergrad who says: 'I think the biggest thing about coming here is that once you graduate you go into an amazing network of alumni who can set you up.'"

The word *student* derives from the Latin: to direct one's zeal at, as in one who directs zeal at a subject. In its widest use, student is used to describe anyone who is *learning.* Yet being set up is what this student considers to be "the biggest thing" about Princeton. This means, of course, that he is graduating from one of the world's great universities fundamentally unable to reflect, essentially unable to think.

I also look at *Forbes* magazine once in a while, although not as much as I used to, and saw recently that it had come out with its own very different kind of *Best Colleges* rankings based on such criteria as how good a college is at helping its students finish on time, the number of awards won by students and professors; "students' satisfaction with their instructors; average debt upon graduation;

and postgraduate vocational success as measured by a recent graduate's average salary and alumni achievement." For those blinded by
the lure of prestige, the results might be surprising: Harvard is not
number one. The United States Military Academy at West Point is.
In fact, only four of the Ivy League schools make the top 25. Washington University was 45th, far behind Wabash. Penn (83rd) placed
lower than Hillsdale College (76th), Dartmouth was 98th behind St.
Mary's. The most popular choices among my students didn't do so
well either: Ithaca was 145th, a hundred places lower than DePauw.
University of Michigan was 200th, Cornell 207th, Delaware 217th,
Penn State 324th, NYU 355th, Maryland 387th, George Washington
429th, Northeastern 593rd. Our kids practically kill to get into SUNY
Binghamton, as if it were some panacea, yet *Forbes* ranked it 202nd.
And Geneseo, now considered the most prestigious SUNY school,
ranked 399th behind Albany, 385th, but ahead of Buffalo, 468th.

"If college is primarily about securing a profitable future," Felten
asks, "why not just judge schools on that criterion? That's the thinking behind a recent addition to the campus ranking follies: *Forbes*
magazine has produced a rating system specifically designed to
gauge get-ahead-ability." In conjunction with Payscale.com, *Forbes*
also ranks the Top Colleges for Getting Rich, which include the likely suspects: Dartmouth, Princeton, Stamford, Yale, MIT, Harvard,
UPenn and Notre Dame. But interestingly they were followed by
Polytechnic Institute of NY, and Worcester Polytechnic. RPI is tied
for 14th place with Cornell and Georgetown. Brown comes in at 19th.
At 12th UC Berkeley is the only public university to make the top
twenty. But what is also interesting is that while Harvard and Penn
rank highly in producing potentially rich people, they score relatively lowly (98th and 83rd) on *Forbes* list of Best Colleges, below both
Hillsdale College and Macalester College. (Brown comes in at 72nd.)
Does this kind of inconsistency deserve such avid devotion?

Parents' urgency then, often bordering on panic, seems not to
be so well thought out at all. Herd mentality rarely is. For example,
if only one public university made the top 20 list of schools most

likely to make their children rich, why do so few of my students' parents pay for them to attend private schools? Yes, of course, the expense. But if the parents' no holds barred mission is to provide their children with a lucrative career path, why haven't they saved enough money to pay for it? While the parents seem capable of doing everything possible, to the point of behaving outrageously, to enable their children to get good grades, in the end many don't seem willing to pay the price for the most obvious advantage. These same parents drive Mercedes and Audis and send their kids to camp every summer and buy them new cars and pay for their insurance. Do they know that one of the most important things they can do to help their kid get into a good school is check *No* on the application next to the line that asks of them if they are in need of financial aid? A customer who pays full price is always the most desirable customer, in spite of what the colleges claim about blind admissions. Running a university is big business. But when it comes to the bill, these Me Decade parents selfishly want it both ways: they want their child to get into a good college yet they want someone else to pay for it. So, again, perhaps these parents' top priority isn't their children after all, but themselves. If parents are primarily interested in sending their children to college for career advancement instead of for the enlightenment of an education, yet falter when it comes to making the necessary sacrifice, then perhaps they too have not been educated, become wise—which is the result of a true education—at least in the Aristotelian sense. Perhaps they too are victims of our ever wavering, diminishing educational standards.

Here is something else to consider: "A growing number of students accepted by the nation's top colleges are postponing their long anticipated freshman year," writes reporter Tracy Jan in a *Boston Globe* piece entitled "Worn-Out Students Choose a Timeout." It seems that after all the stress of preparing for and then applying to these colleges, these accepted students now don't want to go, at least not right away? "The students say they desperately need a timeout after spending their high school years building impeccable credentials for entry into selective colleges. 'I was consumed with doing well and didn't sleep a lot the last two years,' said Gaby Waldman-Fried. 'I would have five or six hours of homework almost every night. The last thing I wanted to do was more school.'" Instead of enrolling in college Ms. Waldman-Fried will be volunteering at an organic farm in Maine. "'As the anxiety that surrounds the admissions process has increased, getting into X college has become an end in itself rather than a means to an end,'" says Robert Clagett, admissions dean at Middlebury College. Of course nothing butters the bread of admissions deans like Mr. Clagett better than all this anxiety. "Backpacking through Europe remains popular, but admissions deans report that more students are choosing internships in their academic fields of interest in hopes of getting a leg up in a down economy. Whole cottage industries have sprung up to help match students, for a fee, to the right gap year experience as the practice becomes more prevalent. Harvard has seen a 33 percent increase in the number of those taking gap years over the last decade." The gap year is something I heartily encourage my students to consider, because I know too well how unready many are. "I was pretty driven and high-strung and hard on myself to get straight A's," says Victoria Thomas, an MIT junior, who says her gap year was the best thing she has ever done. "Now I want to do well because I want to really understand what's going on in my classes and not just taking the test to get good grades."

There is a website called Whatwilltheylearn.com, which describes itself as a guide to what the college rankings don't tell you. It provides information on whether colleges make sure their students learn the things they need to know, outside their chosen majors. Of course my students have never heard of it. Nor have our guidance counselors. I spent some time on it:

"Even as our students need broad-based skills and knowledge to succeed in the global marketplace, our colleges are failing to deliver. Topics like US government or history, literature, mathematics, and economics have become mere options on far too many campuses. Not surprisingly, students are graduating with great gaps in their knowledge—and employers are noticing. According to a recent study, only 31 percent of college graduates can read and understand a complex book. In another recent survey, only 24 percent of employers thought graduates of four-year colleges were "excellently prepared" for entry-level positions. College seniors perennially fail tests of their civic and historical knowledge. Our colleges have largely abandoned a coherent, content-rich general education curriculum. If our colleges don't get general education right, students will get a spotty education that will not prepare them for a life well lived."

This is what the college cult blindly strives for.

What grades did the elite schools earn when the standard of making sure their "students learn what they will need to know" was applied? Princeton and Dartmouth scored Cs; Harvard, Penn and Georgetown scored Ds. Brown, Cornell and Yale scored Fs. The colleges and universities favored by many of my high school's best students fared similarly: Washington University, F; University of Michigan, D; American, C; George Washington, C; Penn State, D; SUNY Buffalo, D. The A list? Baylor University, Brooklyn College, Hunter College, Texas A&M, University of Arkansas, and University of Texas-Austin, colleges my students would never even consider applying to, let alone attending.

It could be argued that Brown and Harvard and other *most competitive* colleges don't need to require their students to take general courses in literature, history, economics, language, sciences and mathematics because these "smart" kids have already "mastered" these core disciplines in high school. Yes, many of these students have been *taught* these subjects, but, because of the cult of college that emphasizes, reinforces, even mandates "playing the game" to get into these good colleges, the students haven't *learned* these subjects at all. Instead they have only *used* them. What isn't arguable is that these colleges offer a pedigree: what does it matter if your son or daughter goes through life not knowing enough about or even having a relationship with literature, art, science, mathematics, history, right vs. wrong, good vs. evil, as long as his alma mater has an active alumni group to help set him up with his career.

Another book I suggested to my students for their independent reading, and what started out to be the most popular choice, was Craig Brandon's *The Five Year Party*. But of course instead of playfully documenting the debauchery that goes on at most campuses, which my students eagerly await, Brandon casts serious aspersions on the myth of college, arguing:

> *College campuses have been deliberately transformed into havens of adolescent hedonism, where student misbehavior has become the norm and college administrators allow it because they don't want their student customers to take their tuition money somewhere else. In an all-out effort to attract and retain as many student customers as possible, administrators have given students exactly what they said they wanted: more parties and less education. Dining halls have been enlarged and reinvented as gourmet food courts and campuses have been tricked out with hot tubs, climbing walls, workout centers, water parks, and wide-screen television sets. Dormitories have been torn down and replaced with luxury condominiums. The hard work that used to be required has been eliminated because students said they didn't want to do it.*
>
> *Focused on increasing their revenue stream, today's party school colleges squeeze as many students as possible onto their campuses at the highest tuition they think they can get away with for the longest possible amount of time. Where does all that tuition money go? Only one dollar out of five is spent on instruction. These unnecessary frills push the costs up year after year, while national surveys show that students are learning less and less, and many of them are functionally illiterate. Party schools operate more like adolescent resorts than higher education*

institutions. Students get away with doing as little work as possible while still earning As and Bs. Half of the freshmen class drops out before graduation."

Brandon offers some chilling statistics: 44 percent of college students are classified as binge drinkers; 599,000 college students are injured yearly as a result of alcohol abuse; 1700 people are killed each year by intoxicated students; 20 percent of female students are victims of rape or attempted rape; college students spend eight hours studying and attending classes per week; 31 percent of college seniors can understand a newspaper editorial; 50 percent of college seniors can interpret a simple table; college tuition has increased 439 percent since 1982; the average amount of student loans graduating seniors must pay off is $23,000; and 50 percent of recent graduates move in with their parents. Even though Brandon's excellent book began as a popular choice, largely because of its title, once my students discovered it wasn't about kegs, they quickly abandoned it, especially once it began challenging their perceptions.

Another choice my students had for their independent reading was *Higher Education?* by Professors Andrew Hacker and Claudia Dreifus. None of my students attempted this one. Its subtitle must have given it away: *How Colleges are Wasting our Money and Failing Our Kids.* The book describes, among other disturbing trends, the dramatic increase of non-tenured, adjunct and graduate student teaching that goes on in undergraduate classrooms. For example, when I graduated from college in 1973, less than 40 percent of college teachers were temporary instructors; now that rate is 70 percent. About America's dream school, the authors, write: "The mediocrity of Harvard undergraduate teaching is an open secret of the Ivy League." Instead they recommend such schools as Ole Miss, Cooper Union, Berea College, Arizona State, and Western Oregon University, colleges none of our students have ever applied to.

Loren Popes' *Colleges That Change Lives* was another choice but the students who attempted it complained it was boring, even though, as Pope writes, "this book will help youths of many levels of different academic aptitude find catalytic colleges that will help them find themselves, raise their aspirations, and empower them. In doing so it will free them from our system's obscene obsession with academic aptitude, which does not determine achievement, satisfaction with life, or the merit of a human being." Of the 40 colleges he researched and recommends, only one, Clark, has ever received an application from a student from my high school.

This is what the college cult causes. Why don't we seem to care that for an enormous, life-altering cost, our children will drink until they vomit and when they do attend class, which is less and less often, they won't be "taught" by the professors we are paying for, learning little if anything that will allow them to be citizens of the larger world? Because we've been indoctrinated. All that matters is the diploma. This is the kind of dogma that characterizes the college cult. "Colleges have been redesigned for partying rather than studying," Brandon writes. "And parents and taxpayers, the people who pick up the tab for the five-year party never question the value of higher education, even when the price increases at three times the inflation rate."

As an antidote, parents might want to consider that the jobs their children think they are preparing for won't even exist ten years from now. Advances in technology, business, health and most segments of the global economy are changing at such a fast pace that whatever our students think they are learning today won't apply tomorrow. Instead of blindly competing for grades, what our children need to develop is the primal ability to adapt. The Bureau of Labor Statistics reports that the average number of jobs workers have between the ages of 18 to 42 is eleven. Employers increasingly cite that a basic knowledge of writing, reading comprehension, mathematics, science, and a foreign language is crucial to the meet the challenges of constant change, yet all our students seem interested in pursuing is some mythical good job that probably won't be around for long.

Talking about this in class the other day, I called on three students to tell us what they planned to study in college.

"Pre-med," Zoheir said.

"Is your father or mother a doctor?" I asked.

"My father."

"What do you know about medicine?"

He shrugged. The class laughed.

"What kind of car does your father drive?"

"A BMW 750i turbo."

"It seems you know a lot about that."

He shook his head, beaming with anticipation of his own Beemer someday.

"Let me ask you a question: have you ever thought about what practicing medicine will have become by the time you are ready to do it, ten or twelve years from now?"

He looked at me strangely, not even understanding the question, let alone having ever raised it himself.

"Our current health care system is unsustainable. It is going to break, smash, come crashing down. It won't look anything like it does now. It is quite possible that when you are ready to be a doctor, doctors will be middle level government employees, overworked and underpaid. Have you been following the national debate we are having on your chosen profession?"

He shrugged again. The class laughed again.

I called on another student.

Teacher

Accountant.

Engineer, because my parent read that that is a field with lots of job openings.

"Maybe now, but what about later, when you are ready?"

None of them had thought about any of this. They hadn't thought, period. This is what happens to kids in the college cult.

Another thing that happens to them is that somehow they seem to learn a whole brave new worldly way of behaving.

Because I'm a ski coach (and not getting any younger) I get banged up now more than I used to, and my latest injury was a torn hamstring. My friend, Chris, owns a string of physical therapy clinics specializing in athletes. The other night after rehab he and I were talking and I mentioned my research on the Gen Me'ers.

"I have an employee," he said, "a young lady who has worked for me for three years as an assistant trainer. She graduated with a degree in physical therapy. She is working on her advanced license. She didn't show up for work during those last two snowstorms. She assumed we would be closed. Never called. Just assumed. We were understaffed badly."

"How old?" I asked.

"Twenty-seven. To reprimand her I asked her to make the daily calls to our clients reminding them of their appointments and she said she wouldn't do it, that it was below her. Usually our office staff people do it. I made her, but then I found out she only called about half of them, then stopped."

"Why do you think that is?" I asked him.

"Some bizarre sense of entitlement, like the world revolves around them. I call it bizarre because it is so undeserved. I am only thirty-four," he said, "not that much older, but even in that short age difference, I already see such a difference. A lot of the day to day routine of living is beyond these young people," he said.

"You are a small business owner. Your business is growing, expanding, in a dynamic field, one I understand that is increasingly popular as a major in college, physical therapy, sports medicine. You are offering these young people the golden opportunity, experience, training, a career path. The good job they have always strived for. They could even own their own someday."

"But too many of them, once they are here, they don't know what to do with it. I have another employee, a young man. I had to fire him and he could have been good too. He repeatedly called in sick. The last time he did it I decided to go on Facebook. He and I had *friended* each other. And there on his Facebook page he was bragging how he had called in sick to work to go snowboarding. Didn't he know? I had access to his page, for God's sake. It is almost like they are oblivious."

As unlikely as acceptance at most elite colleges and universities is, parents push anyway, possibly fearing their children will succumb to some low-level job when they could have been bankers or lawyers. But the failure of these young employees came from lack of character, not lack of prestigious degree, and that same failure awaits anyone without character, no matter what college or university they graduate from. But parents and schools like mine push on anyway, emphasizing results over process, demanding good grades instead of good character, in spite of the evidence that the education their children would receive might be suspect, even inferior to the education they would receive at a less "prestigious" college. If, statistically, your son has almost no chance of being admitted, and the education he would receive is questionable, why ruin him in the process? Just because Junior hit two home runs in the Little League all-star game doesn't qualify him to play for the Yankees someday, does it? But then again Gen Xer parents were raised to believe they could have it all. This belief is so unsubstantiated and unreasonable that it is naïve and therefore forces the conclusion, once again, that their drive is not so much about doing what is right for the child but about doing what is right for them. What will people think of me if my daughter is the only one of her friends who doesn't have the latest Blackberry? What will it say about me as a parent if a good college doesn't accept my son? Schools ask a similar question: what will our reputation be if a high percentage of our graduates don't attend the best colleges? Even though the education offered there might be flawed and flagrantly overpriced. This all leads to the same end: a college cult that caters to the needs of parents and schools more than the needs of kids.

What children absorb, I think, is a belief in doing what is right for them, instead of doing what is right. I've discovered in my longish life that the two are rarely the same. Yet relativism has pretty much eradicated that quaint notion.

A few summers ago my daughter was offered a job taking care of a young couple's two- and four-year-old children—a boy and a girl—during their family vacation in Montauk. It was explained that Lesley would get up with the kids each morning, usually around six. She would give them breakfast, drive them to the beach, play constructively with them until lunch, bring them home, feed them, take them back to the beach, play with them, read to them, bring them back home for dinner, feed them, read to them some more, bathe them and then put them to bed. The mother was very clear that my daughter's duties would last well into the evening because she and her husband would be busy. The pay was $250 for the week. We talked it over and agreed it didn't sound like a very healthy situation. Isn't the point of family vacations to be with your kids? When Lesley declined the offer, the mother asked her if she had any friends who might be interested.

A few weekends ago this summer, my wife and I were in Vermont hoping to enjoy a quiet meal at a popular hangout near Stratton Mountain called the Outback. We sat at the bar and ordered pints of beer, a burger and pasta. Seated around us were a few people we recognized, golf school pros, other ski instructors. It was very much an adult scene. In fact, this was more a saloon than a restaurant, darkened, the Red Sox game blazing from flat screen TVs. But at one of the tables nearby three forty-something mothers sat swirling their chardonnay while their children played pool. It was obvious they weren't locals but second homeowners from Fairfield or Westchester, like us. With them though were their five or six children, a combination of boys and girls ranging in ages from nine to twelve. But they weren't really *with* them. Instead their kids, who had finished eating, ran around the saloon as if it was their personal playground, conspicuously loud, banging balls on the pool table, constantly bothering the busy bartender.

"The white ball is stuck," one boy with his baseball cap on backward said interrupting her as she took a drink order from one of the waitresses.

"The coins won't go in," another kid said a few minutes later.

"I need change," a girl little said, waving the ten-dollar bill her mother had just given her.

The mothers, obviously friends, couldn't have cared less. They were enjoying their time together, leaning in over their wine, occasionally laughing. The tough duty of issuing discipline to their misbehaving children was just not something they were interested in, or worse, didn't feel was necessary. Even in the bar room din, I could overhear part of their conversation. One mother was explaining to the other the importance of picking just the right summer camp for the kids. A performing arts camp, for example, would show her child's interests beyond academics. It wasn't too soon to begin building a "narrative" for colleges.

I got up and went over to the pool table.

"Hey, guys," I said unthreateningly.

The kids looked up wide-eyed.

"Can you keep it down? I'm trying to eat my dinner over here."

Their expression told it all. It was as if I had spoken to them in a foreign language. They had no clue what I was asking of them. They were so comfortable in their consequence-free, characterless existence that they couldn't understand this simple request, and from a stranger no less. They shrugged me off and went right back to playing noisily.

But the mother, ever vigilant of a potential predator, hadn't missed my intervention. She eyed me like tigress protecting its cubs.

The kids played on, screeching, darting back and forth to the bar, nearly causing the waitress to stumble while the moms remained locked in conversation, dangling their stem glasses between delicate fingers. This was not being *with* their kids.

I was mad now. My wife was trying to rein me in, but the main reason I was so mad is because she was mad. Her evening had been ruined. I started toward the kids again, but was cut off by one of the mothers who, having seen me get up, beat me to them.

"Now children," she said in some kind of calm Oprah inspired tone. "We must lower our voices and play appropriately." She was watching me the whole time, doing this on my behalf. "Please be quieter now."

She then returned to her friends. The kids gave her the same look they had given me.

"You really think that's going to work?" I called over to her.

The mothers ignored me.

These mothers and the millions like them allow their children to interrupt other people's evenings so they don't have to bother being parents, yet, on the other hand, they manage their kids' college tracking so tightly that we teachers have begun referring to them, after watching the recent Olympic games, as curling parents, beyond hovering or helicopter parents. When it comes to college, their kids are those big dumb rounded stones and the parents are the curlers, first taking careful aim at the target, then gliding on the ice, releasing, barking orders, directing the frantic sweepers until the stone has bumped its competition aside.

A telling scene is a school concert. Elementary, middle school, high school, it doesn't matter. Go to one, pay attention, and you will see: the end is near. Here is what happens: While the orchestra wails on, the video cameras whir. Dads and moms look on in rapture as their child saws her cello bow across the squawking strings. In the meantime their younger children, bored, tear around the gymnasium as if it's recess. And the minute the piece is concluded and future Yo-Yo Ma no longer has a starring role, the parents pack up their gear and leave, unwilling to pay respect to whatever ensemble comes on next. The rudeness has become so unmanageable that now schools schedule their concerts at different times. The chorus sings on Wednesday, the band performs on Thursday, the select chorus on Friday.

When I owned my advertising sales company one of our clients was *Commentary* magazine. I had the high honor of sharing an elegant lunch one day with its legendary editor, Norman Podhoretz. I've read the magazine ever since. When I was about to sell my company and go into teaching, a piece appeared in the magazine that caught my attention because it was by Chester Finn, then Assistant Secretary of Education. In the piece Finn considered various trends in contemporary parenting, from aiding and abetting bad behaviors to the failure to shape good ones and their impacts on education: "Heirs or alumni of the 1960s counterculture, they (parents) tend to be ambivalent about the exercise of authority, fearful of upsetting children or of quashing their self-expression, eager at all costs to appear 'supportive.' This style of 'passive parenting' comprises equal parts incompetence, feel-good psychology and the remnants of 60s ideology. The combination is deadly."

In a nearby town similar to the towns I live and I teach in, two hundred intoxicated high school students, including five later hospitalized for alcohol poisoning, showed up for the homecoming dance. After twenty-eight were suspended, a few of their concerned parents called the school to complain, but not about the binge drinking that left the kids as young as fourteen "vomiting, incoherent, or on the verge of passing out" and not about the two families that hosted alcoholic pre-party festivities in their homes. They called to complain that "suspensions would mar their children's college transcripts."

In a nearby town a high school junior was killed at an unsupervised party.

Last year at our own school's annual Winter Formal, so many kids were vomiting all over the gymnasium floor that the principal had to suspend the dance. I asked my students how this much drinking could have happened.

"It's the 9th and 10th graders that are the problem," a senior told me. "Someone gets a handle of Grey Goose and sneaks it into her room. Then she has friends over. They go up to her room and there is a set price for shots. Two shots cost $5. Five shots cost $10. These kids can't handle their liquor. They need to be older to do that, like us."

"Where are the parents while this is going on?

"Probably downstairs. They were in this case. I know."

"And they don't notice that there is a parade of girls going up to their daughter's room?"

"They think they are getting ready for the dance."

"They are," another student adds, causing laughter.

"They don't notice the girls coming back down all tipsy, giggly? Don't suspect anything?" I ask.

"Nope."

I found out that one of my 9th grade students was responsible. I asked her about it.

"Yeah, my mom was home. She didn't know what was going on."

"And you charge for shots. Do you make money this way?"

"Yeah."

"Your mother has called me three times this year wondering how you are doing in class, making sure you are on time with your assignments."

"Yeah," she said, uninterested.

"So she is all over your grades but not your selling vodka from your bedroom," I said.

"I guess."

One of my closest friends, recently retired, who helped me become a teacher, was the athletic director at a large school district on Long Island. Before that he himself was a teacher, coach and assistant principal. A few years ago he found out that while in Florida at their annual Spring Break training camp a few of the players on the varsity baseball team and two of the coaches had gone drinking at a strip club. My friend fired the two coaches and suspended the five athletes for the remainder of the season. Three of them were seniors and were being scouted by division one colleges and universities for potential scholarships. Their parents were apoplectic, not at their sons' and coaches' behavior but at my friend for the punishments he had levied. They first complained to the superintendent who backed my friend's decision. They then petitioned the school board, which also backed my friend. Finally, like vigilantes, like a lynch mob, the parents took matters into their own hands. They called nightly, threatening him. They left obscene messages accusing him of ruining their sons' college chances. They went on a rampage of personal assault. They hired a private investigator to tail my friend hoping to catch him in any untoward behavior. They conducted a background check on his finances, any legal problems he may have had in the past. After an exhaustive search they finally caught my friend at something they could hurt him with. In college, forty years ago, my friend had been a bartender at a tavern near the college he and I attended. There he had invented some kind of chugging game. The parents found a sympathetic reporter and somehow got their discovery published in *Newsday,* the stretched upshot being that my friend was a hypocrite.

Like children these parents, when they don't get their way, want blood. They want instant gratification, the trophy—acceptance to a good college—not the slow-cooked good character that will well serve their children for a lifetime. Typical of their Me Decade generation, they want the success now, not thirty years from now, when their children will be parents themselves and have progressed in careers and have had the occasion to demonstrate character, all of which are true measures of success. No. These child-like parents consider their job done when they can tag the back window of their Mercedes SUV with a decal from a "good" college. If parents were truly concerned with their children's well-being they would not allow them to have cell phones in school, video games in their rooms. The "family" computer would be placed in a centralized location and supervised. Kids would be allocated specific times to use it. We wouldn't allow them these secret lives, this iconic "privacy," so ironic when these lives kept from us are splashed all over the web. But now their rooms are not bedrooms, under our supervision. They are separate apartments where friends of both sexes gather at all hours of the night. Can anyone remember the quaint rule when at this age boys and girls weren't allowed in the same room alone with the doors shut. Does anyone remember parietals in the college dorms? Does anyone remember when a telephone call used to come in through the landline phone, when the dad or mom would answer and it would be someone wanting to speak to their kid, when the dad or mom would then ask, who's this? Now the parents never know who is calling, what is going on. When did parents become incapable of saying no?

In her *The Demoralization of Society*, one of my favorite historians, Gertrude Himmelfarb, writes, "we have abandoned the idea of virtue and have adopted instead what we now call 'values'. Value is a subjective, relativistic term; any individual group, or society may choose to value whatever they like. One cannot say of virtues what one can say of values, that anyone's virtues are as good as anyone else's, or that everyone has a right to his own virtue. This shift from virtues to values represents the true moral revolution of our time." Our civilization has redefined what it means to be virtuous. In the college cult it is a virtue to get into a "good" college even if it means doing whatever it takes. It is now a virtue to cheat if it results in a good grade. This may sound extreme to what few reasonable minded grown-ups still remain, but consider that my seniors would almost unanimously agree that to tail-gate a slower driver in order to push him off the road so they could go faster is commendable, virtuous in fact, because they are getting what they want. They would agree because there is no stigma, no shame attached. Their behavior is applauded. Winning at any cost is sanctioned, condoned, justified everywhere they look, certainly by the scandals of celebrities, athletes and politicians. In fact, even many parents cheat, lie, deceive, distort, right in front of them; parents actually help their children cheat and then get away with it, which signals encouragement not denouncement. Really, isn't it a form of cheating to hire for more money than most Americans can afford SAT prep companies and tutors? Even the colleges look the other way at this inherent unfairness, actually encouraging it, only too happy to maintain their averages, allowing them to promote their "selectivity." The only judgment comes in the form of the college acceptance letter. The only stigma is rejection, which could mean they didn't cheat enough. In the college cult parents and their indoctrinated children *valuing* getting into a good college has become the *virtue*. It is now *virtuous* to be willing to pursue the end with whatever means are necessary. Instead of saying no to their children's bad behavior like real grown-ups would, parents behave badly too, excoriating teachers, threatening lawsuits, doing their kids' homework, seemingly oblivious to the obvious human consequences.

In the college cult *bad* has become the new *good*.

14
THE PURSUIT OF HAPPINESS

ONE DAY A FORMER student showed up after school to ask me for a letter of recommendation. He was a sophomore at large state university and wanted to apply to its prestigious business program. Apparently students take general courses during their first two years then must qualify for acceptance.

I write many recommendations for former students, but this request came as a surprise. When he was in my English class I often called on him and challenged him, hoping our discussions would awaken his better angels, and perhaps he mistook my interest in him for approval. He was an active participant, espousing candid views, but he was also cynical and shifty. He was bright but misguided, and I figured he knew I didn't like him much. During one of our conversations on Aristotle's *good*, he described proudly how he had cheated all the way through high school, in any way he could, and his high GPA and his acceptances to many good colleges and universities weren't the only justification; everyone did it. It was the new way to achieve.

And then there was his insensitive remark to one of my first generation Chinese students following her presentation to the class that she should learn how to chill out. She had shared how, as the only daughter, she was often overwhelmed to the point of deep sadness with all of her family obligations and rigid expectations and had no time for the normal things teenagers do.

I hoped that perhaps he had changed enough so that I could help him.

"Well, tell me how have you gone about your first two years there? What courses have you taken? What have you learned?" I asked him.

"To get into the business program you have to have at least a 3.5 GPA. I have a three-nine."

"But what courses have you taken? What has interested you?"

He laughed. "I don't really remember. Now I am taking... I don't know. I am taking any course that is easy. There is a rating system the students have. It ranks professors for difficulty."

"So you will take any class, regardless of its subject and your interest or lack of interest in it, so you can get a good grade?"

"Exactly."

Again, I don't know why he came to me. To this day I wonder about it. Anyone who takes my 12th grade class would know how I feel about these things. What could he possibly have been thinking? But then that's it. He wasn't thinking.

Of course I lectured him on how he was belittling his own education, that a university like the one he was attending must have amazing resources and professors and endless opportunities to grow intellectually, the goal we set for ourselves in 12th grade.

"It doesn't work that way," he said with such self-assuredness it startled me.

"You are hurrying to get into this business program only because you think it will make you money, yet in the process you are losing yourself. We talked a lot about this in class. The examined life. True human happiness. You are still cheating."

"Happiness is relative and cheating has always gotten me what I want."

"Is this the real you talking?"

"My parents are spending a lot of money to send me to that school," he said. "My education needs to have a practical purpose."

I felt badly for him. After all, in spite of his attitude, he was still only nineteen and desperately entangled in vicious net of contradictions, although he didn't know it.

"I won't give you a recommendation."

He looked at me quizzically, as if in a million years he never would have expected this response. Then he got up, tilted his head lost in a feeble attempt to understand, then walked out without saying anything more, and I never saw or heard from him again.

I can't stop thinking about how this young man continues down the wrong path and I wasn't able to prevent it.

He was one of the students who hated Wilson's *Against Happiness,* and he was vehement about it, as if he took the book's thesis as a personal attack, way too negative, he'd pontificated, which of course, unbeknownst to him, validated Wilson's point.

Two people I know who love the book as much as I do are my daughter and her fiancé, which doesn't surprise me. They are both profoundly original people who live simply so they can immerse themselves in the miracles of nature. They have moved to Utah where they explore Anasazi ruins and camp in the desert in the stark cold of winter, climb walls of ice and rock, raft down the Colorado days on end with nothing to entertain them but each other's thoughts, their survival, the endless stars, the intricate interchange of the subtle wildlife, and the indescribable colors of the canyons at twilight.

Wilson writes that in America we have created a culture that attempts to subvert the sadness. Yet sadness, or melancholia, as Wilson prefers to describe it, is fundamental to our being connected to the essence of our human existence. It comes, of course, from awareness, the heightened consciousness of learned people, the wise, and the liberally educated, of being in touch with the truth, whether that truth be the ragged beauty of a lone butte in Utah, a Beethoven sonata or the mysteries behind the forces that both motivate and manipulate us. Is that one of the reasons we are backing away from the classics, from colleges devoted to the humanities, because the minds they will produce will be saddened? So instead, like my students, we prefer vocational tracks, training, that will produce good jobs and lots of money, distractions, really, which we assume will assure our happiness? But Aristotle insisted that only the virtuous could be truly happy. He went on to associate wisdom with virtue. Socrates said there could be no virtue without wisdom.

This real happiness is not what parents want for their children. If they did, they would put urgent emphasis on creating wise kids instead of furiously pushing them to get into good colleges so they can get good jobs. Maybe it is because Aristotle's seed for happiness, wisdom-inspired virtue, can't take root in America. Maybe selfishness and ambitious materialism, what Wilson calls "crass happiness," are ingrained in our uniquely American psyche whereas Wilson's melancholia is a feeling we Americans try to expunge, exorcise. If we know better we won't have as much fun. But it is from this sadness, this wisdom that comes from woe, as Melville identified, that so much of our civilization depends on. Compare Aristotle's virtues to their contemporary counterparts. Which list is more descriptive of our way of life?

Loyalty	*Disloyalty*
Responsibility	*Irresponsibility*
Honesty	*Dishonesty*
Courage	*Cowardice*
Perseverance	*Vacillation*
Work	*Play*
Compassion	*Indifference*
Self-discipline	*Self-indulgence*
Commitment	*More Indifference*

Wilson's essay warns us of our roots, namely that our sacred Declaration of Independence, which proclaims our inalienable right to life, liberty, and the pursuit of happiness is connected to John Locke's original decree that everyone has the right to life, liberty, and property, possibly meaning that inherently we are a shallow people, or as Wilson puts it: "America was and still is the place where one can find happiness through acquisition. There in the distance, let us say, is a thriving forest. What is this to the typical American, the American bent on discovering happiness through securing stuff? This forest is to the American entrepreneur a reservoir of resources, a space containing materials just waiting to be bought and sold. He trades quality for quantity. He thus loses reality." Is the gradual erosion of our humanity, as evidenced by what we are doing to our students, merely an unavoidable consequence of who we have become collectively? Is it so ingrained in our cultural DNA that there is nothing we can do about it? De Tocqueville wrote that "Not only does democracy make each man forget his ancestors, it hides his descendants from him, and divides him from his contemporaries; it continually turns him back into himself, and threatens, at last, to enclose him entirely in the solitude of his own heart." At heart, is American democracy selfish? Is our culture about winning at any cost?

By shunning Wilson's book for their independent reading assignment, my students unequivocally showed their lack of the most basic critical thinking skills, especially self-awareness. They couldn't recognize and evaluate their own bias. A noteworthy author was challenging their status quo, but instead of entering into an intellectual exchange, opening their minds to new possibilities, they kept them closed.

In our schools our students are not learning, they are competing. A competition implies winning and losing, with prizes attached. Our students are not pursuing learnedness. They are being ambitious. But the Founders importantly, purposefully decided to change Locke's phrasing from *property* to *happiness*. Why? I think because there is something more to the American Dream than merely winning by acquiring more and more things. It is the *liberty* part of the phrasing, the freedom it implies, again uniquely American, that should intrigue us. Without liberty, there can be no happiness. We humans once yearned to be truly free, originally from religious persecution, then governmental intrusion, but finally to be free essentially to shape and guide our own individual destiny. To do this we need to be able to *think*. This is what the Founders meant when they warned us that having an educated electorate was the only way to keep our new Republic. But do we still have that powerful yearning today, or has it given way to complacency?

Thomas Aquinas, who was profoundly influenced by Aristotle, believed that choice includes judgment as well as desire. But judgment requires thought. There now seems to be too much will (to the end that justifies the means) and not enough reason to complement it. All appetite, little intellect. Therefore, today's young people (and too many of their parents) are not truly free because they are not reasonable, in the classic sense. They are missing out (or they missed out) on the learning that produces reason and wisdom. How can a young person (or his parents) make an informed choice without an intellect? He can't, according to Aristotle, Aquinas and their army of philosophical disciples. If the tempering of appetite by intellect is the "beginning of the essence of man," as Aristotle indicates, what do we have today? This is our current curse, maybe our eventual demise.

Too many people simply can't decipher the truth, can't even recognize when they are being disloyal, irresponsible, dishonest, lazy, cowardly, mean, or self-indulgent. Being able to think critically derives not from following the mindless rubrics teachers too often dispense or mastering the SAT, but from the wisdom acquired from sustained serious liberal study as opposed to vocational study. Yet our culture increasingly devalues liberal education. In fact, high schools race faster and faster toward releasing their 12th graders earlier and earlier in the year to pursue "internships" where they can experience the workplace instead of "confining" them to the classrooms where they might take, say, a philosophy course.

My brother, the one who was my business partner and bought my shares allowing me to become a teacher, has done a nice job of growing the company and one of his clients is an online journal called *Insider Higher Ed.* He sends me articles from time to time that he thinks I might find interesting. One was called "The Case of the Disappearing Liberal Arts," by professors Roger Baldwin and Vicky Baker, stating that in the last twenty years the number of liberal arts colleges has decreased by half and predicted that in ten to fifteen years from now there will be even fewer truly liberal arts colleges. There is no denying that traditional model of education based in humanities and sciences and offering a common intellectual canon is dying out.

The consequence of this, of course, is an *illiberally* educated electorate, which we already see evidence of, beginning with many parents who can't control themselves and their newly minted high school graduates who can't think. My students can't stand the silence when their iPods are turned off because they depend on music to stir them, not their own thoughts. They are afraid to be left alone with their thoughts because they have none. They then become parents who can't make decisions based on classical notions of right vs. wrong and good vs. bad. What they can do is buy the metaphorical liter and a half of Grey Goose Vodka for $50, share it with the kids and their friends, and find nothing appalling about that. Their decisions and the actions that follow become secular and therefore relative. They depend, not on ancient empirical truths, but on whatever feels good: If my kid feels good socially networking all night long on her computer, then that's fine with me; it means I'm a good provider and keeping up with the Jones's and my kid is happy; I would feel terrible if I had to tell my kid no and isolate him from the crowd, no matter how harmful it might be; she might not like me anymore. If students never read the *Picture of Dorian Grey* or *Babbitt*, then how will they ever be able to recognize bad behavior when they become parents? Majoring in Communications doesn't teach someone right from wrong. But parents insist on pushing their kids toward jobs instead of developing character.

I was delighted to learn recently that a fraternity brother of mine, Bill Fox, had been chosen to be the 18th president of our alma mater, St. Lawrence University, one of the few colleges remaining dedicated to a liberal arts education. Foxy was loved and respected even back then for his brilliance, humor, serenity, and perspective. He was a serious theology major who went on to earn a divinity degree from Harvard and a PhD. In addition to being an educator he is a philosopher, a writer, a devoted father, and husband. In an interview after his appointment he was asked "what he really knew for sure." He said: "The beginning of wisdom is the desire for discipline." When asked what a liberal arts education means to a graduate and how its very high cost could be justified, Foxy said: "The best reward of a bachelor's degree earned at a liberal arts college is, of course, intrinsic and personal. It is the self-confidence in self-education that this particular kind of college career gives a person. All gaps in knowledge can be bridged when you enter the larger world with a liberal education."

High school's job was once to provide its students with a liberal education; now it is to train them to get into college. This has dire consequences when the colleges, too, avoid the responsibility of educating students and merely train them for jobs instead. And by training I don't necessarily mean the professional undergraduate tracks like business or nursing or education. These are fine along with any undergraduate degree, as long as the student is also required to study and embrace the liberal arts, so he can complete his person.

A couple we know is divorcing after being married for thirty years. The reason is because the husband is addicted to Internet porn, so his wife is leaving him. I did some research and was shocked to discover that, according to a professional association of divorce attorneys, pornography is now the leading cause of marriages failing. Not infidelity, not abuse, not alcohol or drugs or money problems or gambling. Porn. And what to me is even more horrifying about this is that 70 percent of pornography is viewed between nine and five o'clock, at work. Sixty-five percent of all companies now use porn detecting devices, up nearly 50 percent from the beginning of the decade. Yet so many porn viewers are willing to litigate to defend their *right* to this behavior under the Americans With Disabilities Act that their employers are fearful to crack down on it.

It seems our civilization has sprung another leak.

This is what's so important in the debate over what has happened to our children. We may have arrived at a place where not only are we okay with our self-indulgences, we also feel we are entitled to them morally, even legally, which implies that character, and the virtues and reason that create it, has degraded and devolved into something entirely different.

When my youngest daughter was a junior in high school, she asked us if we would host the cast party following the musical. I said sure, but she needed to understand a few things, such as there would be no alcohol, and if I found any I would embarrass anyone I found in possession of it. She agreed.

That night we had over seventy kids in our house. My wife and I were in the kitchen busy preparing food for them all when I looked up to find two police officers standing in my family room.

"What are you doing here?" I asked them.

They were busy themselves, looking all around.

"You have no right to be in my house," I said, sternly.

"Sir, we asked that person over there if we could come in and she said yes."

They pointed to my daughter, so legally they were allowed to enter.

"I know what you are looking for," I said. "I appreciate what you are doing but as you see I am here and my wife is here. There is no alcohol anywhere in my house."

"We can see that, sir, but unfortunately this is not what we usually find, even with the parents home. They just don't know any better."

Our TV screens are inundated with commercials for diets and exercise machines that don't work and which, after bought, are rarely used. Why are we drawn to them? Because we don't *know* any better? Where is our sense of dignity? I read an article in *The New*

Yorker recently and learned that according to Center for Disease Control and Prevention, in the early 1960s 24.3 percent of American adults were overweight. During the 1980s, 33.3 percent of adults qualified, and since then the proportion of overweight children has doubled, while among adolescents it has tripled. "Something big must have changed in America to cause so many people to gain so much weight so quickly. A food scientist from Frito-Lay relates how the company is seeking to create a lot of fun in the mouth. Another product development expert talks about the effort to cram as much hedonics as you can in one dish."

Hedonics, as in hedonistic, as in hedonism, usually marks the end of a civilization. Brian Wansink, author of *Mindless Eating* and director of Cornell University's Food and Brand Lab "has performed all sorts of experiments to test how much people will eat under varying circumstances. These have convinced him that people are—to put it politely—rather dim."

And there you have it. Many sophisticated scientific theories abound as to why people have become obese, but aren't they just more examples of our culture looking away? In spite of the excuses that attempt to justify America's gluttony, there is really nothing at all complicated about it. The reason is quite simple. We have grown "dim." Americans are much fatter because we have much less self-discipline (and certainly no desire for more of it), and the reason for that is because it's no longer taught, not even touted. We're fat because we have no will power, or, worse yet, we don't care. We lack discipline because we don't care about the wisdom that comes with it. Whatever happened to *judgment*, to saying to yourself: "This is not good. This is not right. I shouldn't be doing that. I should do this instead." On a popular TV show called *Cooking Thin,* the gorgeous host in an impeccable British accent tells her two overweight guests, "Just because you want to drop a dress size doesn't mean you can't have chocolate, chocolate, and more chocolate!" It doesn't? Since when?

I was working out the other day on one of those funny-looking elliptical machines at my club when I felt a poke from behind. I turned around to find a forty-something Gen Xer glaring at me, holding a water bottle.

"How much longer will you be?" she asked.

I had just gotten on the thing. "Well," I started to say, but there was something about her, in her eyes. She looked almost panicked, as though if I didn't get out of her way something bad would happen to her.

"Give me five minutes," I finally said.

She was like an emergency vehicle, lights flashing, so I yielded. She needed to get that workout done in a hurry because she had to move on to the next item on her list. She was wound so tightly there could be no compromise to her schedule. It wasn't that she was rude, although it would be easy to dismiss her as such. The truth was that she was tortured. I imagined her day had gone something like this: Her landline phone rings, which is rare, because everyone she knows calls her on her cell, so she panics that something terrible has happened. She races over and picks it up but, even though she's asked to be added to the "no call" list, a pre-recorded voice solicits her for new credit card or cheaper mortgage. The interruption to her life isn't merely frustrating. It is invasive, an assault. Now she needs to make a hotel reservation for an upcoming trip and dreads it. Reluctantly she logs on to the chain's web site, follows the tedious prompts, typing in all the necessary information. When she gets to the final instruction she clicks purchase. A message appears instructing her to wait, that her reservation is being processed. Ten minutes later she is still waiting. She calls directory assistance, gets the hotel chain's reservation number and attempts to call it, but is told by a recording that the call could not go through. She calls back and reaches a young woman in Manila who has trouble understanding her English. After repeating three times all the information she had previously typed onto the computer, she finally has her reservation, but now she is double booked. That afternoon she is driving to an important appointment but as she rounds the bend on the New Jersey Turnpike she sees a sea of red taillights and becomes entangled in an inexplicable traffic jam with no apparent cause. After crawling along for two hours the traffic just as suddenly dissipates, and of course she is so ecstatic to be moving again that she too quickly forgets what pain she has just been in.

But the damage has been done, to her soul. And she is not alone. Over time, these daily assaults wear away at whatever patience and compassion we have left. The more we find ourselves lost in phone mazes mindlessly responding to mechanized prompts desperately navigating toward some human being only to discover at the end of the line that we must now return to the main menu, the more we lose ourselves. Like the George Washington Bridge these things extract a heavy toll, quietly relentlessly eroding our common sense, our strength, our dignity until, desperate just to get through another day, we can no longer resist, so we give in easily to the lamest temptations. We don't say no to porn, to overeating, to numbing ourselves endlessly with video games and NFL football polls and social networking sites because we need to be in a perpetual state of being entertained, so we can escape.

But there is more to it. We are also a nation of bread and circuses because we are not aware enough, in other words not educated enough, to recognize it. We don't say no, not because we can't, but because we don't want to, and we don't want to because we find nothing wrong with giving in to our destructive indulgences, to listening to our lesser angels, because there is no right vs. wrong anymore. Those distinctions come from deductive and inductive reasoning, from studying history and literature and philosophy and theology. Drawing lines between good and bad is the soul of being educated. We should say no to porn and road rage and self-indulgent obesity because they are sleazy. They are squalid, sordid, immoral, corrupt and bad. We display too little of Hemingway's grace under pressure. Why has doing what is wrong become so easy, so acceptable? The only possible explanation, because this behavior is so widespread, is because it is not perceived as being wrong. It is almost as if the notion of self-discipline has been laundered in the political correctness washing machine, that if we demonstrate restraint, if we don't give in to our whims, our impulsiveness, and our impatience we are somehow inhibited, uptight. Discipline, after all, is the antithesis of doing your own thing.

It is a deadly combination.

A recent *Newsweek* cover story asks "Is America Losing Its Mojo? Like a star that still looks bright in the farthest reaches of the universe but has burned out at the core, America's reputation is stronger than the hard data warrant. The United States has made the least progress of the thirty-nine countries analyzed in improving its innovation capacity and internal competitiveness and has fallen far behind in one key resource: human capital." America's prowess has always come from its ability to invent, to improvise, to create. We have always been a nation of dreamers. The American Dream comes from imagining, yet instead of imagining, we are entertaining and *unthinking* ourselves to death. Americans now seem to be pursuing happiness by getting good grades so that we can go to a "good" college so that we can get a good job so that we can visit porn sites, then go home and watch the *Bachelorette* and *Jersey Shore*, eat until we are overweight, Twitter, then post it all on Facebook and YouTube.

15
THE ANTI-CIVILIZATION

MANY CONTENTIOUS ISSUES CONFRONT public schools—tenure, charter schools, teacher evaluations to name a few. Debates rage. The problems seem insurmountable. Davis Guggenheim's disturbing film "Waiting for Superman" covers the near total failure of poor urban schools, wagging a finger at unions. Vicki Abeles' eye-opening documentary, "The Race to Nowhere," deals with the sometimes lethal pressure put on the super kids, more relevant to the problems at my school, although it too doesn't address what concerns me, which is that good schools, our last best hope, and the parents who ultimately control them, actually impede the intellectual growth of all the students, instead of stimulating it. Ironically, we slow kids down, or worse, we stunt them permanently.

My school and high achieving schools like mine unintentionally do this in more than a few ways. First schools systemically distort the reality our children must face as adults if they are ever to become truly successful human beings. One way they do this is via incessant quizzes, tests, and quantifiable assessments of all kinds, falsely reinforcing in our young people's minds that life is a competition, a zero sum game that somebody wins and somebody loses. Because of this constant judging, our unlucky students (those who are deemed less "smart" than the others) "learn" they are not meant to be learners, while we prepare our luckier "gifted and talented" students for a life in which they feel like constant winners, who will someday feel comfortable and complacent and even proud when they are the *haves* when there are too many *have nots*, merely because they possess more quantifiable stuff, bigger homes, longer vacations, fancier cars. This becomes the only way they know how to keep score, because early on we have justified their empty victories. Schools contribute, then, not only to the polarization of society, but to the desensitizing of young people who may never know or care about the other ways to keep score in life, such as a long and happy marriage, interests in things outside of work such as art, music, literature, current events, the human condition. Steve Jobs' last words, said in the presence of his beloved family, were "Oh, wow. Oh, wow. Oh, wow." I'll bet this almost divine display of ecstasy, proclaimed at the moment of death of a man who through his creativity, vision and passion changed our world for the better forever, was not caused by how much money he'd made. Sure, some of life is winning, a small part. I was a salesman for many years and always had a hard number attached to my success. If I didn't make that number I wouldn't have made the money I did, nor would I have been able to buy the things I was able to buy. But a good life, a life well lived, is not a competition, is not gathering lots of good grades, whether it be on a math quiz or the good grade of making lots of money. A good life is *examined* and worked at to make it "rich" with meaning. It is a reckoning, a making the most of our brief existence, and that doesn't necessarily mean having to beat someone, especially at the accumulation of material things. Being a successful human means not only being successful at a career but also being a good human being, living a fulfilling and fulfilled life. It means being enriched, not rich. It means not only knowing who Beethoven and Kant and Huck Finn and Rembrandt were and what they did, but why they are important to us and how they make us feel, of how they verify us, not just owning the newest iPhone.

This requires more intellectual rigor than our children are getting, less enabling and less reliance on keeping score. The only stimulation that appears to go on in schools like mine is the adrenaline rush, the anxiety, the near obsession students have about their grades, especially when they are about to get back a graded test or assignment. They will pester a teacher days on end to return their work, rushing our desks, crushing up against us, and once we do, they look only at the grade on the top of the first page, rarely at the comments, competing against each other, collecting their ribbons to show mom and dad how well they are doing, for what? So they won't get grounded?

For years I couldn't figure why 9th graders are especially eager, demanding to the tipping point of rudeness, about getting their silly grades back. They are only fourteen years old, for God's sake! They couldn't possibly comprehend the cause and effect relationship of grades and college. They have no sense of the future, of long-term consequence. They have enough trouble simply managing their day. They fall out of their chairs, they get gum stuck in their hair, they lose their hundred dollar history textbooks, they would forget to breathe if someone didn't remind them to. They are appropriately clumsy adorable little oafs. But when it comes time for them to get a grade back, or think they should get their paper or test back, that the teacher has had "enough time," they aren't so adorable anymore. They are more like are mercenaries, or attack dogs, trained to be cold-blooded, to kill. I don't exaggerate. I have had children, their mouths stuffed with multi-colored braces, look up with indignation and tell me to my face that I wasn't doing my job because I hadn't gotten their grades back to them quickly enough. This is a perversion. But I think I understand it now. And it is this: they are just kids. They are responding, primitively, in an almost primal way, as kids do, to their environment. When they get home at the end of the day, the first thing their parents want to know is if they got "any grades back" and if they are able to say yes, what follows is what serves today as post-modern family conversation:

"What did you get?"

"B+."

"How come only a B+?"

"It was hard. The teacher didn't teach me. The rest of the class did worse. I don't know."

"I don't like Bs. You can do better. I expect more. This is not good enough."

"It wasn't B. It was a B+."

"If you don't get As, you won't get into a good college and you won't get a good job and you won't make a lot of money and your life will be ruined."

Getting that grade back with the expectation that perhaps it is what mom hopes for is how these kids relate to their parents. At the deepest level, kids want to be loved, and in our upside-down world this is how they accomplish it, by bringing home a good grade. And even if the grade is not so good, at least the parent and child are communicating, in some twisted way. The grade forms their relationship. In too many cases, school and extracurricular performance is all parents and their kids have in common. They certainly don't seem to share dinnertime or discussions or excursions to museums or concerts. Maybe an outing to a Yankees game. But what really bonds families these days are the As, Bs, and Cs. This is what they *have*—grade togetherness. It's what they *share*. No wonder kids crave grades. It is today's version of affection.

Once, on the last day of school before the long Christmas break, I decided to bring in cupcakes and cookies and candies and soda for my 9th grade class and throw a party, and instead of teaching a lesson I would read them a story. The kids were all excited. They grabbed for the treats as I passed them around. But then one asked if I had graded their essays yet. I said I had, but I wanted to wait until after the break to pass them out because I wanted to talk about them. They kids protested, telling me I wasn't fair, that they wanted to know their grade. I said that today I wanted to read them a story about winter and snow and ice and I began, but noticed they weren't interested. The mood of the party had shifted. They sat list-lessly, having lost interest. In the middle of the story a boy got up and asked to go to the bathroom. A girl put her head down on her desk and sighed. Today's kids would rather get a grade back then have story read to them.

Hoping to make a returned paper or test mean more to my students than simply a grade I began telling them that if they wanted to discuss their performance and learn how to improve, they could come see me anytime they wanted during our ninth period, the last period of our day, designated solely for student/teacher conferences. But none ever showed up. What for? Once they got the grade back that contest was over. As determined by the grade, their race had either been won or last. Now it was time to anticipate the next event. For more than ten years walking the hallways of my school between classes as students swarm by I have never once heard one talk with another about something that interested them in the previous class. Instead, hundreds of time I have heard the following:

"What did you get?"

"I got an 87."

"I got a 90."

"What do you think Seth got?"

"Oh, he probably got a 100 again."

"Do you think we will have a quiz in Global?"

I don't have the narrative skills to describe what the hallway outside my room looks and sounds like on report card day. The best I can do is to say it resembles the feeding frenzy of sharks lured by chunks of bloody bait. They actually push each other over in an attempt to see who got what.

Sure, it could be worse. They could be talking about drugs instead of grades, and at first glance these might easily be described as motivated students. But motivated by and to do what?

I have new policy now. The only time I hand back grades is when a student makes an effort to come to see me during ninth period, and when they come, I force them to sit and conference with me about why they earned the grade and how they might improve.

This suggests the other way schools distort reality for our children. By pampering them we inoculate them from individual responsibility: review sheets before each quiz, review sessions before each test, the necessity of posting homework assignments on e-chalk so parents can monitor them. The result is that the existence students experience in school is also a virtual reality, like Facebook, like a video game, impressively simulated but certainly not what they will inherit in the real world. In essence, our schools, then, keep our kids pinned inside Plato's cave, rewarding them for sitting passively and watching the shadows on the wall, forever unaware of the bright light that burns right outside. The reason for this is that, in a swarming sea of mandates and parental and cultural pressure and politics and political correctness and ever changing policies, pedagogy and curricula, our schools have lost their way. We're bogged down. Education is just not as complicated as we allow it to be.

Shortly after I became a teacher, I wondered what had become of the once simple purpose of a high school education, which to me had always meant teaching kids stuff and opening their minds so they could think with the stuff they learned, because the high school I found myself in certainly didn't look like what I remembered it to be. Very few if any of the kids seemed to want to be there, especially for the sake of learning. They were bored and indifferent and went along with the flow only because they had to, memorizing stuff long enough to take the quiz or test but rarely remembering it, and never using it to think with. Many of the kids felt they had outgrown school, the juniors and seniors, for sure. The younger students had learned to regard school merely as an obstacle course. Does high school have a purpose in the twenty-first century, other than to babysit kids while their careerist parents work? The high school graduation rate in America now is lower than it was 1969, the year I graduated.

I came to realize sadly, of course, that the purpose of high school in most of America today is to host a four-year college acceptance competition. The only enthusiasm I see is for grades. Kids are only stimulated by what they "earn" instead of what they "learn." This makes the experience—the game, the rules—acceptable to some, while it completely alienates the others. Of course this game has very little to do with our children becoming educated during the process. President Obama has upped the stakes, declaring recently he wants the United States to have the world's highest percentage of college graduates by the year 2020, as if this is some panacea. Why not the world's best educated citizens? The two are not necessarily the same.

Certainly, the unapologetic purpose of my high school is to get the students into "good" colleges. One day I went to the guidance counselor of a student I was concerned about. This student, like too many of the great middle portion of our students, seemed to be drifting through, unmotivated, relegated to the back burners of the non-AP and non-Honors tracks, disenfranchised. His counselor told me unabashedly: "You need to understand that our school's success depends on what colleges the top 10 percent get into, because that's what drives everything else. The bottom 10 percent is taken care of by mandates from the state. The middle just doesn't get that much attention."

What also strikes me as strange is that the way we go about teaching kids in public school is always changing. Why? Wouldn't you think in the 2500 years since Socrates we would have figured it out by now? I am deeply suspicious of this constant need for "reform." Something is amiss here, maybe even sinister. Education is continuingly, incessantly, almost neurotically being reinvented all the time, yet it never seems to get anywhere, get much better. In fact, it could be argued that it gets worse. But it always gets more expensive. Part of the problem, of course, is the complexity of the ever-changing American landscape, for example, shifting demographics, the redefining of family, savage income inequities, along with numerous other dynamics, and the unending parade of national initiatives to address these. During the years I have been teaching just a few I've seen include *No Child Left Behind*, then *Race To The Top*, now *Common Core Standards*. It seems like a race, all right, all this change, a rat race. In the last five years New York State, the second largest educational system in the country, has changed its standards so many times I've lost count. Its signature examination, the Regents, required of all public high school students in all academic subjects, has undergone numerous transformations. One year they make it easier so more kids will pass, the next harder, then easier again in a never ending attempt to address the needs of children, but are state officials really more concerned with their own political needs?

This vacillation, this inconsistence, this incompetence, this bumbling and stumbling should tell us all we need to know about those who are supposed to be minding the educational store. It's almost like the professional educators have the ADD/ADHD we treat our children for. One trend follows another: Twenty-First Century Learning, Global Thinking. I give them credit for their clever buzzwords. The edu-crats must have copywriters! In my district "new initiatives" such as *curriculum mapping, standards-based report cards, differentiated learning,* and *responsible classroom* are too many to keep track of, and at any given time they are entirely different from the myriad initiatives pursued at neighboring districts. In one school kids are taught X and in another they are taught Y.

My home district once adopted something called *Habits of the Mind*, hiring guru Bena Kalick, who, at significant expense, trained our teachers at all three levels—elementary, middle and high school—in sixteen such ostensibly desirable practices as persistence, empathy, meta-cognition, and life-long learning. But when the district hired a new assistant superintendent with ideas of her own about education, *Habits of Mind* was quickly discarded, relegated to the trash heap of other well-intended trials, replaced by the next educational flavor of the day. All that's left of Bena are the posters on the wall. This is what I've become accustom to as a teacher. Education is a whirling dervish of reform, a circus of flip-flopping, yet it always seems to lead to the same unenviable result, the same unintended consequence: the kids aren't learning what they need to, such as how to become informed, interested, interesting, engaged and engaging citizens of the world, in other words, how to think. In this relentless search for the magic bullet, educators, it seems to me, are overlooking the obvious, that somehow whatever we do we can't be counted on to get the job done.

I found this news item in the *Wall Street Journal*: "Erasing years of educational progress, state education officials on Wednesday acknowledged that hundreds of thousands of children had been misled into believing they were proficient in English and math, when in fact they were not." Then later on, this from the *Journal*: "Middle schools fail kids, study says. In the year when students move to a middle school or junior high school, the data show student achievement falls substantially in both math and English, relative to that of their counterparts who continue to attend K-8 elementary school. However, instead of bouncing back after an initial transition year, achievement continues to decline throughout middle school." This is absurd. Off we go again, to quote Vladimir in *Waiting for Godot*.

Maybe all the constant change leading from nowhere to nothing is because the public education industry involves way too many vastly well-trained very smart people all tripping over themselves to make something complicated out of something that essentially is quite simple, losing sight of the real goal. It is almost as if we are trying to make it complicated, to justify all our advanced degrees. But what it looks like from the inside is that we just keep throwing stuff against the wall to see what will stick. Does all our erudition make us clueless and inept, like the super brain who has no common sense? Or, because we educators think we are so smart, do we keep reinventing the wheel simply to stay engaged and avoid boredom? Another possible explanation, far scarier, is that public education is a racket, serving not so much the needs of children as the needs of teachers, administrators and state and national education officials, that it is a vast public works program, and the constant change is fueled by the need to justify the bureaucracy's existence. Follow the money.

What, specifically, does this have to do with kids not learning to think, with students' sorry state of malaise? This: Kids sense when they are being scammed. They've figured out by now that either the grown-ups aren't sure what they are doing or worse, they are corrupt. In either case, too many of our students decide early on that they shouldn't take their education seriously, so they end up uneducated.

An issue that drives much of the public education debate and will continue to do so is teacher accountability. Currently property taxpayers and, by default, elected and appointed officials, are roiled with the expedient notion that somehow, as in the private sector, teachers need to be measured, quantified, to make them more accountable, and what seems to be the measurement of choice is kids' performance on tests. In fact, Albany has just handed down new teacher assessment guidelines that must become normal practice within the next two years. The most controversial aspect is that 40 percent of a teacher's evaluation must come from how well that teacher's students perform on standardized tests. What this means, obviously, is that now, looking out more than ever before for their own self-interest, teachers will teach more than ever before to the test, compounding the problem I am writing about. This book aims to describe a serious omen: according to Aristotle, we are busy graduating students from high school who are unable to think and reason, which predicts problems ahead maintaining our way of living. Yet in my school, at least, the vast majority of the students do exceptionally well on all the tests. All pass easily, most at mastery level, or else we would not have a graduation rate of 100 percent. Sadly I know that this is not the case in too many schools across America where too many of the students fail the tests, and surely that is the well-intended purpose for the new teacher assessments.

But what is universally true is that all schools fail when they inadvertently teach kids how to take tests rather than provide kids with lifelong knowledge and teach them to think with it, to internalize it. In too many schools kids are prepared by their teachers to take the tests; the kids then take them and immediately forget whatever it was they so briefly "learned." They certainly rarely learn to apply what they temporarily learn, because if they did, they might not forget so easily. This is not teaching, nor is it something we should use to measure teachers.

New York State law now links teachers' pay increases to how well their students perform on tests. Because this complies with federal initiatives to leave no child behind and race to the top, our state will now receive hundreds of millions of dollars in aid. Again, I understand the impulse. Tragically, too many kids are not passing even the most basic standardized tests and something needs to be done about it. But what should be held accountable is not how well schools teach kids to take tests—because that is what's going on, to facilitate the contest—but how well we teach them to think with the information they are learning, so that they will be able to reflect and be more complete and deeper human beings. I doubt we have become so crass that money only is behind this mess. I think instead that we as a culture and a society are no longer able to ascertain just what crass money or any of our other earthly temptations are doing to us, largely because we also no longer possess the critical thinking skills—the ability to think reasonably—to figure all this out. What we educators are doing isn't working, in both rich and poor school. This is a reasonable conclusion, a cause/effect, problem/solution argument, a syllogism. If x, then y. But we seem to have lost the ability to make deductive leaps like this, to connect the dots, to reflect on our own behaviors this way. We are all becoming unreasonable, unenlightened, thoughtless. As a reflection of us, our schools are missing the point of their existence. Even though on graduation day in June we may be able to parade forward students who have passed or even mastered the tests, if we were to test them on the same material a semester later they would fail. I know, because I have researched this with my own students. One year I had seventy seniors retake parts of their tenth grade global history Regents exam. I made sure to incentivize them: I told them whoever passed would not have to write a second research paper. While all had originally passed and most had achieved mastery level, with many scoring in the 90s, they all failed this second time. And it was the exact same test. It came as no surprise: once the test is taken, the information is gone. As a result of this false emphasis, we are becoming a civilization of contestants, not thinkers, an anti-civilization.

16
"The Betrayal of the Mentors"

The vast majority of teachers, at least the ones I know, sincerely believe they place the needs of their students first, despite all the obstacles laid down before them. Of course there are teachers who don't, who don't like teaching, who don't even like children, who don't read their students' work, who get through their days sitting at their desks while their students attempt to teach themselves from some contrived lesson downloaded from a distant Internet site. And more than any other factor, these teachers damage children forever by killing any interest they may have had in the subjects these teachers are hired to teach. Every parent has experienced them. I saw two of my daughters "learn" to hate history because of their teachers. But they also learned to love biology because of another teacher, and they went on to study nursing in college. One is now an acute care nurse practitioner, the other a neonatal intensive care nurse. My colleagues, with the exception of maybe two or three, work remarkably hard, much harder in fact than my colleagues from my other jobs. They put in more careful effort, make more sacrifices, and are unarguably more committed. It is commonplace for teachers to work through their lunch periods providing extra help to needy students, stay late revising lesson plans, call parents, advise and supervise extracurricular activates for a "stipend" that if amortized amounts to a paid wage of about a dollar an hour. I know a social studies teacher who recently spent her entire weekend visiting museums in New York gathering (at her own expense) materials for a history lesson that would include a scavenger hunt.

This is dedication.

But herein lies the question, as I see it: A scavenger hunt?

One of my colleagues, a charismatic young science teacher, prepares his students for quizzes and tests by playing "Physics Jeopardy" on his Smart Board. He has worked hard to create this "technology-based learning," which leads to "desirable outcomes": his students do well on the tests. Another respected colleague of mine teaches 12th grade AP literature and spends hours organizing costumes and crafting dramatic scenes, which result in her students wielding elaborate cardboard rapiers in the hallway enacting Hamlet's final duel with Laertes. No, I am not concerned with lazy teaching, because I see the exact opposite. What I am concerned about are the implications of a rampant pedagogy that insists that learning must be fun, that to be effective, teaching needs to be entertaining. The point we all seem to be missing is that learning is a discipline, and discipline, like saying no to porn or chocolate, isn't necessarily fun or easy. You see, it is *how* teachers think they are helping kids and *what* teachers and administrators perceive to be the kids' needs that are suspect. Our schools are hurting kids because they no longer "teach" the virtue of self-discipline.

Because they are required to teach to state standards so their students can pass state exams, teachers also occupy much of their students' minds with content, "the facts of the external world" instead of "the inner life," the soul, the activity of knowing, which leads to the practical activity of doing. These teachers then hold their students accountable, not enough through sustained serious reasoned discussions, but by predictable quizzes and tests, probably because the skills of the inner mind that Socrates and Aristotle wanted their students to possess are so difficult to assess, and of course without tests and their incumbent scores, we teachers couldn't referee the contest. And to prepare them for those quizzes and tests we do the following, all under the guise of effective teaching: first, we announce the date of the test, which seems an anathema to me; second, we review the material that will be on the test, and finally we hand out actual review sheets of what will be on the test. The students quickly learn that all they have to do during the weeks of class time discussion leading up to a final assessment is wait us out; they don't even have to pay attention, let alone process the lessons. In the end the caring teacher will provide an escape route: meticulous review. Then the student crams the summarized information into her head the night before the test, and once the test is taken the content is as quickly gone. Somewhere along the line we teachers and parents came to believe that sheltering our children from the unhappiness of failure would be good for them. In doing so we failed them.

We ski coaches tease our young athletes that if they're not crashing, they're not learning. One time the mom and dad of one of my new skiers approached me early in the season after our morning training session. Their daughter was unhappy in our group, they told me. She wasn't making any friends.

"We're talking about Olivia?" I asked them. "I don't believe that. She gets along fine with everyone. The kids all like her. Her skiing needs work, but she is keeping up."

"Well, that is what she says," the mom insisted.

"The truth," I told them, "is that she is afraid. The program she skied in last year was recreational and fun. Our program is competitive. I have to push the kids outside of their comfort zone, make them do things they don't want to do. And Olivia isn't going for it. She won't jump. She doesn't like to do some of the high speed drills. But that is fine. I have seen this a million times coaching. The kids are eleven years old. It will click. I will get her through her fears. But not without her failing, a lot."

"But what you are doing is safe, right?" the mother asked.

I looked at her in disbelief.

"Safe? This is freestyle skiing. Of course what we do is not safe," I told her. "We won't let kids try something unless we think they are ready. We prepare them, coach them, avoid unnecessary risks, but everything we do is very risky. Kids get hurt. But they also become world class skiers."

Olivia did not come back.

One day I got a phone call from a mother about a progress report I had sent home indicating her son was failing because he was not turning in his homework assignments. I explained this to her.

"But you don't post your homework assignments on e-chalk, do you?" she said.

"No."

"If you did, I would have been able to check it. I would have known."

"Your son knew."

"Do you at least write assignments on the board, so he can copy them down?

"No."

"Well, then how do you expect him to do his homework?"

"I expect him to listen when I am telling his class what the homework is, then write it down in his agenda pad."

"But my son is not an audio learner. He is a visual learner."

"Someday soon he will need to be both, so I feel it would behoove him to learn now."

She hung up. Her son not doing his homework was my fault. What the mother has provided him with is a built-in excuse.

Report cards have been issued twice a semester, once every 10 weeks, forever in my school, but recently that proved not to be enough. Grades, the Holy Grail. It was decided that electronic progress reports (the written ones were being intercepted by the students) needed to be completed by teachers and sent home in the *middle* of the marking period. This, in addition to the traditional report cards. Rumor has it that teachers soon will be required to post all their assignments daily on e-chalk, an online "blackboard" parents and students can access at home on their computers. There goes the method to my madness. Soon it will be official: kids won't have to listen when I'm talking. "This will be on e-chalk?" they yell over my directions. Next year "Parent Portal" will be opened. We teachers will then be required to post our grade books! "A committee is being formed to determine what exactly will be seen," we have been told by our administrators, but the intent is obvious. Since grades are all that matter, access to them on a daily basis will give parents more power to control them, by complaining about them, taking invasive action. When this happens a child of a portal parent will never again receive a C or D or F on a report card, because long before that happens, the parent will have successfully intervened to prevent it. The contest of high school is heating up. Maybe sometime soon the soccer moms will be allowed to stop play when their children miss a pass, overshoot the goal. Maybe they will get a do-over.

When she was in 10th grade, my youngest daughter received an F one marking period in English. When we asked her what happened she told us she had not turned in two papers. We asked her why and she said she hadn't wanted to do the work, that she had no interest in it. Lesley was a good kid. She never got into trouble. But she was stubborn. The fact was, all she was interested in was music, so that's all she wanted to do. When she was very young she would spend hours singing, memorizing Broadway show tunes, playing her piano. At the time she had become a fine young classical singer and she worked hard at it. (She also loved to cook. She would watch cooking shows for hours then go into the kitchen and prepare amazing meals.) While creative and talented, she was never much for academics, and her grades showed it. She was one of those low B, high C students these "award winning, excellent" schools couldn't care less about, whose talents don't show up on the radar screen. In other words, she was a non-conformist. If a student is not a high maintenance "AP" or "Special Ed" kid, they systematically become part of the fall-through-the-cracks pack, the great silent majority overlooked by teachers and administrators, victims of the squeaky wheel syndrome. But they are also the backbone of our society, and our Arts. Why these kids' parents don't complain about the lack of attention their kids receive is beyond me, but then, we, my wife and I, didn't intervene much on Lesley's behalf either, preferring instead to let her figure things out for herself. As her parents, we respected her interests and understood how they often conflicted with her responsibilities. But nonetheless we expected her to be a good school citizen and learn and respect the requirements of her teachers. After disciplining her, I made an appointment and went to visit her teacher who confirmed that indeed Lesley had failed because she had not written two papers. My purpose for the visit, I told her, was to ask for the assignments.

"I will give Lesley lots of extra credit next marking period to make up for this," the teacher immediately responded, apparently not listening. "And since this happened late in this marking period, it was too late for a progress report."

"All I am asking for are the assignments," I said.

"Perhaps I should have called."

"Yes. But this is not your failure. It is Lesley's and she is going to make up the work."

"But I can't change the grade. I can help her next marking period though, by giving her—"

"I just want the assignments."

"The marking period is over. I can't go back and read her papers. What I can do is give her the chance to earn lots of extra credit next quarter so we can get her a very high grade, if, of course, she does all her work. This will offset the F."

"That's generous of you, but I just want the assignments."

"But why, if she will not get credit for them?"

The teacher was genuinely perplexed. She wasn't inexperienced. She had been a teacher for dozen years.

"Because I am assuming that the work you assigned her was valuable."

She hesitated, thought for a long moment, and was clearly uncomfortable trying to decipher my motives, which, I thought, I had made clear.

"I simply want Lesley to do the work," I continued, "so she will learn the lessons you were trying to teach her through the assignments, and also learn that she cannot just do or not do anything she wants. Right now she has missed those lessons. And, more importantly she was disrespectful to you and to her classmates by not doing what was required. And she was dishonest to us. And I don't care about the extra credit. She deserved to fail and she needs to pay the price."

The teacher shook her head. "You don't want the extra credit? Let me say this one more time, Mr. Baird. I don't know what you are up to here, and if you want the assignments I will provide them, but I will not read them and under no circumstances will I change the grade. I can make sure she gets enough extra credit to make up for it, so it won't affect her final average. You can go to the principal if you feel that is necessary."

While I had been a teacher myself for three years by then I still didn't understand where she was coming from. "Listen, I don't expect you to do any more work. She had her chance and blew it. This is her fault. All I want is for her do the work and to apologize to you for not doing it when you asked her to."

"Well, I still don't understand what you want," she said, annoyed.

And she truly didn't, and now, these years later, I understand there are two reasons why for it. The first is that her experience with other parents had intimidated her and therefore left her slanted to being so obsessed with giving kids a way out that she could not imagine another parent who was interested in something else. But much worse, her *own* focus was results, the grades, and their consequences, not only for her students but for herself, instead of inspiring learning, inspiring Lesley to do the work. This is the biggest problem with our schools today. This teacher, like her students, was restricted by a narrow lens, trapped inside the immediate, the relevant, the practical. What she had in sight was the destination, not the journey. Her mind had been closed to the possible, the universal.

Driving to school each morning I first must pass the school in my own town. Invariably I get stuck in a traffic jam. We have no school buses in our district. The kids walk. Cars crawl, then are stopped, one by one, by the crossing guard to allow kids to cross the street. What is interesting about this is that the crossing guard never makes the kids wait at the crossing. He only makes the cars wait, driven by busy adults like me who are trying to get to work. Even for one kid, he will hold up his hand and stop the traffic. And the kids never look up, never look out at the cars, never look the proverbial both ways. They just know the guard is making it safe for them, so at full stride they lurch into the street, backpacks bouncing, earphone cords dangling. Every morning I witness this spectacle, the real world grinding to a complete halt in order to allow one precious kid to pass, and never once does the kid ever assume the individual responsibility of seeing whether or not it is really safe, because he knows all that is being taken care of for him.

At our school, the board is now considering requiring that all teachers offer extra credit assignments to all of their students on a regular basis. Of course extra credit is a standard teacher tool, but usually only given in very special cases, something severe, like when a child has missed lots of school because of an illness or just can't grasp the learning and has tried very hard but will fail without it. I have offered it a few times, in rare cases like these. But I fear we will soon be asked to offer to all of our students, because "it is inherently unfair to make it available to just a few," one school board member opines.

Is handicap parking inherently unfair too?

With extra credit for all, now everyone will be able to get As! It reads like some Orwellian slogan.

A parent stopped me the other day and asked my opinion on

the subject. I had her son in one of my senior classes. He is heading for Tulane in the fall even though he is an unoriginal, unimaginative, thoughtless student. But he has made the Honor Roll every marking period since freshman year. In fact, he told me once that making honor roll had been his only goal in high school, and he was proud to have achieved it. But because of two failed tests in my class his winning streak was in jeopardy. His mother wanted me to give him something to do for extra credit so he could raise his average.

"I can't do that," I told her. "It would not be fair."

"Then give everyone a chance to earn extra credit. I understand there is talk that it should be policy."

"Extra credit for everybody?" I asked. "On a regular basis?"

"Yes."

"Well, it is fine with me under one condition."

"What's that?" she asked.

"That on our students' final transcripts their grades have a little asterisk, you know like the asterisk after Mark McGwire's single season home run record."

She gave me a funny look.

"You remember. He was on steroids. The little asterisk on their transcript will let the colleges know that these weren't really their grades, that they have been juiced. What do you think?"

She walked away without answering.

Teachers play the game too.

"I need to give another test," teachers say to each other, "because I don't have enough grades for the marking period."

"Yeah, I need to assign another paper. I need more grades in my book too."

I hear this all the time, in the faculty lounge, the hallway, yet no other teacher or administrator ever seems bothered by what it implies, that we are ringleaders conducting circus acts. This is just one of the school practices that distends cynicism in students like Lesley, who don't want to play the game. Students are not fools. They know what's going on. The grade game shows them in no uncertain terms that their worth, like trained animals, is jumping through contrived hoops, measured in As and Bs and Cs and Ds. It promotes parents to ask their kids "What did you get?" when they come home from school instead of "What did you learn?" Do you know what many teachers do when they see that their students' averages are not as high as they would like, believing they are doing the right thing? They throw in a few easy quizzes to inflate the grades. What does this "teach" our children?

The problem is that when we enable them, kids begin to think that no matter how much trouble they get into there is always a way out, a second chance, a reprieve. Yes, there may be some small consequences to their mistakes—a detention here, a grade of C there— but never long-lasting ones, nothing permanent or fatal, except, of course, when they crash their cars driving too fast while texting. That has happened to more than a few of my students, and when it does there is the initial mandatory expression of grief, but what is telling is that the kids are more surprised that something like sudden death can happen than they are saddened by the unnecessary, careless loss of a classmate's life, as if the accident didn't follow the rules, was so far beyond their expectations that they slough it off as something that could only happen to someone else, never them, wrongly assuming they will always be protected. And their naivety goes beyond the classic youthful delusion that they are impervious. Their audacity is something new, troublingly different, a kind of willful defiance of the laws of the universe. Unlike their predecessors, they have been *taught* to believe they are invincible. Who needs self-discipline when, like a super hero, you're a super kid!

One Monday morning a student came into class wearing a neck brace, her face bruised. I'd heard rumors there had been an accident but hadn't been able to confirm it. It turned out Becky had been in the car with a boy who had graduated the year before. Speeding, he had crossed a double line, passing another car on winding road, and when a truck loomed into the lane he rammed his car into a tree to avoid it. He had almost killed her, yet she wasn't mad at him. It was a joke. She laughed at it, as the rest of the class did. They were impressed with the playfulness of it all. It was as if she had been in a video game. Even the pain she felt was a virtual reality.

You see them driving on the highway, young people with no more than a few years experience behind the wheel, weaving through traffic at breakneck speeds and you know they have no sense of the danger. They go by you so fast it takes your breath away as if they think they are back in their bedrooms playing X-box. They play in our classrooms without much real fear as well, maybe a bit worried about the occasional B- on a paper or 78 on a test. But even that disaster can be quickly remedied by another easy quiz, extra credit, a phone call from a parent. Certainly our students are not afraid of being unable to read and think deeply, a condition with actual consequences. Because grades have paramount importance, we have erected for our children a make-believe world, a paradise, an academic Garden of Eden without any real danger, a thriving lie.

Again, the root cause of this was the 60s youth movement, which led to Me Decade parents spawning Generation Me children and endowing them with way too much attention and esteem, then demanding their teachers to do the same. Schools capitulated. Youth now is to be celebrated, not educated.

In *The Dumbest Generation* Mark Bauerlein, calls this "the betrayal of the mentors." He writes of teachers' and parents' overindulgence of children, alleging that our endless interference is achieving the exact opposite effect of what education intends: we are actually making our kids dumber. "The attitude marks one of the signal changes of the twentieth century in the United States. It insists that a successful adolescence and rightful education entail growing comfortable with yourself, with who you are at age 17. Many generations ago, adolescent years meant preparation for something beyond adolescence, not authentic selfhood but serious work, civic duty, and family responsibility, with parents, teachers, ministers and employers training teens in grown-up conduct."

Before this new attitude, before this betraying of our children under the guise of helping them, it could have been said of education that a desirable intellectual goal for young adults was to be *uncomfortable* with themselves and who there were at age seventeen, so that their intellectual and emotional pain would prompt them to explore, yearn, learn, and create pathways to greater understanding in order to endure. But we teachers are failing at educating our young at what matters because, ironically, we are too youth-centered, too student-centered. We care too much about kids. We are trying so hard to teach that we are accepting *their* responsibilities. With all of our elaborate rubrics and review sheets and methodologies and layers upon layers of special education services and ever-changing pedagogies and assessments, we are smothering them, preventing them from learning the basics, from how to think for themselves, to self-discipline, to English grammar, stunting their growth, when this is exactly what we had hoped all our progressive pedagogies would avoid. Worse, we are getting in the way of them learning how to handle failure. Bauerlein tells us "in a traditional classroom from way back when, a youth-centered approach might have appeared iconoclastic and provocative, triggering disputes over learning, maturity, and selfhood. Now it passes without a murmur. Spend some hours in school zones and you see the indulgent attitude toward youth, along with the downplaying of tradition, has reached the point of dogma among teachers. Pro-knowledge, pro-tradition conceptions strike them as bluntly unpleasant, if not reactionary and out of touch."

A *good* teacher is no longer a sage on the stage. We mentors have abdicated center stage to our children, at school as well as at home. Being the sage—in other words sagacious, level-headedness, prudent, wise, learned, judicious—is no longer fashionable. In most schools it isn't even tolerated. If, for example, during a formal observation, a teacher takes too much class time lecturing (the word itself is now taboo), she is instantly reprimanded. If she is untenured, her future in education is seriously endangered. Far better for the teacher to show how she can get out of the way and allow her students to self-instruct, to make their learning "student-centered" and fun. So we experts step aside to foster the foolishness of such youth-affirming strategies as peer editing, a practice in which one student critiques another student's writing. Teaching is based on activities instead of thinking. Of course teachers believe that by performing in an activity, instead of sitting passively at their desks listening, students are thinking. But are they? I see a whole lot of doing going on, getting the "job" done, but not much thinking. "Today, boys and girls, what I want you to do is..." This is how many teachers begin every lesson. The object is to do what you are told, not think too much about. At least that is how it's perceived by the grade-conscious students. "If I do this the way my teacher wants it done, I will be rewarded." And so they are turned loose to perform a task. During their performance I see a lot of socializing and some productivity, certainly worthwhile goals, teamwork, collaboration, although predictably, as in life, a few of the kids lead and work while most of the others goof off and, at best, follow. But we shouldn't mistake these behaviors for introspection, for analysis, for evaluation, for invention, for the stuff of critical thinking. In fact these consensus-building activities could be seen as edifices to induce conformity, preparing out students for the march toward becoming a cog in the great American machine. I don't see conspiracy here. I think it would be going too far to accuse our schooling of existing merely to grease the capitalistic engine, but even so, capitalism requires innovation more than regimentation. Our system needs creativity more than it does institutionalization. What I see is the students' self-instruction becomes self-destruction. But not to worry: the kids feel *good* about themselves. Why don't we understand that thinking is the grandest activity of all, that what is fun is rarely good for us, that what really is good for us is usually really hard?

One worry I have, although unsubstantiated, is that schooling has turned so voraciously toward activities-based learning because being a sage on the stage and teaching students to think is a lot harder than being a social director. Instead of being concerned with helping students learn, perhaps all this deflected teaching has found its way into our curricula because we teachers simply don't want to do the very hard work of standing before a class all period long commanding their attention and demanding that they learn by listening to us and thinking independently about what we've said, so instead we turn them loose in the name of the latest progressive pedagogy. Let's face it: walking around the classroom refereeing their group work is less demanding than knowing so much about our subject matter and having such a deep and abiding passion that a teacher can talk movingly about it for a whole class period and inspire. Remember those teachers we would have listened to, spellbound, for hours?

This is not to say that the children run around unchecked. They don't, not in schools like mine anyway. We have rules, although not so strict. Kids receive detentions, although they are perceived to be more like afterschool playtime than punishment. They can even receive suspensions, although they are rare, and, in many cases, welcomed: far better to be at home than in school. In fact, the school is required by law to provide a tutor so a suspended student won't fall behind.

The other day two teachers overheard a student taunting a gay student with vicious slurs. They immediately referred him to the principal who recommended he be suspended. Our school has a very strict policy against this kind of bullying. In fact, just the week before we had an assembly at which an authority spoke to the entire student body about homophobia and the horror of the recent suicide of a Rutgers student. But the bully's parents appealed the suspension to the superintendent. To her credit the superintendent backed it. The parents then took their appeal to the school board, which overturned it, citing that there wasn't enough evidence to justify the severe penalty. Two eyewitnesses—teachers, professionals—weren't enough. In this Never-Never Land of make-believe it is the teachers' word against the bully's, and he wins.

What does go unchecked is our students' false sense of confidence. They slouch in their seats. They leave their empty water bottles behind. For a long time I thought this was just laziness or faulty upbringing, but I've since come to see it more as a distorted, undeserved, dangerous form of arrogance. How in the world can a seventeen-year-old be arrogant? Arrogant adolescence. Adolescent arrogance. This is oxymoronic. Teenagers are supposed to be adrift, lost, floundering, and therefore uniquely ready intellectually for much needed help from the likes of Melville, Hamlet, and Homer. Yet they feel completely comfortable describing Wilson's elegant *Against Happiness* as "dumb." They are at ease proclaiming that "all that guy does is keep referring to things nobody knows anything about, like William Blake, whoever that is, and who cares, and besides, he uses big words just to impress us." Never once does it occur to them that they are dumb for not recognizing Wilson's allusions, not knowing about romantic poetry or understanding vocabulary. They are too used to being the stars, too sure of themselves. For those of you who have never been inside a classroom, replay in your minds celebrities like Sean Penn and Ben Affleck and Susan Sarandon pontificating about politics, how, if you are like me, you cringe at their unearned audacity, at how pathetically unqualified they are, yet they believe their views are not only legitimate but important and profound simply because of who they are. It would be like me lecturing them about acting. It would never occur to me even to consider it. It would be too absurdly foolish. I would be afraid of being laughed at. That's how our students look, spewing random opinions on Franz Kafka such as, "this book sucks," ridiculously *un*-entitled to say whatever they please without reasons or evidence or experience to back it. But no one is laughing at them, even though their arguments, if you can call them that, are specious, vague, replete with fallacies such as *ad hominem, post hoc,* straw man, *tu quoque,* over-generalization, slippery slope, circular reasoning. They don't care. Why should they? They have never been taught the necessity and beauty of logical reasoning. All they've been taught is they "have a right" to their own opinion, not that their opinions need to be scrupulously, meticulously defended. How far will these undisciplined, unexamined minds take them?

"None," the vast majority of my seniors say when, upon first meeting them, I ask them what books they enjoyed in grades nine, ten and eleven.

"None?" I reply. "Come on. You had to read a lot of books. Not even one? Not even *Catcher in the Rye*? How can you not like Holden?"

"I hated him," one girl says, cringing as if she's just tasted something bitter.

"I can't stand that book," another adds. "I hated having to read that thing."

"Why?" I asking, hoping for a good debate.

"I don't know. Because. I just did."

End of debate.

"I'll tell you why," a senior will inevitably say. "Because we had to. We were forced to read them. I don't like any book that I have to read."

"What does *having* have to do with it?" I ask. "Either it's a good book that you like or it isn't."

"Yeah. I hate it when it's an assignment," another student adds, allowing my question to evaporate.

Sadly, I go through this with them every year. At first I dismissed it as age-appropriate rebellion, again some laziness, the coolness factor—yes, it is now cool to hate learning, especially reading—but now I know their disdain for assigned texts has a much more serious vein. They despise *duties*. They loathe requirements. It causes me to wonder if the school, we teachers, might be the last place where kids have authority figures, or quasi-authority figures, anyway. Do they "have to" do anything at home anymore, mow the lawn, wash the dishes, take out the garbage, clean their rooms, or is all of that done for them? Do they ever have to *obey*, except to get good grades? We elders have engendered a very serious attitude problem: our children not only believe they can do no wrong (except get bad grades), but that they know better than their mentors. It seems that a few generations ago, adolescents, even if they didn't admit it, were confused, perplexed, unsure of themselves, which, of course, fostered growth. If I am weak, then I need to get strong. If I am dim, then I need to get bright. But that logic isn't relevant any more either. This means that when we, and society, and natural law require something of our young people, say, don't tailgate when driving or do read this book, they feel entitled to say no. What they are is unafraid and therefore disrespectful. By celebrating them so much we have driven away their awe, their capacity for wonder. They have been permanently reduced to the very dangerous state of insubordination. At my high school and many like it we routinely teach the likes of *Hamlet* and Melville and Homer but we avoid insisting to our students that if they don't really read and understand and internalize them, they will become incomplete people and lead incomplete lives, as Baulerlein puts it. We don't threaten them, make them squirm with uneasiness and self-doubt. And God help a teacher who suggests they actually might be dumb as my teachers frequently did to me. "Ouch," is what kids say if a teacher chooses to challenge rather than coddle, attempts to put them in their place. "I'm going to tell my parents." We never scare them, because we can't. They are immune, untouchable. We are not allowed to tell students in no uncertain terms that they are still profoundly unaware and if they don't stop believing they're all that, they will soon find themselves in unspeakable trouble. Instead we indulge them, and, in doing so, we betray them.

School Spirit

ALMOST AS soon as the school year begins, the seniors receive clear but misleading signals (which quickly descend through the ranks to underclassmen) that what happens outside the classroom is as important, if not more important, than what goes on in the classroom. "See, it's true," the 12th graders sigh with relief. "Senior year will be different. The work really is over." On the Friday of the very first week they are allowed to leave school around noon to attend their class B-B-Q, which, like so many of our indulgences, is well intended. But the unintended consequence is that instead of the bonding that is supposed to occur they stay for an hour or so, eat a burnt burger, then cut away in their cars to the beach or to cruise the malls, all sanctioned by school policy. What this event tells them in no uncertain terms is that class time is no longer as important as their other senior activities, reinforcing the notion that high school merely exists to get them into college, something that does not go unnoticed among the younger students.

Following hard upon the Senior B-B-Q comes Spirit Week, something akin to a school wide week-long beach party. Monday is Pajama Day. Then Tropical Tuesday, then Wacky Wednesday, followed by Thursday Night Fever. Try to imagine teaching chemistry or Spanish to a class full of kids dressed like Lady Gaga. Friday is Blue and Gold Day. The classes are shortened to accommodate the traditional home coming weekend pep rally, which can't be held after school, of course, because too few kids would attend or it would interfere with practices. The quieter students cower in the bleachers, forced to behold a spectacle that celebrates the loud and popular. The pep rally perennially deteriorates into its most anticipated moment, the senior girls doing sleazy dances wearing short shorts and cleavage exposing low-cut skin-tight shirts with clever obscene slogans such as "Senior girls do it better!" Allowing school to be reduced to jungle of bizarre, hurtful primitive rituals like this also sends a message to the students about the building they occupy, that it is not special. Remember: these are not critical thinkers. They can't analyze and evaluate the distinction between these rare outbursts in the gymnasium and the quiet lectures in the classroom. All they can do is lump the activities together and assume they are somehow compatible. And so the shouting and immaturity reinforce their misguided notion that school and all it implies is a game to be played, not a hallowed place of learning to be respected.

Sure, I know why there's a Spirit Week, but does it set the appropriate *twenty-first century* tone for the school year? Yeah, it promotes enthusiasm for the school, and after the week of ramping up (rendering too much class work irrelevant) the students sure do make a lot of noise in the gymnasium when the football team is introduced. But where is their spirit the following Monday morning back in the classroom, where, as usual, the seniors (and too many underclassmen—they may look like they are paying attention but all they are concerned with is the next quiz) sit disengaged from the learning, watching the clock, texting below their desks, waiting for the group work to begin so they can goof off? What kind of *spirit* (i.e. strength, soul, courage, character, determination, moral fiber, heart) is that? What, exactly, are we educators trying to accomplish here?

Not even a month of the new school year goes by when I am in the middle of teaching a lesson and a senior gets up from his seat and heads for the door. I look at him, but before I can ask where he is going and he self-assuredly replies: my senior photo. The school actually allows these photos to be scheduled during class time, because, again, if they were scheduled after school, not enough students would show up for them to produce an acceptable yearbook, signaling that they are not so much interested in traditions as they are in missing class. Does that lead to educated graduates?

When the college representatives start visiting, my senior classroom would be better served with a revolving door. "Where are you going this time?" I ask a senior girl. By now they have so many excuses to leave class—blood donor day, the wrecked car out front of the school to caution against drunk driving—that I can't keep up. "Guidance, the guy's here from Princeton." The guy. This girl's average hovers just below a B. "You are considering going there?" I ask. "Yup," she lies, and there is nothing I can do about it. Otherwise her mother would call and accuse me of preventing her child from getting into an Ivy League school. And the kids know it. So with a smirk she leaves. The school has provided yet another irreproachable excuse for them to disrespect learning.

Then there is the day the guidance counselors come and take over all the senior classes to talk to the students about college applications. The reason why this meeting can't take place some other time eludes me. I guess I don't have my priorities straight. So whatever lessons we teachers of seniors have planned must wait. It doesn't matter what we're doing with them at the time, what momentum we've created, which is vital to sustain any learning that is going on. It is interrupted. These are seniors, and what the teachers are covering just isn't as important as the college talk. And ironically, it looks like this:

"Those of you who have begun the application process, please raise your hands?" the guidance counselor asks.

I have twenty-five students. Four hands rise. It is late September.

"How many of your parents have begun the process," the guidance counselor asks wisely.

Three times as many hands rise.

My seniors know someone else will apply to college for them. Why shouldn't they? For seventeen years someone else has been doing everything for them.

Then the guidance counselor attempts to bestow some discipline, but it backfires woefully.

"Keep in mind that you may think you are done, that your senior year grades don't count, but they do," she warns futilely. "We have had students who were border-line at their top choice schools but didn't get in because their first semester grades were significantly lower than their GPAs. You shouldn't goof off too much third quarter either."

Goof off? Too much? What about fourth quarter? Thanks for your guidance.

What is so remarkable, no, so incredible, is that this interruption, as much as it annoys me every year, is necessary. These seniors need this meeting, a wake-up call to remind them that in a few months they will be graduating from high school. My seniors wait for this, showing little or no initiative, the way they wait for everything else.

For seniors the year drags on, rife with distractions, interruptions, and excuses for abusing learning.

For many of the years I have been teaching, commencing in May, (or as soon as AP tests are over—APs seem to govern just about everything we do at my school) the seniors, our finished products, so to speak, were no longer required to attend their social studies classes. Instead they performed "internships," not academic or scholarly ones, by the way, such as working with a local historian or at the office of their state or national congressional representative. No. These internships are vocational. The students interned with local businesses, restaurants, auto dealerships, law offices. They would file papers, fold boxes at the local pizzeria, roll balls across the gymnasium toward kindergartners at the elementary school, ostensibly learning something about the nature of work or the profession, in case it proved to be something they wanted to pursue as a career. Following their internship they then were required to do a presentation on it for their grade.

Then a few years ago our principal expanded the program, adding what he calls the Senior Externship, allowing qualifying 12th graders not to come to school at all for their last two months of high school. Their grades had to be C or better, with no disciplinary issues. They submitted a proposal and if it was accepted they were free, again to pursue some alleged vocational interest. At first, twenty or so students were allowed to participate.

This past year, though, well over half the senior class applied, and they were *all* accepted, regardless of their grades or past transgressions. The principal confessed it was just too difficult to be objective about choosing one proposal over another.

Now we have a new Senior Externship program, following the model of most high schools across the county. Commencing this spring all seniors must participate, even though many don't want to, which means that during the months of May and June we 12th grade teachers will be staring at empty class rooms.

Aristotle very carefully warned about the dangers of substituting vocational training for academic instruction and inspiration: "The meaner sort of artisan is a slave, not for all purposes but for a definite servile task." This is what happens to our children when they are schooled only for the purpose of work, instead of for the enrichment of their minds. They become enslaved, shackled to the ordinary, the mundane, the routine, the surface of things, like the prisoners in Plato's cave.

School is an academic institution, not an employment agency. Schooling should provide an education, not a training program. I understand the argument that it is valuable for these young people to go out and get a taste of the real world, report to a boss, all that everyday stuff, but our students will get to spend their entire adult lives waking up and reporting to a job. Now is not the time for that, when they are making ready for four years at college. How many of our seniors would have submitted proposals this year if their externships needed to be scholarly, say researching a topic and writing a dissertation on it, instead of vocational? None. Which might suggest how motivated our graduates are to pursue real learning, ostensibly the reason why they should be going to college in the first place. It seems to me we've got things upside down here. I just don't believe that what these young people are doing out there in these externships is more valuable to them at this time of their lives than continuing their education, and the evidence of that is their disinterest in anything academic. What the vaunted senior externship program tells the entire student body in no uncertain terms is that what goes on inside the classroom—mathematics, literature, art, history, music, science—is not as important as what goes on in the outside world, that education is not a highly desirable end to itself, but merely a means to a practical end, the world of work rather than the work of the mind.

Group Play

THE GOOD news, I suppose, is that even through all the interruptions and disruptions students still have to show up for class, most of the time anyway, if for no other reason than to review for the barrage of quizzes and tests they take. But even inside the class-room, they are indulged with practices that pamper rather than push them, providing them with "good grades" they don't deserve, also serving to undermine their self-education.

Take "group work," for example, the most common form of activities-based learning. Group work is, by now, ubiquitous. How? Why? What is it, really?

Almost immediately after I started the process of becoming a teacher, in one of my graduate education classes, I was taught what I now know to be the core of public educational dogma, that people retain 10 percent of what they read, 20 percent of what they hear, 30 percent of what they see, 50 percent of what they see and hear, 70 percent of what they say or discuss, and 90 percent of what they say and do. My professor told me emphatically about the ancient Chinese proverb that goes: "I hear and I forget, I see and I remember, I do and I understand." This mantra guides nearly every aspect of teaching today, to the point where asking a student to listen is almost forbidden, which, of course, is producing legions of young people who can't. Have you noticed how many times you have to re-peat yourself to store clerks, airline reservationists, waitresses, who, after you have had to give your instructions multiple times still get it wrong? A growing number of educational researchers now consider the method of *doing* rather than *listening* to be more myth than science. Yet it prevails. In fact, even when I myself am a student, say attending a post-graduate class to improve my teaching, I am subjected to it, put in a group to work. I hate it. I learn nothing. I have paid for the professor to teach me something. I have paid for expertise. Yet I am forced to sit with a group of peers in an awkward Darwinian struggle over who will take charge. Since when are we supposed to emulate the Chinese? Why not emulate Ben Franklin, who said:

> *A republic, if you can keep it.*
> *An investment in knowledge pays the best interest.*

A man wrapped up in himself makes a very small bundle.

Being ignorant is not so much a shame, as being unwilling to learn.

Diligence is the mother of good luck.

He does not possess wealth; it possesses him.

Honesty is the best policy.

There never was a truly great man that was not at the same time truly virtuous.

Group work is an example of the widely practiced methodology of differentiated instruction, a form of teaching which attempts to accommodate various learning styles and abilities. It is serious-minded and well-intended, but too often it is too predictable; kids know the formula so well they can recite it and so they abuse it. They have been told what kind of learners they are: visual, like my young homework-challenged friend, or maybe kinesthetic. So they can justifiably dismiss all other kinds of learning as unavailable to them, irrelevant. "Oh, Mr. B. is going to talk now," they say to themselves, "but since I only learn from doing, I don't have to pay attention until he breaks us up into groups." That is the problem with these methodologies: by providing our students with a whole set of elaborate excuses we enable them to avoid the hard work that learning usually requires. We justify their inattention. They "learn" how to avoid being self-starters, being self-taught.

Group work, also sometimes known as collaborative or cooperative or team learning, is a teaching tool used, not only to accommodate learning styles, but to facilitate better learning because it is universally believed that students learn more and retain more by being directly involved. Teachers prepare students with the important skills necessary for groups to function properly. It is believed that students are better motivated when they know their group members depend on them. A task is assigned and the groups have at it. But too often what actually goes on during group work, just as it does in life, is that one kid—the leader type—does most of the work. The others know this so they let him. They follow. They *learn* to follow. We teachers are indoctrinating them to become middle managers, employees rather than employers. When I ask my seniors about group work they laugh.

"We love it. Usually you don't have to do anything until the teacher comes around with her clipboard and rubric. Then we pretend we are doing what she asked us."

This is what group work too often results in, more cynicism.

It unfolds this way: After about ten minutes of a lecture that leads to Socratic questions that lead to a whole class discussion (in which too few participate), I can palpably detect their squirminess. My students' body clocks are telling them it is time for them to get out of their seats. Some actually do, to throw something away that doesn't need to be thrown away until after class. Too many ask to go to the bathroom. To them, it is time for the teacher (and them) to stop talking; they want to be excused from having to listen and think quietly. They want to be divided into groups. (Many of those who chose not to participate in the whole class discussion did so on purpose, to speed it up so we would move on to the less rigorous task of not having to listen, of not having to make sense by themselves of what they were hearing.) So a task and groups are assigned. They get up. This means five lost minutes of chairs and desks squealing as they are moved around, languid body shuffling, giggling. They love this part. What they really love is to be exiled to the hallways where they can practice, say, their Shakespeare scenes, unguided. I know of one teacher who keeps an egg timer on her desk. The kids watch it, nearly salivating, conditioned like Pavlov's dogs. When it rings it's time for them to be turned loose. They simply cannot sit still and listen for even 40 minutes.

What becomes of them a year later in the large university auditoriums (as in audio, as in auditory, i.e. to listen) where they must sit with two hundred other freshmen while a professor's assistant or a graduate student or, if they are really lucky, an actual professor, lectures them for two hours? It is well-documented: they occupy the time texting or Facebooking on their laptops pretending to take notes. Or they transfer or drop out and go home.

But why should they have to listen, it might be fairly asked, if students can learn by doing? Because even in the twenty-first century human beings will still need attention spans. Our mental endeavors cannot be condensed to the intellectual equivalent of a sound bite. Concentration is not a thing of the past. Yet every day we teach as if it were; we eager teachers offer up to our students a dizzying, delicious array of exciting diversions from the hard job of sitting still, paying attention and allowing the mind to engage intellectually instead of being stimulated, by sights, sounds, motions. Our academic classrooms often resemble physical education classes. I'm surprised the balls and mats haven't come out. (My wife tells me they already have.) The hallways are always crowded with kids doing projects. Administrators glow, satisfied that much great learning is happening. The more outrageously different a lesson is from the traditional classic lecture the more it is celebrated. "Wonderment and awe" is one of the desirable "habits of the mind" Bela Kalick and all of us teachers strive for, but too often we fall for the latest 'initiative' passed down from administrators' offices because they have recently attended some conference or read another edu-speak book. Technology for technology's sake! We need to use more of it in the classroom because, well, it's there! Children, Kalick contends, need to be amazed, for example, when they behold a spider web.

The trick is how we educators get kids to accomplish this. Kalick and her disciples insist we need to instill a passion in them for learning, to be curious, to want to reflect on the formations of a cloud. This is the good intention of the bells and whistles. But maybe to do this we need to slow the kids down first, free them to roam around inside their own minds for a while, and this requires a skill they sorely lack, imagination. And they must want it, not because their teacher has told them to, but because they really are passionate everywhere that learning is available, not just in groups. Passion is a contagious thing. Our kids can catch it. But we teachers, and the administrators who guide us, seem to be relying too much on external stimulation, when our kids are already over-stimulated. Our kids already have too many things on their plate. Their brains can't handle it all. Yes, we need to amaze them, but not so much by the fancy animations on our Smart Boards as by our own commitment to and knowledge of and enthusiasm for the subjects we teach, by the look in our eyes as we stand before them, by our body language. But instead we always seem to be dismissing them, getting them up out of their seats every ten minutes or so, or spicing up our lessons, say with the latest gadgetry—blogging, tweeting, video conferencing— serving the noble end of differentiating learning and implementing technology. But we've gone overboard along with those moms. All this stimulation does more damage to our students' attention spans than a thousand text messages, because we the mentors are sanctioning it. The result is that kids have developed selective hearing. They hear what they want to, then they zone out, exonerated. We are teaching kids that they cannot learn unless the experience is as entertaining as their video games. They are addicted. They cannot function without sizzle. Or they are like athletes who load up on steroids and hit lots of home runs. What is knocking the ball out of the park, their skill or their artificial musculature? What about the quieter wonderment and awe of Hamlet's soliloquies, Chamberlain's heroics at Little Round Top Hill during the Battle of Gettysburg, the chemical composition of a strand of DNA? What about the ultimate wonderment and awe of an amazing teacher?

I am not advocating a return to chalk and talk, but I am advocating that we stop discouraging teacher-centered *teaching*. We have drifted too far from traditions that work. Yes, there is a value for group *work*, but not for group *play*. And it can never replace the truly gifted teacher who as tour-de-force can bring a whole class to its collective knees. "I'm going to major in biology," a student says proudly. Chances are group work and techno-wizardry didn't inspire this. A teacher did. Students simply cannot become that inspired off in the hallway by themselves. They need a mentor on the stage, a role model, exciting them, exposing them to their civilization's great ideas and making them relevant. This is difficult to do, to be sure. It demands a special kind of person. Is that perhaps another reason why we have abdicated the stage, because we're out of talent? I don't see any evidence of that, at least not in my school. I see lots of talent and dedication, enthusiasm and passion, but they are too often misdirected.

The Rubric Rube

ANOTHER EXAMPLE of overdoing it is the rubric rube. During one of our department meetings, a colleague shared with us a new strategy to help her students better focus on what they needed to improve their writing. It was another rubric she gave to the students after their initial rubric. For example, a student turns in a writing assignment, say a paper or an analytical paragraph. We English teachers read the paper, comment on it, both in the margins and between lines, then make general comments at the end of the paper. We then attach to the paper a detailed rubric, offering criteria on thesis to punctuation to paragraphing to overall content and meaning. We meticulously check each box, offer more comments per specific criteria, and then at the end of the rubric once again offer general commentary, including the grade. But my dedicated colleague believed this still wasn't enough. On the second rubric the student was required to record the areas of his writing he had done well on and those that still needed work. The purpose, my colleague explained, was so the student wouldn't just focus on the grade he got for the first paper. He would be forced to read the comments and first rubric.

The department applauded the concept.

But I wondered about it. Of course I use rubrics, mainly because I believe they made teaching and learning easier. But suddenly the image of one assessment attached surreptitiously to a second caused me to question once again if we were going overboard here.

I asked my wife if elementary school teachers use rubrics.

"We are mandated to use them, so the parent can see exactly who is best. I am required to use them too, in art. Imagine a rubric for artwork. Rubrics kill creativity. It would be like you giving out rubrics for your creative writing kids, a rubric for writing a poem. So they follow the little directions making sure all the parts are in place according to what is expected. Is that creative? But parents seem not to care so much if their kids are allowed to be creative as they care about performance. 'Johnnie got a 2 instead of 3 on the rubric. Why isn't he the best? What can you do to make him the best?' Parents are desperate for their kids to always be the best or among the best, and I think we have caused this by providing all these tangible measurements. What makes a rubric easy to use is also what makes it easy to abuse. The numbers are right there for everyone to see, a 2 instead of a 3. Whatever the highest score on the rubric is, that's what they want."

We even have a rubric for our Socratic Seminars. The students sit in their respective groups responding to a Socratic question guided by requirements on the rubric. Even the language they must use is written down for them to emulate. Imagine what Socrates would have thought.

Rubrics have even invaded the sanctuary of skiing. After twenty years as a coach, I must now issue rubric-like "report cards" to my eleven-year-old "athletes." My sport is reduced to this. This is what the rush, the thrill, the dance with inertia and gravity, the smiles and shrieks, the indiscernible joy of sliding down a snowy mountain on a pair of thin plastic boards then becomes to the kids, a grid of criteria and descriptors, a code box of "desirable outcomes" and goals, another test to pass or fail.

Busy Work

EARLY EACH morning when I walk through the hallways of our school on the way to my classroom I come across the same sight, students huddled earnestly in groups of five or six sitting cross-legged on the floor, leaning on the lockers, furiously copying each other's homework. I see the same sight at lunchtime when I wander through the cafeteria.

Another way we betray our students is all the unnecessary homework we assign, usually because we think we are supposed to, that it's the right thing to do. Imagine a job you work at every day for eight hours, but your boss sends you home every night with more work to do, most of it without much purpose. In fact, you soon realize that the work you are forced to do at home is more to help your boss look good than it is for you to do a better job. You would feel used. You would start looking for another job. This is precisely how our students feel, and what they do is turn cynical. They give up on their job of learning and replace it with the other job of faking it, of cheating to get by.

Almost every teacher in high schools like mine assigns homework every night, for many reasons. Even the kids will admit that some homework is necessary, especially in certain subjects such as math and foreign languages, because they require lots of practice, like learning how to play a musical instrument. And other subjects require some work to be done at home simply because there aren't enough hours in the school day, such as English. Longer novels can't be ready during class time, although in my class we read shorter novels and plays to avoid the problem. The same holds true with history textbook chapters. But most homework is actually destructive, mainly because it isn't necessary. It is another way schools destroy the idealism that is the necessary foundation of education because so much of it is phony and abusive and corrupt and no one knows this better than the kids, and so, tragically, they transfer this disgust and cynicism to the rest of their learning. And what teacher really believes in this era of Instant Messages, Facebook and texting that their students, alone in their control and command centers, really concentrate enough on their homework for it to do any good? An assignment that should take twenty minutes now takes over an hour because of the constant interruptions. Students call homework "busy work" and this is what they tell me about it:

"Teachers give us homework only as something for them to do."

"Teachers don't have enough confidence in themselves not to give homework."

"Teachers don't read our homework. They pretend they do. They will walk around the class and glance down at it, then check you off in their book, but there have been a million times when I just put anything on the paper and the teacher nods at me and says good job and gives me a check plus."

"One time I handed in a homework assignment that was supposed to be who knows what, but all I did was write about Zombies and how Hitler was a great guy and when the teacher it handed back she had written good and interesting on it in a few places and gave me a B+."

"We copy homework assignments from each other word for word and no one ever catches us because teachers don't read homework."

"One time for homework I wrote the lyrics of my favorite song over and over again."

"Homework is 30 percent meaningful and 70 percent bullshit. The problem is that because 70 percent of it is busy-work bullshit we don't care about the 30 percent."

Review Sheets

FINALLY, A last word about those ubiquitous review sheets! Review sheets are also dispensed with the intent of helping, a noble goal, but to what end? I think of them as little gnats stinging the resolve out of students. "We are having a test on Friday. Here is your review sheet." When a teacher does this it tells the students that up until this moment they really didn't have to do all that much. Sure, the teacher insists there might be thing or two on the test that is not on the review sheet, but thematically and significantly, this is it. And the kids know that if there is something on the test that was not on the review sheet, they can tell their mothers who will surely call to complain about it.

At the beginning of each year I tell my classes that during the course of the unit we will be having tests.

"Will you be giving us review sheets?" I am asked immediately.

"Why would I do that?" I ask back.

They look at each other puzzled.

"I mean, why would you need review sheets?" I continue, playing with them. "Shouldn't I assume that you will be paying attention and taking appropriate notes, making your own decisions about what is important enough to warrant being part of an assessment of your learning?"

Their faces go white, blank.

"Oh, and by the way, I don't announce tests. I just spring them."

"You mean pop quizzes?"

"No, I mean pop tests, big ones."

We teachers baby them because we are afraid if they don't do well it somehow reflects on us.

"Did you give out a review sheet?" asked an irate parent once after her daughter scored a D on one of my tests.

"No. I don't think it's right to encourage my students to wait around until someone else does the job of learning for them," I said.

She disagreed.

What does the long practice of review sheets and announced tests look like when our students become seniors and the hand-holding is supposed to be over and they should be able to think and learn for themselves?

Senioritis

DURING THE teaching of my 12th grade English course I try to search for whatever truth is available by raising questions and asking my students to respond, yet most choose not to. I will introduce a topic related to our reading, then narrow it into a specific inquiry:

"Hamlet's antic disposition, his feigning craziness," I say. "It might be that he really is just putting on an act to catch the king. But it also might be that he is going insane. If he is going insane the cause might be the death of his father by the hand of his uncle. It might also be Hamlet's discovery that life is meaningless. Does life have to have a meaning? If it does and yet you can't find one, is that unsettling? What do you think about all this?"

My classes have on average twenty-five students. Having now taught for eleven years, I can accurately predict the number of hands that will rise after posing a question like this. None. Zero. It used to bother me, a lot, until over the years I came to understand why. Some of it has to do with fear. Even at age seventeen and eighteen, students are still worried what their peers will think of them. Some are afraid that by responding to my questions they might sound dumb. And remarkably, some are terrified of sounding smart, of going along with the teacher, instead of resisting. "Whoa, what did he have for breakfast?" I've heard them say sarcastically, insulting students who choose to participate. What these students want is for the teacher and his dopy questions to go away, not be encouraged by some eager student's willingness to answer him. But most of their silence, their collective unwillingness, is apathy and indifference. Unless there is a grade or rubric attached, the students feel no need to participate.

To combat it, I wait them out.

My question posed—'What do you think?'—I stand before them, unmoving, unflinching. I scan them, one face at a time. When eye contact is made they lower their heads. Time drips by. One by one they begin to squirm, shuffle in their seats. I say nothing more, just watch. It can take five minutes before someone finally breaks down and responds, sometimes longer. But no matter how long it takes I don't back down and answer the question for them, which is what they all want.

So I wait.

"Well, I guess I think that…" a student finally begins.

And with that one student's defeat, which of course is really his victory, the rest of the class capitulates.

"You were the subject of the pre-class kids' chatter," a science teacher told me once. "They are in utter amazement at your stamina."

"My what?"

"I overheard them saying how you waited over half the class period for someone to answer a question. They were quite impressed."

The problem is it hurts to wait them out. We teachers have a lot to get done, so too many of us lose our patience and give in. Instead of waiting for them to respond we answer the questions for them, which accomplishes nothing but them sighing with relief. They won. The teacher backed down and did the intellectual work for them.

Each year I ask seniors the following questions and each year they are more and more shocked when I tell them the answer:

"How many of you want jobs that will pay you a lot of money?" I ask.

All their hands go up.

"Okay, I am going to describe two different situations to you. Pick which one you think will lead to you making the most money. The first is this. You are making your way through your career at a company you like. You have had a couple of assignments and you've done pretty well and now you've been promoted. On the first day your new boss calls you and says the following: 'Here are ten things I want you to do. Do them well and you will get a big bonus.' Or your boss says the following: 'Congratulations on your promotion. From now on no one will be telling you what to do. You need to be telling us what to do, so we can grow our business. Now get out and make something happen.' Which scenario can you expect to make more money at?"

Everyone shouts out, "The first one!"

"Why?" I ask.

"Because you are following directions exactly, doing what you are told to do and doing it well."

"Well, I've got some bad news for you, although that is what you have been trained to believe. That's not how success really works, if you want to make a lot of money. It is the second one. To be successful you have to think for yourself."

They vehemently disagree, try to cite examples of why I am wrong, deny the truth because it debunks the myth their school has promulgated, that subservient followers win over independent-minded leaders.

For as long as I've been teaching here, our district's main initiative, admirably, has been to improve student research. Committees of parents, administrators and teachers meet to try to improve the way our students conduct and formalize research. The committee recently determined, after reviewing hundreds of research assignments, assessments, and projects that the progression from elementary school through middle and high school was consistently more rigorous, with the exception of the senior year English research paper, which seemed, by comparison, less substantive, the task much less demanding. There is something quite telling here, that the committee seemed to overlook: the devil is in the details. They alleged that the 11th grade English research paper was more complex, citing for example that the assignment consisted of an entire elaborate *packet*, over eight pages of explicit instructions, complete with sample rubrics and formats. The instruction packet was longer than the students' papers needed to be! By comparison the 12th grade assignment consisted of a mere declarative statement: write a research paper on *Hamlet* on any topic of your choosing. Minimum length: six pages. But here's the rub: The 11th grade students know exactly what to do: do this, do that, do this and that. Because of the girth, the weight, the size and scope of the 11th grade teachers' dictates, the project appears formidable, and the results— the papers—appear comprehensive and commendable, but only in so far as how well they follow the teacher's directions. The 12th grade English research paper, on the other hand, includes no packet, no explicit directions, and no dictates. Instead it is purposely vague and open: write a research paper on *Hamlet*, minimum six pages, no maximum. I repeat for emphasis: no maximum. This, after the students have studied the play for well over two months, in all its myriad complexities and possibilities. In fact I refuse to provide them one more time with proper MLA formatting guidelines, because teachers have been giving them these since the 5th grade. That responsibility, along with creating a suitable topic and conducting correspondingly suitable research and finalizing the paper according to MLA standards, is entirely their responsibility. "Figure it out," I write on the board. And these are their final instructions.

Which, then, is more "rigorous" and more "demanding," the 11th or the 12th grade assignment?

Let's ground this in the everyday: to an 11th grader you say that his assignment is to mow the lawn. You then provide him with his *packet*: he must use a Lawn-Boy mulch mower to improve fertilization of the soil by recycling organic matter. Each blade of grass must cut to exactly three inches. The pattern of cutting should not be circular but back and forth to avoid skips. Goggles and gloves must be worn to avoid injury. The meticulous rubric lists and carefully describes these and ten other criteria including the time of day he is allowed to mow. The 11th grader will be able to see exactly how his performance is being measured, how well he either exceeded these explicit expectations, merely met them, or failed to meet them. The 12th grader, however, a year after his comprehensive 11th grade assignment, is merely told: mow the lawn.

During twelve years of "education" kids have been taught over and over again the right way. Why, then, do the seniors usually fail so miserably? Most of their papers fall short of even the minimum required six pages. The others, miraculously, run exactly to the required page count. Their thesis statements are missing or incoherent. Even their papers' formatting is incorrect. Clearly this is what the committee is responding to, but its analysis doesn't go far enough. Its knee-jerk reaction is: we need to make the 12th grade assignment more rigorous and demanding, code for more handholding in the form of related assignments, conferences, revisions. But not only wouldn't that solve the problem, it would exacerbate it, by continuing to coddle them. We could easily and expeditiously and irresponsibly blame it on senioritis, that the seniors know how to write a research paper; it's just that they don't care. But I argue that if by age eighteen our best and brightest don't care about the quality of their intellectual output as they make ready to depart for college, we have Beckett's "catastrophe" on our hands. Worse, senioritis is not only about not caring about schoolwork, it is about not caring about anything, especially something intangible, such as why they should do a job well if there is no reward. The schools, we teachers, have simply overindulged these kids—done the thinking work for them—to make ourselves look good, perhaps. It is another tragedy that by the time they are seniors they have still not learned how to "figure it out" for themselves, and that the most important thing to figure out is how to be proud of their own accomplishments, not for some teacher's recognition, but their own. We have not taught them the most important lesson of all, which is how to take ownership of a responsibility and find dignity by doing so.

17
THE PUBLIC PRIVATE SCHOOL

LAST WINTER I ATTENDED a town-hall-style meeting presented by the principal, conducted in the high school auditorium, on the contentious issue of whether our current system of weighting AP and Honors courses should be eliminated. Weighting works like this: when students qualify for these more challenging courses and elect to take them, the grades they receive are inflated. An earned grade of B, say, is counted as an A-, which, of course goes a long way toward elevating their final GPA and improving their class rank, allowing them a better chance to advance into higher quintiles, giving them a distinct advantage when applying to colleges. Microphones stood on each aisle. The school board was in attendance, along with the superintendent and a hundred or so community members. One by one the parents got up to present their case, speaking mainly from prepared statements:

"Damage will be done if the school district abandons the current system," one father read forcefully. "I have met with several parents who share the same concern. Without incentive to take AP or honor classes, many students will take an easy route out. It would hurt the national ranking of our school district. The number of students taking AP classes is one of the metrics in the *US News* Ranking."

A mother stepped up. "It feels so wrong to be talking about education in quantifiable terms. I look forward to the day when we can focus on how we can our make coursework and teaching so compelling that students will want to learn and reach for the sake of learning. When will schools like ours recognize that critical and creative thinking is crucial, rather than memorization? How can we engage and motivate students, rather than put them into rankings?"

Another father took the microphone. "I am very concerned about the unweighted GPA proposal," he said. "Instead of de-incentivizing students from taking more challenging courses, the administration should be doing more to incentivize them. I'm afraid the unweighted proposal will result in dumbing down our kids. This is in stark contrast to the globally competitive environment. It would ultimately disadvantage our kids. When the school lumps all the high achievers into mediocrity by taking away competition, trust me, it will surely devalue our investments in our homes."

"I support maintaining the current GPA system as a matter of basic fairness," began another mother. "If you work harder, you should be rewarded accordingly. Our students have done very well in terms of college admissions under the current system—why would we want to do anything to jeopardize our success?"

"I would hope that ours is a community where students and parents recognize that the rewards of learning are intrinsic and not some inflated number on a transcript," a father offered.

A man in half glasses read, "I urge people to consider that high school is a crucial educational and growth experience in itself, not simply about getting into a competitive college and certainly let's keep property values out of the discussion. The focus on scores and ranking is insidious, and blinds us to the rich intellectual, creative, and personal differences in our students. Just as the entire senior class should not be lined up top to bottom along one numeric scale, so too we should keep in mind that college options should not be presented to kids like some mathematical chart where you simply plug in your numbers to determine where you belong. It's a rare and fortunate student who approaches the end of high school with some degree of self-awareness and an idea of what kind of college might be right. We should provide as many opportunities as possible for kids to explore their interests, experience real learning, and develop skills and tools for college and life—and make good choices for their next step."

"Let's face reality here," another mother said sternly, waving her papers at the audience. "What that man just said is a pipedream. In high school we prepare our students for life after high school. College is competitive, as is life in general. Having had three children go through our schools I can tell you that if students want to succeed at top colleges, they need good and sound knowledge in core academic subjects and they need rigor. The argument that eliminating course weights will allow students to take courses they love rather than core subjects they need doesn't make sense. They do not need more excuses to kick back and take electives which are less challenging courses. The idea that switching to an unweighted GPA would free our students for course selection toward interests rather than weight is not realistic. These weighted courses are what the college admission counselors looking for. So if a student wants to apply for excellent colleges and stay competitive, he or she has to take these courses no matter what and they should be rewarded for it. Sometimes, principle just cannot 100 percent catch up with reality."

Since when? I went up to one of the microphones, adjusted it and began to speak:

"My name is Mr. Baird and I teach English here at the high school, mainly to seniors. I am here tonight to speak not only for myself, but on behalf of the faculty in urging you to do away with our current GPA weighting system. I have spent a lot of time observing what happens to our students as a result of policies designed to help them, like weighted GPAs, and it can be summed up in one word: senioritis. Although most people don't take it seriously, senioritis has bothered me ever since I began teaching here ten years ago, until I began to understand it, and it is this: our 12th graders' disinterest in learning is direct evidence that we are somehow undermining our children's education, and in the process hurting our children. While our graduates might look good on paper, too many of them are unable to think, and the GPA weighing issue is just one way we're culpable. A student once told me: 'High school is when the Olympics begin.' But the study of Shakespeare, the American Revolution, biology, geometry are not hurdles to jump over. High school should not be an obstacle course, a race, with teachers as timekeepers, referees. This corrupts learning. Worse, it makes cynics of our children. By emphasizing scores and outcomes over thinking we are sending the wrong message, that what matters is not learning, not growing, but only the gold star, the trophy. It breeds a selfish culture of 'What's in it for me?' Do you know that most of our students perform community service or do charity work only to add it to their college resumes? This is a perversion. It subverts not only the noble purpose but also the child's impressionable mind. Motivation to do good, to succeed in life at what truly matters, at work, at home in relationships, even at recreation, doesn't come from external rewards. It comes from within. There is something much bigger and more important than the college acceptance race, and that is acceptance into the human race. But from where I stand, in front of a hundred seniors each year, the final products of our educational system, produced not only by the schools, but by the parents and their priorities, I don't see that happening. A few weeks ago I was talking to one of my classes about the devastating pain in the famous "To Be or Not to Be" soliloquy. In it Hamlet equates choosing to live a life without thought or introspection as a kind of suicide or deep sleep, devoutly to be wished for because thinking, being awake, can be painful. It is one of the most important and moving passages in our language. While I was speaking a student raised his hand. I called on him, eager for a discussion. It's exactly noon, the student said, pointing to the clock on the wall. Our report cards are on now up on the school website. Can I go on my iPhone to check them, he asked? Yeah, the rest of the class yelled out. They hadn't heard a word I'd said. They were too distracted thinking about their grades, if you can call that thinking. I gave a poll the other day to all my seniors, offering a hypothetical choice. They could get an A in a course but remember nothing from it after the course was completed. Or they could get a B in a course and retain all the learning for the rest of their lives. Every single one of them chose the A. There is an old saying: the true measure of someone's character is what he does when no one is looking. What our 12th graders do, when the colleges are no longer looking, is nothing."

I left it at that and returned to my seat. There was genuine applause. I was thankful for it. I had taught many of these peoples' children and they were respectful and appreciative. Then a small, intense woman took the microphone.

"I think it is a disgrace that Mr. Baird thinks so little of our seniors, has so much disdain for them that he could say those things." She pointed at me as she spoke. "When my daughter and her friends were seniors they most certainly didn't fit his description. They most certainly did not *do nothing*, as he alleged. It is shameful that he, a teacher no less, feels that way, and I am here tonight to say that he is wrong, that weighting system most definitely should stay. Our best students deserve to be rewarded for their extra hard work. They deserve to be singled out and recognized."

I didn't make the connection at first. It had been five or six years. But then, gradually, it occurred to me who the speaker was. I had taught her daughter as a 9th grader.

Another parent rose to speak.

"Mr. Baird may have used some journalistic license in saying our seniors do nothing," he joked, "but he is not too far from the truth, and we should all be thankful for his candor, his comments and his warning, and what is most obvious, that he cares for our kids."

I hope what he said is true. As a teacher, I got lost often in the emotional discharge of what whirls before me every day, a hundred and twenty young people and all that implies. The highs and lows are dizzying. I think I care, but I get so angry from time to time and need to remind myself that the kids are the victims of this crazed urgency that has descended, that denies decency and common sense, and I suppose the parents are victims too, to a degree, even this mom. I remembered now. Yes, she had come into my classroom during one of my free periods waving a paper I had returned to her daughter that had earned a B+. 'She has never had a grade lower than an A. What do you intend to do about this?' she demanded. By then I was used to dealing with parents like this, so I did what I always do. I took out an A paper from my file and gave it to her. 'Here. Read this. If you think your daughter's essay is as good and can tell me why, I will change the grade.' She read the paper quickly, then put it on my desk and left.

As I was making my way out of the auditorium after the meeting, she stopped me.

"You are wrong, Mr. Baird. My daughter certainly did not *do nothing* her senior year, as you put it."

"That may be true. She was pretty driven," I replied. "But all the evidence says we have a problem here with most of our students. They don't care about anything but grades."

"The weighting system, these measurements, this accountability that sets good students apart from the others needs to stay. The good ones need rewards," she repeated. "And they need to be recognized."

"Do they?" I was suspicious. "Do you still have children in the school?"

"Yes, a 10th grader."

"And she is bright and hard working too. She is taking Honors and APs?"

"Of course."

"Do you remember what you said to me when I gave your daughter that B+?"

She folded her arms.

"You said: 'Mr. Baird, you have ruined my daughter's life forever.'"

She glared at me.

"So," I asked. "How's she doing? Is her life ruined?"

High-achieving high schools like ours are really two schools, a public school and an exclusive private prep school. There is no cost differential though. The district's citizens pay, depending on real estate values, more or less the same price, subsidized by taxpayers from all over the state. But the education their children receive, and its incumbent advantage, is not exactly the same. The college-cult parents are keenly aware of this, of course, so they attempt to choreograph their children's path through school in order to maximize their chances of gaining the upper hand, and they are usually successful.

I suspect this was this mother's goal when she strongly resisted changing our school's weighting system. She wanted to retain the elite private school vista that resides within the larger public school, so that it would continue to provide her children with a head start, a jump in front of the other less capable students. What she didn't want was her children sitting in a classroom with "just anyone." She wanted her children safely ensconced in an exclusive environment of high achievement, where no "slower" students or trouble makers with disciplinary problems would impede their "learning," in other words, her race to gain acceptance of her children at top colleges. Too bad for the children left behind in the mainstream classrooms. Let them eat cake.

When I was in school educators believed separating students according to their academic aptitude was desirable pedagogic practice, for the very pure reason that while some kids wanted to go to college many didn't. Our high school offered machine shop, auto mechanics, typing and home economics classes. While there was no such thing as AP classes back then there were honors classes for each subject. This was called tracking.

Years later, educators begin to believe in heterogeneous classes, where the brightest and the less bright were grouped together, where even the special education students had a place. The pedagogy was complicated, but made sense: the kids could all learn from each other, and for a few generations it was widely applauded.

Now tracking is back, with a vengeance, but this time pedagogy doesn't drive it, because we educators all know the undeniable value of heterogeneous classes, for all students. No. The parents drive it, and even though the schools know better, they capitulate to the parents' demands, often with disastrous results. For example, the most horrific unintended consequences of the new tracking (never referred to as such, because the term still carries a taboo) is that it reinforces in all the students' minds that their education is not about learning but about competition, and once the competition is completed, their education ceases. It makes a mockery of what public education is supposed to be.

"Who here likes science classes or math classes more than English or history classes?"

Most of the hands go up.

"Why?"

"Because they're more important."

"How do you know that?" I ask.

"The school tells us."

"How?" I ask.

"Because those subjects have Honors classes and English and history don't."

"I don't understand."

"Well, those subjects must be better, if there are Honors classes."

Unlike most high schools, our English and History departments continue to hold fast against the rising tide of demand for adding Honors classes for our subjects, but each year it gets harder for us to resist.

Our students, guided by the college cult and their counselors, also perceive that math and science are, in their own words, more useful, more practical than the Humanities, because they lead to good jobs.

I teach a creative writing elective but many of our school's most talented writers don't enroll, even though they want to take the course. Many of my English and social studies colleagues have created and proposed other electives, fascinating ones, but they often don't run because of lack of enrollment, and again, it is not because students don't want to take the courses. It is because their guidance counselors and their parents often discourage them from taking these electives because they will look "bad" on their college applications, or certainly not as "good" as other course work the colleges will recognize, such as Physics, AP Environmental Science, AP anything. What does it matter if these APs are of no interest to the student? That is not important. Getting into a college is.

"If you are serious about getting in, then you need to take Pre-Calculus instead of this Creative Writing thing," students say they are told.

AP, of course, is the white hot core of the private school within the public school, signaling to kids all kinds of nefarious things, such as what (and who) is important and what (and who) isn't, who is "smart" and who isn't, and most devious of all, who will succeed in life and who won't, as if a young person's future is somehow cast in stone because he or she took so many of these contrived courses. Certain kids, and their parents, will kill to get into them, mainly because they "look good" on their transcripts.

Each year I must schedule valuable class time in the computer lab for my seniors to work on their *Hamlet* paper because they wouldn't do it at home, even though it is a very important assignment. The reason: many of them take one kind of AP course or another, and their homework for those classes takes priority. A student once told me that her AP Psychology mid-term was scheduled the same day her *Hamlet* paper was due. She said she was sorry but there was no way she would be able to devote much time to it. She said she felt badly. She would have liked to write a paper she would be proud of but there wasn't enough time for it. She was thankful that she could at least do some of the work on it in the lab.

Advanced Placement courses have almost a strangle hold on every aspect of my high school's life. Their scheduling, the test dates, the inclusions and exclusions, dictate in too large a measure how we as a school go about our profession. Their presence has a profound effect on all of our students, not just the kids who take them, and this is especially true in their junior and senior years. For example, the 9th and 10th graders are suspiciously more diligent and enthusiastic with their studies than they are when they become 11th graders (and certainly 12th graders). They feverishly wave their hands eager to be called on. Their class participation is rarely a problem, unlike it is with seniors, who can sit in their seats for a whole period and never once add so much as a word in an attempt to provoke a discussion. Worse, when called on, they shrug and say, "I don't know." One of my colleagues who teaches 9th, 10th and 11th grade English explains the radically different behaviors this way: "The younger ones, they aren't really interested in school work. What 9th graders and 10th graders are doing is trying really hard to qualify for 11th grade AP and when they don't, they feel their chances are over, that they will never get into the better colleges, so the game is over." If it's late in the fourth quarter, why try if you are behind thirty to zero? Character, that's why, but our children have too little character because of the college cult. If they are not selected for AP courses, the school has announced in no uncertain terms that academic excellence is not for them. They are not good enough. The kids feel like they are worthless, and so, predictably, they treat their education the way they feel it has treated them: they abandon it. They have been left out, not invited to the party, so they react accordingly. The presence of AP courses actually serves as a determent to the education of the majority of students who are denied access. AP solidifies high school's role as little more than a stacked competition most can't win. In essence, AP courses and all this manipulation to favor the top kids create within the larger public school setting this segregated private school for a select few. Why the majority of taxpayers whose children are left out tolerate this I just don't understand.

Just consider the simple dynamics. In any heterogeneous (i.e. non-honors) 10th grade classroom, you have the high fliers, the great middle, and the slower learners. In high achieving schools like mine the high fliers usually make up about 20 percent of the class, approximately six kids. The slower learners include the special education kids, those enrolled in emotional support programs, any others with IEPs (Individual Education Plans required by state law because the child has been identified with learning difficulties), and of course the disruptive troublemakers who are unmotivated by academics. This is also about 20 percent of the kids, leaving the rest, the great big silent majority, 60 percent. These are the B students who kind of go with the flow, follow. They can either be led upward or downward. In this setting the high flyers usually set the tone: their homework is always done, they are eager to please and participate, and so the silent majority follows suit. The bottom 20 percent too is lifted, and the disruptive ones are silenced, intimidated by the work being done. Call it trickle down education. But in 11th grade the high fliers are removed to take AP classes. There no longer is a top 20 percent, because the best students are gone, separated from the rest and protected in their own homogeneous classes. The percentage of the silent majority stays at about 60 percent and the bottom creeps up to about 40 percent. The shift leaves a vacuum of leadership, which is quickly filled by the loud unmotivated minority. They take over, dragging the rest of the class downward. Very good teachers can dissuade much of this, but inevitably fewer texts are studied, more class time is spent pushing back the disruptiveness, discussions deteriorate, the curriculum is defined slightly downward. The consequence is that the vast majority of our high school students have their education compromised. This, so some students can have their transcripts adorned with AP classes, so that they can get college credit.

Is it any wonder seniors are cynical, that education has come to mean nothing to them? Parents bully and cajole their children's teachers and the administrators to grant their kids entrance into APs, clamoring for earlier Honors courses and Honors courses in the Humanities so they can further segregate their children in the private school within the public school even before AP courses begin. And we educators, who are supposed to know better, accept this: we allow the squeaky wheels to get the grease, even though we know the result undermines other kids. And it does not go unnoticed. The kids know. They are alert to so much we don't give them credit for, how gamed the system is. Something is rotten in the state of Denmark and they are fully aware of it. How could they not callus over with contempt and disrespect for the educational process? Education becomes to them what Elsinore becomes to Hamlet, a contagion, full of petulance, school nothing but a prison with its confines and dungeons.

Sensing the unfairness, our department curriculum leaders meet each year with administrators to review acceptance criteria for AP courses. One year the Modern Language department offered to try open enrollment, but there was too much pushback. The other departments rejected it. The AP teachers wanted to "maintain high standards." It was argued that if AP teachers let in "just any kids" who weren't "qualified," they would slow down the class. A lot has to be covered in preparation for the test and teachers cannot afford to lose any time, they said. But AP teachers wouldn't necessarily have to slow down. They could teach at whatever pace is necessary, and if some of the kids can't keep up, well at least they are given the chance. "The parents would scream if we let them fail," the adamant AP teachers rightly reply, but at least the school wouldn't have been on the wrong side of the issue.

I secretly suspect though that at least a small part of the reason some AP teachers want to "maintain high standards" is that they don't want "the other kids" in the class. That is why they have maneuvered their careers to include the teaching of these classes, so they don't have to deal with differentiated instruction and the exhausting classroom management problems. And teaching AP with high standards supports their egos. It is self-serving. There is a perceived status to being an AP teacher.

Our schools, then, contribute mightily to the malaise, because we educators have allowed what we do to become the handmaiden of higher education, naively assisting colleges with their running of what should no longer be confused as anything other than big, for-profit businesses, helping them with their churn, yield, attrition, supply, our crazed demand diminishing the quality of the product.

18
THE DE-INVENTION OF THE HUMAN

LEAVING THE NEST, STRIKING out on our own, solving problems, thinking things through until we arrive at a course of action then pursuing that action, persevering, failing, succeeding—all these behaviors are rewarding, the nectar of living. They naturally create a sense of independence and with it a sense of genuine self-respect and dignity. Combine this earned self-respect and dignity with the wisdom that comes from learning, combine it with a relationship to all that is genuinely learned—about literature, art, music politics, history, science and mathematics, about life—and the result is called *an identity*. A real identity, one our young people can carry around inside their minds, not the one they artificially wear in the form of caps on their heads or drive or feign on Facebook. This brings the confidence to proceed through the trying states of life. But many parents and schools are denying young people this genuineness, this sense of self, this real identity, by getting in the way of it to such an extent that they never learn how to think. Maybe even worse, our young people are learning how to deny themselves life. "That would be too random," is one of their favorite expressions, used to describe the little, accidental, daily norms and niceties and discomforts that once comprised our lives, our civility, such as casually passing the time with a stranger or calling our friends on the house phone and having to say hello to the mother or father who might answer or going over to a friend's house and knocking on the door and having to say hello to whomever might come to it. Instead, they text, furtively removed from the everyday fray. They are afraid of spontaneity. To them being extemporaneous equates to being awkward, out-of-the blue, out of place, uncomfortable; it's when they have to have a conversation with someone they barely know; it means having no specific predictable pattern or purpose; it's when they have to improvise. What is safe to them is not *putting themselves out there* to be open to scrutiny or question or uncertainty. They want to avoid anything that appears to be chancy. Why? Maybe in part because they have been denied the joy of the unknown, of risk-taking. They are mainly trained to perform predictably, to measure and be measured coldly and impersonally, and that is preferable to being personally and consciously involved, where the consequences are perceived to be greater. It is too random to raise your hand in class in response to a teacher's open inquiry. Better to remain invisible behind the computer screen. Their dignity has come from grades, no matter how ill-gotten. Their self-respect has come artificially too, from their collection of participation trophies. Their identity comes from the photo albums they post on their Facebook walls, enabling them to be temporary media stars with their friends. Their identical peers, of course, take on a sublime almost religious importance to them. Whenever I ask a senior what is unique about her, she answers, as they all do: my friends. I then ask her if her friends have the same friends, and when she answers yes, I ask her what is so unique then about that. She can't answer. In a profound and dangerous way, their incessant social networking has somehow replaced individuality and independent thinking. Their sites are like ghettos, communes, like self-imposed gulags. They are living in the intellectual equivalent of the old bankrupt Soviet Union. This is not an identity; it is false, untrue. None of this is real, but it has real consequences once our young people are expected to behave like adults, if we adults still expect them to be adults, which seems less and less to be the case, especially as we adults behave more and more like them.

Courage, self-discipline, individual responsibility, originality, independence, honesty, and perseverance: these are some of the important virtues Aristotle insisted lead to human happiness, to success, and they can be taught. And so they can be learned. But in too many schools, and in too many families, they are not. Aristotle's is not the happiness and success our graduates have been preparing for. Schools, the college cult, and too many parents inadvertently teach children that these virtues just don't matter all that much anymore. Competitiveness rules. Winning is all that matters. Collaboration and cooperation are more important than creativity. Whenever a game or contest is involved, with stakes that are misguidedly construed as high, there will be cheaters. And that is okay, so says the new order. When the score is all that counts, there will always be a review sheet, homework posted on the school website, a teacher's assistant to keep track of the student's assignments, a parent conference, followed by an intervention, all supplying a source for the kids to blame if something goes wrong, so they inevitably learn that whatever happens is not really their fault. Students internalize this, deeply. For example, they learn that they can wait in their seats for the teachers to "teach" them without ever having to take any initiative to learn for themselves. When this happens the only thing they learn is that learning, as something to be desired unto itself, has no meaning. Through its overindulgences, high schools reinforce the notion that education is merely a route or means to a specific end, acceptance to college, and once that end has been achieved school is over.

And what happens when they do end up in college? Having learned little more in high school than how to maneuver through the obstacle course of classes, they will then join thousands of other students who pay online services to supply them with original term papers, essays, reports, even dissertations. An estimated 67 percent of college students buy at least one paper on line per semester. One paper-writing entrepreneur recently told NBC News he grossed over $70,000 writing papers for students at all levels, high school through professional school. Google the words "college papers to buy" and a dozen for-profit sites appear on the first page. One claims to have 247,000 satisfied customers. Another site claims to receive eight requests per hour. And these students feel no remorse for this. To them, this isn't cheating. It's an old game: pay to play. This is how it's been since they were children. They know no other way. They might join the millions of students who transfer because they can't figure out how to be happy. (Universities and colleges now have Deans of Transfer.) After they finally graduate six years after they started, having paid for their papers, having accumulated little knowledge, they join the legions of other aimless young people who drift without responsibilities from job to job, relationship to relationship, wondering why they can't find anything meaningful in their lives. A few do find someone like them, probably online, then spend a hundred grand on a lavish wedding only to be divorced nine months later. Because of all the well-intended pampering, our young people's reality has been so badly distorted that when they are finally confronted with life's undeniable and unavoidable truths, they are shocked, confused, disillusioned, distracted, and often defeated.

I know of a twenty-something Williams grad who was quite "successful" in the commercial real estate business, making more than $300,000 a year until it imploded in the fall of 2008. Then he lost his job and was out of work for some time. His parents paid for the mortgage on his Manhattan condo. At first he looked for work, but couldn't find anything that "suited" him, then he decided he might as well turn his unemployment into an opportunity and go to graduate school. He only applied to top schools and was rejected. After that he did little more than stay in the apartment and occasionally send out a resume or two, complaining there was nothing more he could do. People suggested that he do anything, get a job, any job, even at a Starbucks or at a restaurant waiting tables to tide him over, or to lower his expectations and apply to B-school at places like Fordham or Pace.

"Never," his wife said indignantly. "That would be way below us."

They continued to go on vacations, though, also paid for by his parents.

He eventually relented and grudgingly attended a graduate school "below" him, and after getting a degree found a job paying $50,000 a year. She is pregnant, and he feels like a failure.

When I decided to become a teacher but needed some graduate education credits to satisfy state requirements, I enrolled at Teacher's College at Columbia University, believing it was the best education graduate school, but I soon discovered I wasn't learning what I needed. The atmosphere at TC was stimulating and engaging, but seemed to be concerned more with politicized issues like race and feminism and gay and lesbian literature, all interesting and important, but not the necessary everyday mundane skills I needed to learn, such as how to keep a grade book, construct a lesson plan, and manage a class. So I also enrolled in a course at Pace University in Pleasantville. A gray-haired retired teacher taught it. The textbook was a neat clear hands-on guide to effective teaching. This was what I was looking for. And I loved the way she conducted the class. No nonsense. She was sweet and precise and proud and loved to lecture and I could have listened to her anecdotes for hours, all filled with wisdom and the lessons I would need. My much younger classmates, though, disagreed. They were twenty-something fresh from undergraduate schools. They would be teachers themselves soon, yet they reminded me of the students I had seen during my student teaching. They often shuffled into class disheveled, late. They were rude, disrespectful. They slouched in their chairs, they chewed gum, their cell phones rang, and they let their chairs squeal. One day, as the professor spoke, one of them called out:

"This is boring. We have been talking and we have decided that your way of teaching isn't working. We don't do anything. We just sit here and have to listen to you. What kind of model are you, for being a good teacher?"

Her classmates agreed with her, unanimously. The professor's jaw dropped.

"Yeah," someone else called out. "Can't we ever do anything in groups?"

"Well," the professor said meekly, "sure we can. It's just that, this is a graduate class. I just believed that…"

"You believed wrong," another one added.

I was shocked. The professor's eyes welled with tears. She didn't know what to say or do. She sat down at her desk and covered her face. The class was nearly over so people began to leave. I stayed behind.

"They are wrong," I told her. "And they don't know any better. And that is really sad. Please don't think this has anything to do with you. Because of you, I am ready to become a teacher now."

She looked up and attempted to thank me but no words came out. She couldn't speak.

These soon-to-be teachers had been so accustom to collaborative classroom fun and games, differentiated learning, group learning, work resembling playtime, doing whatever they liked as high school students and undergraduates that they could not handle this quiet, highly professorial slower pace and structure that required them to listen and relate, make personal connections, analyze, apply, evaluate, think, and create their own meaning. So now when they go off to run their own classrooms someday they will do only what they know, relinquish control in the name of providing their students with a good time.

As a veteran teacher and department head, my wife often sits on the hiring committees when our schools need new teachers. She told me the other day how the district had three elementary school openings. More than two thousand applied. The final twelve were invited in for extensive interviews, all of them twenty-somethings, some of whom already were teaching in other schools. One of the requirements was a writing sample. The candidates were given a prompt, then told they could either submit the sample in their own handwriting or go to a tech lab where they could compose it on one of our computers. It was a hot July day and the labs had no air conditioning, so almost all of them opted to turn in the handwritten sample, complete with misspellings, messy cross-out phrases, poor grammar. They submitted their first drafts, not bothering to take the time to revise and rewrite. The principals were appalled. But they persevered. They told the group that the next step in the process was another session of interviews with the parents' group, to be held later in the week, but most of the candidates complained the date and time weren't good for them, that they had other things to do.

How could they behave this way, I asked my wife, knowing the answer, but always interested in her take. "Because they feel entitled," she said. "But their artificial sense of entitlement gets in the way of the reality. They don't realize that every part of their application, including their attitude, is being scrutinized."

And these are our future *teachers*.

In the early 90s, again about the same time some of my students were being born, my company's business had grown to the point where I needed to add another salesperson. I preferred hiring recent college graduates. I liked giving them a chance, and I'd had good luck from my alma mater, St. Lawrence University. I called my contacts, got a few recommendations and I hired Brian, a history and economics major from New Jersey. St. Lawrence could be referred to as a second tier college, the kind kids go to when they can't get into an Ivy or a Middlebury. I liked hiring graduates from schools like this because they were never too full of themselves. They turned out to be hungry, hard-working, but most of all they had character. Brian dug right in, learned fast, did a lot more than what was expected of him. Our offices were in a loft in Soho.

A few months after I hired him, I came into work one morning and found Brian pacing the office holding his head in his hands.

"What's the matter?" I asked.

When he looked up at me I knew immediately something was terribly wrong. His eyes were blood shot. He hadn't shaved. He looked dazed.

"My father," he started to say. "He died of a heart attack."

"What?"

"In the middle of the night. We found him this morning." He was rambling now.

"Oh my God. What are you doing here? Why aren't you home?" I asked.

My partner came in.

Brian was shaking now. "This is my job. It is my first job. I am expected to be here." His swollen eyes welled with tears. "My father would have wanted me to go to work. He was so proud when I got this job. I was the first in the family to go to college. He said a job was a blessed thing."

"Go home," I told him. "Be with your mother. You are now the man of the family and she needs you."

"Are you sure?"

"We'll get you a car," my partner told him, dialing the phone. "And you need to know something. Your father died a successful man and I will tell you why. Because he raised a son like you. I can only hope someday when I die I will have been so successful. The car will pick you up downstairs. Now go."

We hugged him and he left.

He was back to work the next day.

He worked for us for seven years and was a star. He married a lovely girl. When he and his wife had triplets he approached me one day to say he was being recruited by a major magazine company offering him a lot more money than our small company could afford to pay.

"Take it," I told him. "It's what you need to do."

"But I feel disloyal," he asked. "You gave me my start."

"And you have paid us back many times. I am proud of you. Go take care of your family."

He stayed in touch over the years, inviting me to lunch from time to time in Manhattan, which I was never able to do on my teacher's schedule. But then one day it worked out. For some reason, I had a day off in the middle of the week, so I jumped on the train and met him at his office in a glass tower near Wall Street.

By then he had become an executive vice president and publisher of a group of high profile consumer magazines. I announced my appointment to the receptionist. It was clear from her reaction that our Brian had turned into quite a big shot. I felt strange, almost like I was having an out of body experience. I was peeking into what could have become my life. He came out to greet me. I had not seen him in ten years. He was fit, dapper at forty-two or three, had lost his hair but wore the shaved head thing well, sporting a neat goatee. He carried himself like a boss. On the walls of his fancy office were photos of him with Kim Kardashian and other voluptuous celebrities who had appeared on the cover of one of the magazines he was responsible for.

But it was still Brian, the fine young man we had hired twenty years ago. We caught up on things, then for lunch he took me across the street to a famous downtown retreat for the powerful. We took turns telling funny stories from the frantic days of running our little company. "It prepared me," he said kindly.

When he asked me about teaching and I began describing this book, it occurred to me to ask him about his experiences hiring twenty-somethings, because surely he had to deal with them. I told him about an article I had read in *Time* entitled *Grow Up? Not so Fast* which used the term "Twixters" to describe the middle class and upper middle class young people between twenty-two and thirty who don't seem to have much interest in settling down with responsibilities. Instead, they choose to live at home after college rather than moving into a place of their own (more than double the percentage since 1970). They follow a series of dead-end jobs instead of seeking out careers or attending graduate school. Their social networking includes multiple sex partners instead of a long-term relationship.

The article included the usual social scientists ennobling these new lifestyles as admirable efforts in which these Twixters "search their souls and choose their life paths," doing "the important work to get themselves ready for adulthood." But do they in fact even have souls to search? Or have we teachers and professors (or should I say graduate assistants) allowed them to move on without ever developing them? I mentioned *The Dumbest Generation* and how Bauerlein describes these self-esteemed twixters who "drift through their twenties stalled in work and saving no money, but they like it that way. They have achieved little but they feel good about themselves."

"From what I see, you've got it exactly right," Brian said. "I spend a good deal of time interviewing and hiring young people. I have lots of magazines in my group, and lots of employees and this is a young person's business. You do the best you can to get the right people, then you hold your breath hoping they will stick around long enough to contribute something. Usually they don't. It is very different now. At five o'clock they are out the door. They spend company time networking instead of working. All the job means to them is a temporary stopover. Turnover and absenteeism are huge management problems. They quit after a few months. One sales assistant came in and said she was resigning, that this would be her last day. I told her that was not how resignations were conducted, that normally people gave their companies two weeks notice. She said she didn't care. We had done nothing to cause this. She just wanted to move on, with no other job. I told her because of the way she was conducting her resignation we would not be able to offer her a recommendation if she ever needed one and she didn't care about that either. She told me it would all work out. And hers is not an isolated case. They live in an American Idol mentality, that no matter what, everyone will be a star."

"But even on that show, everyone isn't a star."

"They don't see it that way," Brian said.

"You know what feature of Facebook I really find amazing?" I asked.

"What?"

"Their *status.*"

He though about it for a moment, then laughed. "That is funny. Of course: their status, when they have no status. They are just kids who have accomplished nothing in life. How could they possibly have any status?"

"Does reality catch up with them?" I asked. "I mean, is there still a reality that means that if you don't have a job you can't pay your rent, or your cell phone bill or buy drinks in whatever trendy bar they hang out it? Or is it a new reality, one in which there are no consequences, a virtual reality, like their Facebook pages?"

"Yes, there still is a reality, thank God. I have three nine-year-olds. That is reality. And when these young people come back to it they are hit hard. We do a lot of business with the big drug companies like Merck and Pfizer. We carry a ton of their advertising. You know what they tell me? These young people are the biggest market for antidepressants—Paxil. Stuff like that. They can't handle the normal everyday hardships of life. The Facebook thing goes a long way to causing the problem. These young people make celebrities of themselves, create a whole narrative about themselves that isn't true, but it becomes true to them."

"The giddy, smiling party pictures," I added, "the incessant banter, the self-importance of it all, when they are unimportant, like we all were at that age. So you interview them and then hire them and they come on board, but they are counterfeit. You and your company have been conned."

"It is a big problem," Brian repeated. "And I deal with hundreds of companies from every business you can think of and they are all having the same problem."

In the early 1900s sociologists and developmental psychologists needed a term to describe that strange period in life between the ages of thirteen and eighteen, so they came up with *adolescence.* They have now come up with a term to describe the meandering crowd of twenty-somethings who seem to resist growing up, coined by Jeffrey Jensen Arnett, a psychology professor. They are the "emerging adults." From *The New York Times Magazine*: "No one knows yet what the impact will be—on the prospects of the young men and women; on the parents on whom so many of them depend; on society, built on the expectation of an orderly progression in which kids finish school, grow up, start careers, make a family and eventually retire to live on pensions supported by the next crop of kids who finish school, grow up, start careers, make a family and on and on. The traditional cycle seems to have gone off course, as young people remain untethered to romantic partners or to permanent homes, going back to school for lack of better options, traveling, avoiding commitments. One-third of people in their 20s move to a new residence every year. Forty percent move back home with their parents at least once. They go through an average of seven jobs in their 20s. Two-thirds spend at least some time living with a romantic partner without being married. And marriage occurs later than ever."

If it occurs at all.

At the start of this past summer I did what I do at the start of every summer, loaded my mower into the back of my car and drove it over to the shop where I got the blade sharpened and the spark plugs changed. When I got there the place was swarming with Spanish-speaking crews from a dozen lawn maintenance companies.

"Am I the last guy left who still mows his own lawn?" I asked the guy behind the counter.

"Yup," he said, without looking up.

Maybe twenty-somethings behave the way they do because as safely designated *adolescents* they weren't required to mow their own metaphorical lawns, let alone those of their grandparents. And when was the last time you saw an adolescent shoveling snow? Bauerlein blames this on the emerging adults' lack of intellectual labor in school and points the finger squarely at us, the mentor class:

> *Nobody ties maturity to formal and informal learning,*
> *reading or studying, novels or painting or histories or syl-*

logisms. For all the talk about life's concerns and finding a calling, none of them regard history, literature, art, civics, philosophy, or politics as helpful understanding. As these young people forge their personalities in an uncertain world, they skirt one of the customary means of doing so—that is, acquainting themselves with the words and images, the truths and beauties of the past—and nobody tells them they have overlooked anything. Social pathologists don't tell them so, nor do youth experts and educators, but the anti-intellectual banality of their choices is stark. What is the role of books in the Twixter's world? Negligible. How has their education shaped their lives? Not at all. This is what the Twixters themselves report. The intellectual and artistic products of the past aren't stepping stones for growing up. They are the fading materials of meaningless schooling.

The twenty-somethings resist growing up, as my students tell me, because, like reading Shakespeare, being a grown up is difficult. It means being independent and working hard and thinking and making decisions. Independence and diligence form an intellectual concept, a tenant of the Western canon. Because of what we have done to our young people, through our indulgences and what we have denied them in their education, they have never learned to be independent and enjoy doing what is hard. Instead they prefer what is easy; they prefer *group* work. They don't like challenge. They don't like going it alone. They want to avoid the hardship of adulthood. The hardship? When I was their age, I wanted to be an adult, desperately. I wanted the challenge, the adventure. I wanted the journey to begin. Pick your icon: Huck rafting down the Mississippi with Jim, Natty Bumppo, Ishmael ("A whale-ship was my Yale college and my Harvard"), Nick Adams. Neal Armstrong's one small step on the moon. These are the lessons of the American Dream. We are the inheritors of a rigorous individualistic frontier tradition. Uniquely

USA. We explore. We work hard here and aspire. We are an unambiguously and unapologetically ambitious people, or we used to be. The fancy pandering and psychobabble don't address the real issue, and that is too many young people just don't want that responsibility, because they have never learned how to relish responsibility, to crave it. "I want to be the employer, not an employee." "I want to lead, not follow." "Give me the ball," they should be saying, while instead they won't raise their hands; they shrug, "You can do it." The reason, I think, is their shamelessness. Because we have spared our young people from the sting and stigma, the pain and humiliation of indignation, of losing, they in turn have never really experienced the joy, the sublime satisfaction of truly succeeding, of creating something uniquely theirs, the ecstasy of really winning because their shallow victories have come so cheaply. It isn't until you know how to lose and hurt over something that mattered to you that you know how to win, its preciousness, and it isn't until you know what real winning can feel like that you know you want more of it, and the biggest win in life of all is owning up to one's responsibilities, resulting in the kind of joy Wilson describes in *Against Happiness* as eternal instead of temporal.

What becomes, then, of an America where high school graduates can't think, where traditions and roles are reversed, where adults act like children and children refuse to grow up, where households are run by kids instead of parents, where schools are run by students' neurotic needs instead of passionate teachers, where companies are run by their employees instead of their employers, where "it's not cool to know anything," where the trivial and ephemeral are preferable to the sublime and eternal? Because of one-dimensional parents, because of a culture that bows to false gods like college acceptance and the Internet's omnipresent handiness and schools that train our children for work instead of educating them, we are becoming a civilization of people who may know how to "get" things, for example get into college, or get a job or even get some kind of a shallow life, but who don't know how to "do" it once we get it.

When my students write their senior research papers on *Hamlet*, I make sure they read Professor Harold Bloom, who asserts that Shakespeare invented us. But even he worries that Shakespeare's work too will soon be among the fading materials of meaningless schooling, *Hamlet* reduced to nothing more than an artistic product of the past instead of a vital step for growing up: "Four centuries have only augmented Shakespeare's universal influence. Will this change in the new century, since deep reading is in decline, and Shakespeare, as the Western canon's center, now vanishes from the schools with the canon? Will generations to come believe current superstitions, and so cast away genius, on the grounds that all individuality is an illusion? If Shakespeare is only a product of social process, perhaps any social product will seem as good as any other, past or present. In the culture of virtual reality, partly prophesied by Aldous Huxley, and in another way by George Orwell, will Falstaff and Hamlet still seem paradigms of the human?"

Before Hamlet, Falstaff, Lear, Othello, MacBeth and Iago we were all one-dimensional. But through his characters and their universality, Shakespeare bestowed upon us human beings our depth, our psychology. Increasingly, though, we seem no longer to be the complex humans he invented. Worse, what's left of our civilization seems to demand that we shed the last remnants of complexity, our individuality. We humans are being de-invented.

Before my 12th graders graduate I share with them a prophetic article I found in the *Wall Street Journal* by Jennifer Merritt and Teri Evans. In part it reads:

> *Recruiters who named an Ivy League or elite liberal arts school as a top pick say they prize their graduates' cachet among clients, as well as the 'soft skills' like critical thinking and communication. Other recruiters prefer the big state universities because their big student populations and focus on teaching practical skills gives the companies more bang for the buck. Companies have found [their gradu-*

ates] fit well into their corporate cultures. Pennsylvania State University and other schools' willingness to partner with corporations goes a long way to helping graduates get hired, corporate recruiters and colleges say. Such partner-ships—often in the form of 'master agreements'- typically begin as a means of connecting professors with companies to collaborate on research. Students often get involved in the projects, which may lead to some of them being hired by the company.

But my students don't get it. They simply can't think well enough. In fact, rather than being frightened by the piece they em-brace what it suggests, which to them means that if they go to Penn State they will get a good job. They can't connect the dots: recruited from colleges for their cachet among clients? Critical thinking as only a lesser soft skill? Our students have become mere cogs in the wheel, mass-produced, used only as part of the larger deal. Bloom is right: these "master agreements" smack of *Brave New World, 1984*. This corporate quest for practicality and cachet over wisdom, knowledge and intellect amounts to the corporatization of our young people, and it has spread, like head lice, from the panicked parents and numbed culture to our elementary, middle and high schools, the final warning sign that our future, by way of our most precious asset, our children, will be unenlightened, uninformed, uneducated, nothing more than a dim world of drone-like workers instead of thinking, feeling, *Shakespearean* human beings.

PART THREE
THEIR SALVATION

19
"THE ECCENTRIC, THE IDIOSYNCRATIC, THE ANNOYINGLY INDIVIDUAL"

FRANCINE PROSE CREATED THE phrase. I use her book *Reading Like A Writer* in my creative writing class. I met her once when I participated in a fiction-writing seminar where she was our guest instructor.

When I was still in business I discovered her famous essay "I Know Why the Caged Bird Cannot Sing: How American High School Students Learn to Loathe Literature" in *Harper's* magazine, then one of our clients. To this day I remember taking time to stop from my frantic day filled with complaining advertisers and business travel plans and status reports and meetings to find a quiet spot and read it. Instantly it reminded me of Miss Shupp and of how serious I became in college about literature, and certainly it kindled at least at some subconscious level a desire to switch careers and become a teacher myself, although that would by years away.

Traditionally, the love of reading has been born and nurtured in the high school English class—the last time many students will find themselves in a roomful of people who have all read the same text and are, in theory, prepared to discuss it. High school—even more than college—is where literary tastes and allegiances are formed; what we read in adolescence is imprinted on our brains as the dreamy notions of childhood crystallize into hard data. It is not difficult to find fiction that combines clear, beautiful accessible, idiosyncratic language with a narrative that conveys a complex worldview. But to use such literature might require teachers and school boards to make fresh choices, selections uncontaminated by trends, clichés...Teaching students to value literary masterpieces is our best hope of awakening them to the infinite capacities and complexities of human experience, of helping them acknowledge and accept complexity and ambiguity; and of making them love and respect the language that allows us to smuggle out, and send one another, our urgent, eloquent dispatches from the prison of the self.

Prose's words are not just for literature teachers but for all teachers, and for parents too, if we use her allusions as metaphors. Her "literary masterpieces" are all the subjects we teach—physics, chemistry, mathematics if we are teachers; virtues such as compassion, honesty, self-discipline if we are parents. These subjects demand reverence. We can insist our students and children value them by showing them how much we value them.

But it's not occurring, perhaps because our culture wants it less urgently than we do. Education, after all, is a process intended to produce a product. So we have to ask ourselves: What sort of product is being produced by the current system? And is it really in the best interests of our consumer economy to create a well-educated, smart, highly literate society of fervent readers? Doesn't our epidemic dumbing-down have undeniable advantages for those institutions (the media, the advertising industry, the government) whose interests are better served by a population not trained to read too closely or ask too many questions? The new model English-class graduate—the one who has been force-fed the gross oversimplifications proffered by these lesson plans and teaching manuals—values empathy and imagination less than the ability to make quick and irreversible judgments, to entertain and maintain simplistic immovable opinions about guilt and innocence, about the possibilities and limitations of human nature. Less comfortable with the gray areas than the sharply delineated black and white he or she can work in groups and operate by consensus, and has a resultant, residual distrust for the eccentric, the idiosyncratic, the annoyingly individual. What results from these educational methods is a mode of thinking (or, more accurately, of not thinking) that equips our kids for the future: Future McDonald's employees.

The *New York Times* reported recently that, "Heightening concerns about the value of many of its high school diplomas, the New York State Education Department released new data showing that only 37 percent of students who entered high school in 2006 left four years later adequately prepared for college." The "highly desirable" school district I live in has a 99 percent graduation rate, with 95 percent of those graduates going on to college, but our college-readiness figure, according to the *Times*, is only 52 percent.

During an interview with the *Wall Street Journal* historian David McCullough, author of the best-selling biography of John Adams that became the popular TV mini-series, told the story of a college sophomore who approached him after he gave a speech at her "very good university." She thanked him for coming and admitted, "Until I heard you talk this morning, I never realized the original thirteen colonies were all on the east coast." McCullough thought: What have we been doing so wrong that this obviously bright young woman could get this far and not know that?

What we—her teachers, her culture and parents—have done so wrong is focus on getting her into that "very good university" instead of preparing her for it and for the rest of her life by teaching her how to think. McCullough offers a few possible solutions: "People who come out of college with a degree in education and not a degree in a subject are severely handicapped in their capacity to teach effectively. The great teachers love what they are teaching and you can't love something you don't know anymore than you can love someone you don't know." He also says that, "we're too concentrated on having our children learn the answers. I would teach them how to ask questions."

If you are a parent, this fall when you attend the open house evening at your children's school, instead of asking their teachers the usual questions that signal little more than confused priorities such as how grades are given, which only encourages teachers to teach for the grade, you might want to try being a little bit eccentric, idiosyncratic, annoyingly individual. For example, ask your children's teachers if they hold degrees in the subjects they teach, then follow up with questions such as:

"How will you go about making sure my child loves science so much that she wants to become a scientist?"

"What period of history fascinates you and why and exactly how will you evoke in my child that same excitement?"

"Do you love the literature you will be teaching my child this year and if so, tell me why?"

"What kinds of questions and curiosity do you hope to evoke from my child?"

"How do you intend to teach my child how to think?"

And if their teachers can't answer these questions without convincing you that they have the conviction to change your child's life, then do something about it. Challenge the status quo. But then you must hold yourself similarly accountable; you must ask yourself the same question, because parents are teachers too: do *you* have a "degree" in what you need to be teaching your children, namely Aristotle's ethics—courage, perseverance, and selflessness? Yes, when teachers aren't knowledgeable and passionate to the point of being borderline fanatical, how will they be able to transfer that knowledge and passion and compulsive purposefulness to their students? But at the same time, if parents are not honest, self-disciplined and courageous, how will they serve as examples for their children?

20
DEAD FROGS

IN *AGAINST HAPPINESS*, PROFESSOR Wilson takes a slightly different tack but essentially describes the same approach. "Hallmark
beauty, prettiness: those perfect sunsets on the coastal horizon or
those tranquil panoramas from the rounded top of a mountain or
those perfectly airbrushed faces, wrinkle free and vacant" aren't real
beauty, he writes. Real beauty is "much wilder...you can't discover
beauty when you join the vacationing masses in search of poster
aesthetics. Indeed, these folks—almost all of them happy types—
can't really perceive beauty at all. The novelist Walker Percy argues
that most go through life witnessing not the actual world but their
preconceptions of it."

> *Percy offers a useful recommendation: biology teachers
> should one day surprise their students with sonnets, and
> English instructors should startle their classes with dead
> frogs. Such unorthodox behavior would shock students out
> of their complacency, their dependence on safe abstrac-
> tions, and force them to stare at things unadorned—beau-
> tiful and strange. Denuded of their habitual internal im-
> ages, these students would have nothing to protect them*

from the world's gorgeous weirdness. Once overwhelmed with this torqued upsurge, these same students would likely work for the remainder of their days to surprise themselves, to strain through their familiar grids. They would go to the Louvre in hopes of breaking through their years of T-shirts and postcards and actually experience the enigmatic wantonness of the Mona Lisa.

Teaching today's students to think requires going against the ingrained dogma. It requires celebrating the eccentric, the idiosyncratic, and the annoyingly individual. It requires using dead frogs. It demands that we mentors become dead frogs ourselves: eccentric, idiosyncratic and annoyingly individual. Most great teachers (and great parents) already are. It takes enormous confidence. This is very difficult in a culture bent on eroding confidence. One of my very best students now goes to college in Japan. She could have gone to college anywhere. When she was young her parents would not allow her watch any TV. She had no access to a computer, except for schoolwork, and when she wanted to play she was sent outdoors to invent her own games, no toys, no electronic gadgetry. Her parents allowed her to skip a year of high school to live in Japan where she learned the language. She is remarkably mature, elegant, soft-spoken and brilliant. She either wants to be a pianist or a chemist. It is difficult to imagine how brave and strong her parents must have been, bucking against our insecure, instant-gratification culture, but the results of their wisdom to be weird produced spectacular results.

Being eccentric and utilizing dead frogs is very difficult in public education, where teachers are expected, if not commanded, to conform to bureaucratic standards. What I try to do is constantly create surprises, not with the sizzle of the latest Smart Board technology, but simply by teaching unlike everybody else. In other words, I take chances. I am risky. And the kids pick up on this immediately. And they respect it. This immediately sets the tone that my class will most definitely not be business as usual. I start with how my room appears. It needs to be very different from any classroom my students have experienced before. As soon as they walk in they need to know that they are about to experience something new. The room is lighted only with a collection of odd low yellow lamps, all different shapes, with strange shaped shades that cast hues of red, green, blue. I allow absolutely none of that hard harsh overhead sickly gray florescent lighting, ever. Thanks to my art teacher wife I have provocative art posters tacked all over the walls: surrealists like Magritte and Dali, Austrian expressionists like Klimt and Schiele, Rembrandt sketches, anything and everything to tweak their imaginations. The kids love it. When their parents come to visit it is the first thing they comment on, how my room feels so warm and inviting, like a retreat or salon. Then they say they would like to study there.

But soon after I turned off all the florescent lighting I was visited by our district's grim-faced business manager who informed me that my lamps were not allowed. The incandescent bulbs, he said, generated too much heat and were considered a fire hazard, and I had until the end of the week to remove them and return to the standard overhead lighting. I made a "teachable moment" of it. I used some class time to tell my students what had happened. One young lady was so outraged that she went home and told her mother, who happened to be a mechanical engineer and environmental scientist. The mother got involved. She wrote a scathing letter to the district, and armed with data she provided I proved the florescent lighting was actually harmful, and certainly not conducive to learning. The kids and I won the fight. The lamps stayed.

I also have two sofas in my room and my students are allowed to sit on them during class. For some reason they think that is the greatest thing ever. I also have a circular table where they can also sit. I have area rugs, big beanbags. I never give seating assignments. They are free to sit next to their friends, and so they are free, therefore, to goof around and misbehave if they choose. I will not use some artificial seating arrangements to separate them and combat this. They must police themselves. What I will do, when they are disruptive, is stop the class to discuss what is happening, to shame and embarrass them if I have to, to give them the chance to change their behavior on their own, to learn self-discipline, and over time they rise to the occasion. I have a reputation in our school for referring the least number of students to the assistant principal for disciplinary action, which is a complete waste of everyone's time. We take care of discipline as a class.

Nothing makes students think more than the unexpected. Conversely, nothing makes them think less than the predictable. When teachers are formally observed their administrators look for the same components in each lesson: the "do now," the anticipatory set, the requisite group work, the summary. Each component has a specific recommended length of time. Because of this many teachers are so predictable with the pacing of their lessons the students tell me they can tell the time by it. They come in and tell me this, laughing. This demanded methodological pedagogy serves little end other than to provide a "risk-free" framework that discourages passionate, risk-taking teaching, guised under the notion that it is somehow imparting better learning when all it does is numb young minds. This is how teachers are taught to do it in education colleges. This is what administrators often insist upon when they conduct their evaluations. Teachers are often criticized if they don't conform, don't conduct their classes in a uniform, predictable and "pedagogically correct" way. But teachers must resist.

This is what tenure is for.

21
THE FIRST DAY OF SCHOLE

I sit at my desk finishing another cup of coffee. To remind my-self one last time what's at stake here, I re-read some of my seniors' final reflection essays from last year:

> *I walk into the school for the first day of my last year there and look forward to what is ahead, my senior year. Everyone has told me "you don't do anything... you just hang out and pass the time." I can't wait to party every night and not have to worry about doing papers or tak-ing notes. This year would be a joke for us seniors. I walk into my first period class and know that all I had to do is my current events homework every night to get an A and everyone in my family would be happy. But would I really earn that grade? Work hard. Who cares!*
>
> *But then I walk into my second period class. English. It was a very dim room and the window shadows are down. No teacher had ever taught a class in a room this dark in all my years of school. I am thinking this was going to be my naptime. I was in for a rude awakening. "How many of you actually think you have learned anything through-*

out your high school years?" this old guy asked us. It was by far the craziest yet thought-provoking question that any teacher has ever asked one of my classes. Of course everyone thought they had learned something, whether it be the Pythagorean Theorem or how World War II began. As he saw everyone's hand cautiously raised, he gave us all a funny look and smirked.

It didn't take long before I realized that we had never learned anything in high school, that the school had set us up as robots. Teachers would give us busy work and due dates and grades and that wasn't anything more to it. Is that really helping us to learn? Wow, who would have thought this "blue-ribbon" school would be setting us up for failure. Now I'm not saying that knowing how WWII began isn't important, but we were never brought to a level of thinking that forced us to do things on our own; everything was always told to us. After this class I want to be philosopher now. I want to have a unique perspective compared to everyone else's in the whole entire world.

-Matt

I have always pictured myself as an adult sitting in an old fashioned library drinking tea and discussing history and literature as an educated woman, but I have always been too lazy to read. But this year I experienced English in a way I never have before. There were no tedious worksheets and no busy work dissecting quotes trying to find hidden meaning. I enjoyed how we did it, just reading and discussing, rather than breaking down a paragraph line by line. We were not babied. Yet we read classics that could have intimidated us but didn't because we had meaningful conversations about them. The books we read this year *actually made me think outside of English class. I might be able to sit in that library someday.*

-Domineque

༄

This year I have realized that my view of "being truly educated" was not right. I felt that being truly educated was being a good student and memorizing information to do well on a test. Being truly educated is to enjoy a topic and really learn the material—not just to take a test but for your own personal satisfaction. The material we have read and watched this year has really made me want to change the way I live my life. How many small yet beautiful things have I missed in my short time on earth?

Maybe being truly educated has nothing to do with academics at all. As I am writing this paper I am also looking outside my window and see these trees and bushes and the sun is reflecting off of this one bush in such a beautiful way. I see poetry in it. I am living in the moment. I am not worried about what tomorrow will bring and it feels really good.

-Dylan

༄

Most teenagers and even many adults nowadays act almost as if their minds are part of a collective, thinking the same thoughts and performing the same actions. Education: the imparting and acquiring of knowledge through teaching and learning. In recent years, the meanings of these terms have been largely misinterpreted. "Teaching" has come to be known by my generation as writing notes on a smart board, handing out worksheets, and assigning countless amounts of busy work; while learning has come to be known as memorizing an enormous quantity of information, taking a test on it, then wiping it from our brains. Lucky this English course was run differently.

-Daniel

❧

As a student in high school, I have only ever been in a grade-obsessed environment. When talking about a class to other students, no one ever asks if you learned a lot or if you truly understand the subject. Instead, students ask if it is hard to get a good grade or if there is a lot of home-work. Growing up in an environment like this produces the wrong type of student.

-Sarah

The seniors who will be walking into my classroom in a few minutes won't be able to think like this, but I will have ten months with them. I check my emails. There's one from Amanda.

Dear Mr. Baird,

Hi! first off, I would like to apologize for not contact-ing you all summer. I would like to let you know you will be seeing me first thing when school starts because I am in your first period class. Just a head up, my grade sucks. Already I have heard people saying that they are just going to stop doing work when they find out they get into college, plus they have a lot of ego. Till then. A.

At 7:55 the bell rings. I have four sections of Amanda's 12th grade class this year, nearly a hundred seniors. Amanda takes a seat in the front row. I recognize a few other faces. After the usual ban-tering I hand out my syllabus, which lists the titles of the texts we will be reading.

"Will someone please read the quote," I request, but as usual no one volunteers.

"The first thing you will need to know about me," I tell them, "is that when I ask you to participate I will wait all period long for someone to speak if I have to."

I wait. After about forty seconds they begin to squirm nervously, discomforted by the awkward silence. When a minute has gone by, one of the girls drags herself forward from her sleepy slouch, shrugs and reads reluctantly: "Students cannot become truly educated unless they grow out of and beyond themselves."

"Someone read the next quote," I say. This time the wait is shorter.

"Oh what a piece of work is a man… and yet to me what is this quintessence of dust?" a boy reads.

"Hamlet says this," I tell them, "and before this year is over some of you will be able to answer his existential question, which means you will have grown out of your selves. Some of you won't, which means you will continue residing in the dark, uninformed, narrow space you call your minds. Consider this: in a little more than a hundred years you will be dead, turned to dust, and completely forgotten. Shakespeare once wrote that 'we are such stuff as dreams are made of, and our little life is rounded with sleep.' Your life is only a brief moment of consciousness surrounded by an eternity of nothingness. Now, let me tell why none of you raise your hands when you are asked to participate. Some of you don't because you are still afraid of what other people will think of you. And you are afraid for two reasons, both unacceptable in my classroom. You are either afraid if you speak that other people might think you are dumb, or worse, by speaking out and participating, people might thing you are too smart, too eager, too studious. These fears end the instant you walk into this room."

They lower their heads in recognition.

"Another reason, also unacceptable, is simply that you don't care. You have checked out, either because you've gotten what you want, enough good grades to get you into college, or you have been degraded, embarrassed, demoralized by your SAT scores, your exclusion from Honors and AP courses, so why bother? You just want the period to end. But know this: I refuse to let you. Maybe the school in some way or another has led you to believe that you are a winner, with your good grades and AP courses, or that you are a loser and can't do rigorous intellectual work. No matter who you think you are, chances are you're wrong. I intend to drag you by your hair, kicking and screaming if I have to, toward that wonderful thing called consciousness. Finally if you think you have school all figured out, you're wrong again and in this class you will soon find out why and you will learn something from it. For twelve years you have been quizzed and tested and assessed so much that any genuine interest in learning or even participating, if your participation is not being scored, has been rendered irrelevant. But that ends today."

Their body language gives them away. They fold their arms. Who does this old asshole think he is, they wonder. But from the way they look at me I know they know something new is occurring.

"I want to go over a few rules and I'm not going to speak to you in teacher-speak. I'm not going to bullshit you. First, don't be late. If you are late, but no more than five minutes late, you need to bring me coffee. Strong. Black, half decaf. If you are more than five minutes late I won't write you up. I will embarrass you. Being late is spitting in the face of your classmates. It is telling them your time is more valuable than theirs, but what it really reveals is you have no control over yourself. Next, seating. You can sit anywhere. I want you to relax in this class, so by all means sit with your friends, sit on the couches, sit on that nice rug on the floor, just like you did in kindergarten. Lie down. I don't care. But if you fall asleep I will pour cold water on your head. And if you abuse the privilege of being treated like an adult, something terrible will happen. The worse thing that could ever happen to you."

They look around at each other wondering what it could be.

"I will stop respecting you," I tell them. "Now put your heads down on your desks and close your eyes and think about what I have said. Think deeply and carefully, because it is important."

They do as they are told. After a minute or two I bring them back. "Any questions before we begin?

"What kind of materials will we need?" a girl asks.

"All I require you bring to class each day is your mind. Anything else, notebooks, folders, is up to you. Now, during this course this year, through the literature and our discussions of it, if you choose, you will be allowed to discover the real reason why you are here, not just in school, not only in this classroom, but on this Earth. You will learn how to think. Now let's get to work. For tomorrow for homework I want you to answer on a sheet of paper the following questions—"

"Do we have to write this down?"

"Aren't you going to hand out a sheet?" another student asks.

"Will this be posted on echalk so we can get it at home?"

I throw them a glare. "Do I look like the kind of teacher who holds your hand by doing things for you?"

They start scrambling for pens and paper.

"How old is the universe?" I begin again. "How old is the earth? When did life begin on earth? How long did it take before multicelled creatures appeared? When did one of them finally crawl out of the ocean? When did dinosaurs appear and how long were they around? When did mammals appear and how long have they been around? When did modern Homo sapiens appear and how long have we been around? When did civilization begin? When were you born and how long have you been around."

The bell rings, ending the period.

"Is this English class?" I overhear one boy ask his friend as they head for the door. "Are we in the right place?"

Good. I have them right where I want them.

22
BEGINNING TO GROW OUT OF THEMSELVES

"OKAY, TAKE OUT YOUR calculators," I say to them the next day in class.

They make confused faces.

"You heard right. You all take math. Take out those big fancy things you use in your math classes."

They labor grudgingly through their backpacks.

"Now, I am going to go around the room and ask each of you a very important question, a question you will be hearing all year long. And how you respond to it means everything. You," I say, pointing to the boy in the first row. "Did you do your homework in the spirit in which it was intended?"

He looks at me like I am speaking a foreign language, then holds up a piece of wrinkled paper with some numbers written on it. "I did it. See."

"That's not what I asked."

"Why don't you just go around the room and check it, or collect it?" the girl who asked what materials she needed asks.

"Why would I waste time doing that? You could have copied it, done it in two minutes driving to school in the back seat of your friend's car. No. I am asking you a specific question and I will be asking it all year. Did you do the homework in the spirit in which it was intended, to teach you something, to get you to think? In other words did you give it the time and respect it deserves. Yes or no." I hold up my grade book. "You say yes, you get a check. You say no, you get a zero. Now let's try this again. Did you do the homework in the spirit in which it was intended?"

"No," he answered.

"Thank for your honesty. Do better next time." I mark a zero next to his name.

"You," I ask the next student.

"But I could just lie," she says.

"Yes you could," I respond. I repeat the question.

"No," she answers.

"Why didn't you lie?" I ask.

"I… don't know," she says. "There's just something about the way you are doing this. I don't know. I just would rather have the zero than lie to you."

"Do better tomorrow," I say.

Fortunately enough of them have done the homework so that we can move on.

"Okay, you, how old is the universe?"

"Twelve billion years."

"Close enough. You. How old is the earth?"

"Four billion years."

We go through all the numbers. I have someone write them all on the Smart Board.

"Now, with your calculators I want you to start computing ratios, then translate those ratios into distances in miles, feet, inches. We are going to create a graphic, a time line of existence. We will start in Los Angeles with the Big Bang. Right here, where I am standing, is us, today. So the universe has been around twelve billion years. That represents the three thousand miles between LA and here. Earth began four billion years ago. In what city would that be?"

"Chicago," someone shouts out.

"Don't guess. Do the math. I'll give you ten minutes."

"Can we work with a partner?"

"No!"

Their fingers fly over their fancy machines. They have so many buttons and functions I wouldn't be able to figure out how to add two plus two. It is impressive to watch how skillful they are. Schools like mine take great pride in describing their curricula as skills-based. But what are the skills for if kids can't think?

"Whoa!" a boy in back exclaims.

"What did you discover?" I ask the class. "When, or should I say where, did the earth begin?"

"I think Chicago is right."

"I have Cleveland."

"When did the earliest life form?"

"It's amazing, like not until Newark."

"Dinosaurs?"

"The Bronx."

They laugh.

"Homo sapiens?"

"Like here. Right here in our town, like at the Starbucks," a girl answers.

They laugh again.

"How appropriate. What about civilization? What was our first recorded civilization and when was it? I'm just a goofy English teacher, not history. Who knows this stuff?"

"Rome?"

"Greece?"

I shake my head. "Even I know that's not right." "Mesopotamia," a boy answers. "It started like, in this classroom. Like right there."

"Well, what about us? You and me?" I ask.

"We are like… nothing."

"Mr. Baird, by my calculations we don't exist. We are just too small."

"How does this make you feel?" I ask. "Someone begin."

They are motionless.

"I will wait …"

"Like Chris said, small," a boy calls out. "Like really small."

"Bad," a girl responds. "Creepy. I don't like this feeling."

Like newborns, spitting bits of placenta, sputtering, wet eyes blinking open.

"Like… like…" she continues. "Like I'm worthless all of sudden."

"Yes, this kind of knowledge can be humbling. But what else can it be? Does anyone feel the opposite?" I ask.

Hands shoot up.

"It's weird, but I feel empowered."

'Yeah," someone else adds. "Free. Like what the hell, if I am this small I'm just gonna go for it."

"Go for what?" I ask.

He thinks, looks around for support, like a tag team wrestler reaching for his partner.

"Go for everything. Live life."

"Or just kill yourself," someone comments.

"To be or not to be," I recite.

"That's a famous quote."

"Shakespeare," someone adds.

"Hamlet," I say. "Yes, it is famous, because it applies to all of us. To be or not to be, that is the question. Whether it is nobler in the mind to suffer…" I recite the soliloquy. "Thus conscience doth make cowards of us all. What he means by conscience is consciousness. What you have just done, with this exercise, is expand your consciousness. But does our consciousness make cowards of us? Would you have rather not done this exercise? My plan this year is to raise our levels of consciousness, but is that a good idea? Would you be better off if you were less conscious? Is ignorance bliss?"

We debate these questions for the rest of the period.

23
Open Ears

"I'm going to present a scenario and I want you to respond to it," I tell them.

"Do we need paper?" they shout out reflexively.

"Relax. All I want you to do is think. Then I will call on you."

They sigh, relieved. To them, if they don't have to use paper it means that whatever I will be asking them to do won't count.

"You find a wallet on the sidewalk," I tell them. "No one is around. You pick it up. The wallet has some credit cards, identification, and about four thousand dollars in cash. What would you do?"

They murmur with interest, which is unusual because by now they feel they're done with high school.

"Are you wasted?" one of the boys asks.

They laugh.

"Let's not complicate it," I say.

I urge them to think for a moment, because their answers will reveal a lot about their character. As they write eagerly in their journals, I am reminded how young they still are. Knowing how too many of them will respond, I continue to wonder why this is happening to them.

"Who would like to answer?" I ask after another minute.

"I would give back the wallet," one student calls out. "I lost my license last year and it was such a pain getting another one. I would keep the money, though. I'd just say it was gone when I found it."

"Yeah, my dad lost his wallet and had to cancel all his credit cards and get new ones with new numbers. It sucked," his friend adds. "He was so pissed."

"Would you keep the money, too?" I ask.

"Of course I keep it."

"Me too," a few more students admit freely.

I ask if returning the wallet with the credit cards and license would somehow make them feel less guilty.

"They're no good. You couldn't use them," one of the girls explains, seeming to miss my point. "Whoever lost the wallet would put a stop on them."

While the class is quick to acknowledge her logic, no one speaks of guilt, as if the notion has become obsolete.

"What kind of wallet is it?" another girl asks. "I mean, like if it was like a Gucci or something I would take it too."

"Why?"

"Because it would mean the person is rich."

"Would that make it easier to take it if you knew the person was rich?"

"It would mean I need the money more than he does," she says.

More laughter.

"I'd take it anyway," another student calls out. "The idiot lost it. It's his fault, not mine. I didn't do anything wrong. He did."

"I would turn it into the police," a girl in the front row offers, but she is immediately shouted down.

"That would be crazy! Then they would take the money!"

"The police would take the money?" I ask.

"Are you kidding?" They laugh at what they are convinced is my naiveté.

"Anybody who carries around four thousand dollars is probably a drug dealer anyway, so I take it!" someone shouts over the commotion.

"Would anyone return the money to the owner?" I call out, quieting the debate.

"I would," another boy says, "but I would take half the money, as reward. I'd tell him I didn't know what happened to the rest of it."

"You would reward yourself?"

"Yeah, because what if he didn't?"

As they share their rationalizations I remember that these same students have studied *Catcher in the Rye, Macbeth, The Great Gatsby, The Odyssey, To Kill A Mockingbird* yet they seem to have little sense of right and wrong. What do they internalize?

"What about your honor?" I finally ask.

"As in Honor Roll?"

It seems this is the student's only context.

"Honor as in integrity, dignity," I explain. "These values come from honesty and self-discipline, two of the virtues Aristotle insisted are so important to becoming truly happy. Being truly happy is not the same as having fun, you know."

"Being truly happy is having lots of money!"

I notice a student in the front row lowering his eyes as if to hide. I call on him.

"I wouldn't take the money," he says reluctantly. "I would call the guy and tell him. Then I would give it back. It wouldn't be right to take it."

He is challenged, mocked, called a liar.

"How many of you have cheated in high school?" I continue.

Everyone raises a hand except one girl in the back row.

"You never cheated?" I ask her.

"It's not cheating unless you get caught," she says with such impunity that it implies she believes she has stated an indisputable fact, the twenty-first century's equivalent of an empirical truth. The class spills over in consensus. "And I never got caught."

I point out Aristotle's six categories of human character: the beasts that would rob people of their wallets; the vicious, who would keep the wallet and not only feel justified in doing so, but delight in it; the incontinent, who would keep the wallet, but know it was wrong, feeling guilty, but not having the courage to overcome their desires; the continent, who would return the money knowing it was the right thing to do, but they would feel deprived and angry having to forfeit the money; the virtuous, who would find true happiness returning the money; the super humans, who would give away their own money. When I ask them to place themselves into one of the categories, the vast majority admits unabashedly to being incontinent.

When I first started teaching this lesson I was unsure of my intentions. Was I being hypocritical? Judgmental? These are, after all, children. So to see if there was any validity to it, I decided to test my own daughter, Lesley. She was twelve at the time. I presented the wallet scenario to her.

"I'd call the owner," she said.

"Wouldn't you be tempted to take the money?" I asked.

"Take the money? You mean steal it?" She laughed. "Maybe a dollar. No, just kidding."

"Why not take all of it? No one would know."

She shrugged. "I don't know."

"Come on. You must have an answer."

"Not really. I mean, I just wouldn't take it, that's all. Before you said it, I didn't even think about taking it. Where do you dream up this stuff?"

Because she was already bored with me by then and had no righteous explanations I was convinced she wasn't simply telling me what I wanted to hear. Her indifference revealed that her virtues were deeply rooted. They were habits, not rationalizations, but how had she acquired them?

"It's like the time when me and mom were in this restaurant," she went on. "The waiter forgot to charge us for our desserts. We were in a hurry and mom kept trying to get his attention but he was busy with a lot of other tables, so we had to wait and wait until he finally came over to, and when he did, mom told him he needed to add the desserts."

This is how. They overhear what we say, watch everything we do. What they internalize is us.

"But it was his mistake," I suggested, giving her another chance. "Why didn't you just leave?"

She shrugged again. "Ask mom."

The next day the kids want to "philosophize" some more.

"Yeah, yesterday was fun," someone else adds. "We were talking about it after class.

"Okay," I agree. "Let's continue to talk about dignity. We will be reading Hemingway later in the year. Dignity was very important to him, but what is it, exactly? Let's start with this: tell me about this invention of yours I've heard about, Friends With Benefits."

They snicker and laugh. For the uninformed, FWB is a social system in which a guy and a girl can be intimate without the burden of having to be in a relationship. The unencumbered result? Unemotional sex. Not too long ago that would have been considered an oxymoron.

"It works," one boy asserts.

"Do you intend to get married someday?" I asked him.

"Of course."

"Do you intend to have children?"

"Sure."

He looked at me like I was crazy for asking such obvious questions.

"Open your ears," I said, addressing the girls in the class. "You will want to pay very close attention to this." Then I asked him, "Will you want the mother of your children to have been a friend with benefits?"

The class held its collective breath. The girls inched forward in their seats. The boy squirmed nervously.

"It depends how many times she's done it," he said.

"Let's say twenty."

"No."

"Ten?" I suggested.

"No."

"Three?"

He didn't answer for a while. Then, "No."

The girls lowered their heads in shameful recognition.

"You know," the boy finally said to his credit. "I never thought about it that way."

None of them had. As degrading as Friends With Benefits is, or cheating on homework or endless texting, what is even worse is our young people's lack of introspection, their inability reason, to think critically and creatively about any of their actions.

"Most of you 'never thought about it that way' because you don't think," I tell them. "While you can judge someone for the way they look, you are unable to judge yourselves by the way you act. This is a problem, which we will solve this year."

They can write a literary analysis good enough to master the New York State English Regents exam, they can calculate their way to a score of 700 on the math component of their SATs, but they can't analyze their own motives and behavior. A connection as classic and obvious and easy as the indignity and degradation of emotionless sex? They are like shimmering dragonflies darting along the pond's inky surface satisfying themselves only with the immediate. What they aren't is deep. Worse, they don't care about being deep. What's wrong with preferring "The Bachelorette" and "Jersey Shore" to *Madam Bovary* and *Madam Butterfly*, they would argue, justifying their immediately gratifying easy choices as morally equivalent to the more challenging classics. After all, they insist, isn't life about doing whatever makes you happy? Instead of a passion for bettering themselves culturally, spiritually, and intellectually, this hardy quest for the superficial is what they have internalized. Of course they have never deconstructed what "happiness" means, tried to define the term. How could they? They don't have that ability. They are little more than a spastic bundle of simplified notions and casual, unchallenged assumptions, primitive, almost like single-celled life.

But being deep matters, I tell them. When I was a student I wanted desperately to be deep, I say. To be called shallow was the worse insult you could get. If you were deep it meant you were not dumb. It meant you were smart, but a different smart than grades smart. It meant you were... interesting! It meant had something to say, something to offer. I never hear those terms used to describe someone anymore.

"He's buff," is what the girls now say about the boys. "He's hot. Check out those guns."

One year as my seniors were preparing for their annual spring break to the Bahamas, I teased the boys in the class that the best way to meet girls was to carry around a big thick important looking book, and read it while lounging by the pool.

"Why would that help us meet girls?"

"Because they will see you are not like other guys, that you are interesting."

"What kind of a girl would think that?"

"An interesting one."

They laughed. "Why would we ever want to meet an interesting girl?"

At their age, I suppose I wanted to "hook up" too, but much more than that I wanted to meet the right girl and fall in love.

One boy volunteered to do it.

"Are you serious?" I asked.

"I'll do it, if you give me the book. And I don't have to do anything but lie on the beach and pretend to be reading it."

"Well, you will have to read some of it, so you know what you are talking about."

"And this will attract girls."

"I guarantee it."

"What book?"

I threw him a copy of *Crime and Punishment*.

"Before the period ends, I need to give you your next assignment," I say. "You will give a presentation about yourself that will include a visual component, a poster or collage, a YouTube segment, a PowerPoint, I don't care, anything you want that visually represents you. You are not allowed to use a script. You may use note cards if you want. But your presentation cannot be read."

They look around at each other.

"The tricky part," I continue, "is that this presentation will not be about the surface you, your outer world, where you live, what your interests are, what kind of music you like, who your favorite group is, how you are a cheerleader or football star or that you play the clarinet. I want you to tell us what it *means* to play the clarinet."

This gets their attention.

"What you will do is stand up here in front of your class-mates and reveal your inner world, the real you, the one you guard, hide. You are going to let go. You will reflect, contemplate. You will talk about only what really matters to you, what you think about when you are alone, what keeps you awake at night. What are your dreams, concerns? You will relate the stories of your life. For years most of you have lived behind carefully constructed protective ar-mor. You are an image. Now is the time in your life when you need to begin shedding all of that and come to know and understand the real you. As I've said, that is what this year in this class will be all about. Plan on being up here, alone, in front of your classmates, for at least twenty minutes. In the past I have had kids who have puked, passed out, cried their eyes out. That's okay. When your presenta-tions are through you will remain standing in front of your peers to answer their questions. I will also ask you a bunch of questions too. It will be hard, for a while, but then you will begin to feel dif-ferent, feel alive. And when you are finally done your life will have changed. Your presentations are due in two weeks."

They murmur, squirm nervously. Some fold their arms and shake their heads defiantly as if to announce there's no way they're going to do that. The bell rings ending the period and a crowd pre-dictably stays behind pleading that they couldn't possibly do such a thing, share their personal lives like that with their classmates, that it would be too terrifying. Is there any way they could turn in something else?

"No," I tell them.

When they perform their presentations most feature the usual trips to Disney World, family cruises, summer camp. Sadly, expensive travel seems to be the main adventure in their lives. Either they weren't listening when I gave directions or this is all they have to say. Or they are playing it safe. The highlight of many of these young lives is surviving the mosh pit at rock concerts. One boy's presentation is about how his father took him to Yankee stadium for his birthday and what a nice surprise it was when his name and cake with candles appeared on the giant multi-media scoreboard. He used it for his University of Michigan application and they accepted him.

But then there are the few other presentations, such as the boy who holds up an alien-looking cage-like mask and informs us his father needed to wear it to hold his head steady during his radiation treatments for throat cancer.

Two recovering addicts describe in vivid detail the AA meetings they attended each week.

A student's mom gave birth to her at age sixteen.

One boy's father died just after he was born. They lived in a bad part of Yonkers where he was ganged up on and beaten every day at school. His mother worked three jobs so she could finally afford bring him into our school. Two girls start crying, his story is so sad.

One boy describes home life like this: he goes home after school, his parents fight, then they go on their computers while he eats alone in his room on his computer.

A girl tells us she feels ashamed sometimes when she gets resentful that her mother keeps sending the money they save and clothes and furniture to their poor relatives in the Philippines.

Another boy who likes to work out and has the muscles to show it tells how his father was a drug dealer in the streets of Rio, and when he was arrested and put in prison his mother escaped with him and his sister north to America.

There is the first generation Haitian with three brothers whose father beats them when they don't do exactly what he demands, such as study hard, never give up.

Micaiah is also black. She never met her birth mom, a crack addict who gave her up for adoption though she found out recently she had died. Micaiah tells us how strange it was to learn that your own mother is dead but not feel anything. Then Micaiah starts to cry.

Mohab is first generation Egyptian.

Celia is first generation Romanian.

Laura is first generation Irish and her father is abusive.

Aisha is first generation Pakistani and her presentation is about how her marriage will be arranged by her parents. She does not complain about this. Instead her tone is matter-of-fact, and after tracing the history of this tradition she articulates the advantages. I watch the stone faces of my students as they listen.

"What is the drinking age in Pakistan?" one asks.

Nicole who likes to be called Nickie has some condition in her head that could cause an aneurism and kill her at any minute.

Kristin's dad cheated on her mother.

Jordon, who stutters uncontrollably, made it through her presentation just fine.

Two girls use the occasion to announce they are lesbians and have had affairs with other girls. There is no fanfare to this, no bravado or embarrassment. They present this information straightforwardly, almost with a sense of relief. The class applauds when they conclude.

A little more than half of them come from divorced parents.

Amanda tells how her father abandoned them when she was three.

Alisa describes how her mother and father didn't let her watch any TV when she was younger. They wouldn't let her near a computer either. Instead they forced her to go outside and play or find other things to do. She wants to be either a chemist or a pianist. She studies languages, has lived in Japan as an exchange student.

Lily talks about how as a first generation Chinese she constantly feels pressured into taking on more and more personal responsibility.

They are new American dreams, these children; they are messy miracles, our future. Their presentations reveal that they know, sort of, what's important, but their awareness of meaning, the significance of their existence, their relationship to the world, to the universe, is vague, fuzzy, and indefinable. They just can't grasp it yet. But they are trying, and they need our help. When given the chance they all can "come out." It's like they are delicate ugly infant birds attempting to peck their way free of their shells.

24
Artificial Intelligence

EACH YEAR I MAKE my seniors read parts of Aristotle's *Nicomachean Ethics*. I also make them read the Cave allegory from Plato's *Republic*. Only then, after I feel their minds are greased and they are sufficiently out of their comfort zone do we begin the texts: *Hamlet*, *The Metamorphosis*, *The Sun Also Rises*, *Waiting for Godot* and *The Things They Carried*.

Hamlet of course continues their introduction to philosophy, challenging them to question, to ask why, to look below the surface of their lives, to explore their inner motives, their actions and inactions.

The Metamorphosis is the story of a young man so lost in the self-deception of living according to other people's expectations of him that he becomes estranged from reality, waking one morning changed into a monstrous vermin.

After we study it and watch *American Beauty*, I assign my No Technology project, designed to provoke them into discovering the Kafkaesque surrealism of their own young lives. The No Technology project involves this: For one school week, commencing on a Monday morning the moment they wake up until the bell ends the school day on Friday, my seniors are required to live their lives without the distraction of their technologies. This means they are not allowed to use their cell phones, which means, of course, no picture-taking, and, the big one—no texting. Also, they can't watch TV and listen to music: no iPods, no car radios. No video games. And no computers, which means no Facebook, YouTube. And they must keep a log reflecting on their experiences.

There are some caveats, of course. Although I don't want to, I must allow them to use their phones when a parent calls. They may also use their computers for schoolwork, but they must disconnect the Instant Message feature.

When I present them with the project and announce that it will be graded like a test or essay, they groan and complain and tell me I can't do this to them. I describe the possible benefits, but they are mostly unconvinced. Some are intrigued by it, and begin, predictably to talk it up in class. I count on this small support each year. Somehow it is as if a few students have been longing all along to be set free in this way, to be yanked from habits they somehow know are hurting them. Once the week begins, I don't have to ask them each day how they are doing. They eagerly share their stories, as if they are having some strange adventure. At the end of the week I collect their journals and read them. This is from Aisha, a first generation Pakistani:

> *Monday: Day One*
>
> *My alarm rang at 7am. I had an urge to check my phone. I noticed I already had 7 unread messages. But for some reason I felt a bit … relieved? I've gotten a bit tired, tired of people sending me pointless texts at 2am, tired of people needing me. At school I had to turn my phone off. I couldn't have it in my pocket vibrating at every new text. I couldn't handle the stimulation. I wouldn't be able to resist the urge. Wow, I sound like an addict.*

This is from Mollyanne, who is an addict undergoing rehab for drug and alcohol abuse.

Monday: When I got home it is difficult not to turn on the TV. My family does not eat together so I have to sit alone at the table. I don't like sitting with myself. As a recovering addict it is hard to be placed back inside my own mind. It's a scary place. I rely on these distractions to keep me sane. For me, these distractions help push away dangerous thoughts of using. So I break the rule and use my phone.

Tuesday: It's funny how I can relate withdrawal from substances to the feelings I am feeling now. Someone who has been on drugs so long has lost the ability to be happy without them. And in recovery you are taught to live again happily without them. Now I am forced to live without these distractions.

Wednesday: My mom kicks me out of the house because of an average grade. My grades can't be average, she says.

Thursday: My boyfriend drives me to school and because of this project he doesn't put on the music. We look at the bare trees with the snow on them and there are little black birds on the branches. We agree that it is so pretty we would like to paint it.

Friday: I am excited this experiment is over today but I've noticed that with technology time goes so much quicker. I wish I could continue to slow down the time in the days.

Here is part of what they discover during their time without technology, when they are conscious, alive, about their friends, about their moms, sisters, brothers, girlfriends, driving, walking, the silence, letters, the truth, reading:

I never read for fun, ever! But I read 33 pages and it is an interesting book.

-Jon, who will be attending SUNY Binghamton

I started a book, A Clockwork Orange. *This is something I normally don't do. The rest of my family was watching TV, so it was a bit lonely, but I enjoyed it. It was interesting.*
-Melissa

This from a young woman who will be attending Johns Hopkins, whose mother is Japanese and father is American:

I helped my mom cook dinner for the first time. It was a Japanese meal called tempura udon. I've had it so many times but had never helped her cook it. After dinner I helped my mom wash the dishes and asked her about the recipe and where she got it because I had always wondered why the soup is completely different from the ones at restaurants. She told me that that's how her grandma used to make it. I never knew.
-Alisa

This about boyfriends and cleaning and boredom:

I knew I wouldn't be able to talk to people on the phone later so I went to Starbucks with my boyfriend. I would be able to talk to him there. I found out it's more personal and enjoyable to talk to people when they are sitting next to you.
-Melissa

I am cleaning my closet and halfway done with my room. Cleaning makes you look back at memories and gets your mind thinking.
-Jackie

I am bored, I have been thinking all day and in a sense want to stop thinking so much. However in a sense, thinking is fun. Imagination makes it so.

-Jackie

❧⚶❧

I have come to the conclusion that my life is boring.

-Lilly

❧⚶❧

I have been singing to myself.

-Jackie

❧⚶❧

The project taught me that technology often lures us away from the outside world, keeping us chained to an empty and boring world of electronics. It traps our inner creativity. When I got up this morning, I felt so refreshed that I had no trouble with my morning routine, and the school day went very smoothly.

-Jun

This is what I found in their journals about grandparents:

When I was at my grandma's house I told her about the project, so she turned off the TV. Instead of watching TV like always, she showed me all of the photo albums she had worked so hard to organize. She told me stories that went along with pictures. I could tell she loved reliving those old memories and she liked sharing them. The pictures and the stories taught me about my family history and traditions I had no idea existed.

-Nicole

❧⚶❧

Without technology I had nothing to do today and I had no idea what to do so I looked at family photos from a very long time ago and finally understood why so many people I know say I look like my grandfather. I always imagined him as the 70 year old balding man, but now that I look at his wedding pictures and myself in the mirror the resemblance is evident.

-Jeremy

About the truth:

All technology such as cell phones and music make every minute fly by and they quicken the pace of life. They don't give you the chance to step back, relax and evaluate your situation and decide whether or not you are truly happy.

-Nicole

❧

I feel different. It's like I can see people better, how they act. I listen to my surroundings more than I used to because I'm not as distracted. I see that happiness comes from memories and not just from in-the-moment things.

-Jackie

❧

I now realize that excessive use of technology actually taints your mind sick.

-Jiwoo

❧

Everyone seems so different on Facebook based on their profile page and pictures. My best friend for 14 years has her profile picture of her in a bathing suit and everything

she writes on her page is incorrect and it's really weird. The person on her pages is not my best friend.
                                    -Nicole

This week has showed me that I am so tightly wound and stressed because of an overbearing schedule that I need to learn how to relax. I am going to keep cooking with my mom and learn interesting stories about Japan and I am going to try to save my brother from the "impersonal one." He plays on his Xbox every day and I can't stand it.
                                    -Olivia

About letters:

I wrote a letter to my boyfriend today, 5 pages. It was weird. I didn't know what to write but I am excited for him to get it.
                                    -Lesley

Writing it out rather than typing it means so much more, your handwriting is another form of expressing your personality.
                                    -Jackie

I asked my boyfriend to write me a letter in the mail and he did. It was exciting to receive something through postage. It's nice to be able to hold onto something somebody hand-writes for you instead of reading it on a screen.
                                    -Melissa

I think I might steal Mr. Baird's idea and write my grandma a letter. That would really surprise her, but also make her really happy.

-Brittany

I found out recently that kids do so little actual walking that there is now an official *Walk to School Day*, internationally recognized, with registration, special events, photo sharing. Would all the hoopla be necessary if we simply turned off our gadgets?

I now love just thinking about whatever comes to mind and I love the cold crisp air. It feels pure and clean. As I was walking I passed two cars of people I know who stopped to say hi and looked at me like they felt sorry I was walking, but I felt sorry they were driving. They just whiz past everything. They can't even feel the cold air.

-Nicola

❧

After school Jose, Melissa and I decided to walk home. The last time I walked home was in 10th grade. I think the weather greeted us. It was cold and sunny. The air smelled great too. It seemed to be happy that it saw us walking. We all enjoyed it too.

-Jiwoo

❧

The first thing I noticed was that no one was walking to school. The sidewalk was empty. The second thing I noticed was that everyone who drove by us turned their heads to look at us. I started cracking up and told Jose and David that everyone was looking at us. I laughed. We had tried something that they won't or can't. It was a victorious laugh.

-Jiwoo

Even their sacred driving became something different to them, an intellectual experience:

> *The first thing I noticed is that I drive a lot more responsibly with my radio turned off. I am not speeding or weaving in and out of traffic. I can hear the wind and it is a very soothing sound. But without the car radio blaring I also discovered this strange noise coming from the chassis. I checked it out and found a branch was stuck in there rubbing when I drove. I wonder how long it's been like that?*
> *-John*

❧

> *Without the radio on my friends and I are able to continue a conversation for the duration of our rides, and now that we have gotten through this part of the project we are able to have more intellectual conversations, not shouting matches.*
> *-Jack*

❧

> *I didn't know my car made so many noises.*
> *-Melissa*

❧

> *Without music in the car, we initially played games that required us to pay attention to our surroundings outside. At stoplights, we talked to total strangers sitting in the cars next to ours. Some were very friendly, but most thought we were weird. Our conversations eventually turned very philosophical as we began to discuss the project and then the broader aspects of life.*
> *-Richard*

❧

When not listening to the usual hard rock or metal, I felt more calm behind the wheel and not in a hurry to get to school. I also notice my car makes a certain sound when I come to a stop, which I never realized before. I also heard the sounds of the engines of other cars when they passed me.

-Zak

❧

I was in a car with a friend and he was playing music. I told him to turn off the radio, which he did not want to do. However, I told him about the project and then he agreed to do so. Ultimately, we wound up having a cool, long conversation the whole ride.

-Richard

❧

On the way home we decided to turn down a road we had never gone down before. I don't really know why but I was curious and for once not in any hurry.

-Jenna

❧

I decided to get gas. This is when I discovered the beauty of silence. As I waited at a red light with my radio off and my window open I heard nothing. I heard nothing but the wind slightly blowing and the birds chirping. This calm silence took me away and almost caused me to doze off. While driving back I noticed the trees on my street. I never noticed how the trees from either side touch on the top, creating an arch. I also noticed houses I had never really given a look at. I think technology separates us from childhood. It takes the imagination, outdoors, and the

board games all away with the click of a button.
-Jake

They become alert:

I was more awake than usual in my first few classes.
-Zak

❧

I began doing something strange. I saw my reflection in the window over by the kitchen sink and I just stared at myself. It wasn't one of those stares of whether I looked good or not, but rather it was a stare of who I am as a person. It was weird.

Later, at dinner, my parents, sisters and I had at least a forty-five minute conversation about general topics. Again, I can't remember the last time I had a long talk with my family, and this point I started to figure out the meaning of this project.
-Matt

❧

Noticed some cool things, movement in the pines across my street, the millions of animals that I don't normally see. Not using technology is freeing me in this weird way. It's really clearing my mind and making me look around. I do really like living like this but I know I will not be able to keep this up once the project is over.
-Devon

❧

Something really annoying kept happening to me during this project. Every time I happened to find myself alone with nothing to do, I would consciously try to think about stuff but I could not get past thinking about how I should be thinking.

> *-Jenna, who will be attending*
> *Washington University*

Before this week started I thought it was just going to lead to massive boredom, which would then lead to me smoking a lot of MJ. It's actually been quite the opposite. For some reason I've felt no need to smoke, and my 2-3 times a day habit has turned into none at all! I have no idea why this is.

> *-Phil, who will be attending*
> *University of Miami next year*

Aware of listening and silence:

The second day of the project is here and I am feeling a craving for music. It is the largest part of my life and it is very strange not listening to it. When I got home I turned off my car and just sat there. I sat still and listened. I listened to the silence and looked at the trees. While doing this I felt a strange feeling in my heart. It is hard to describe, it wasn't really a pain, but I felt short of breath. This feeling is interesting to me and I hope to discover what it is before this experience is over.

> *-Chris*

Being in complete silence is strange—you can hear everything.

> *-Melissa*

The breathlessness, the feeling is awareness, the quiet recognition that he exists. It's only been an hour and I can't take the silence.

-Lesley

❧◦❧

Finally the last day without technology. It has been a tough experience, but I made it. Today I decided to sit in silence again and see what happens. I was in my bed and I just took the silence into my body. After a while I started to get the same breathless feeling. It was similar to the feeling that Ricky described in American Beauty. It was as if my heart was going to explode. I am not exactly sure what this feeling is, but it is as if I am sorrowing for those who cannot take the time out of their day to listen. Just listening to what life has to offer. It makes me sad to not have anyone to share this feeling with today. This was indeed an experience worth having and I am a bit reluctant to get back to the real world. Or perhaps I should call it the fake world.

-Chris

❧◦❧

When it's quiet I think too much and I hate it.

-Joan

❧◦❧

I am paying greater attention to the more specific details around me.

-Zak

❧◦❧

It happened at lunch. I was sitting with my friends and they started singing, which made them want to start listen-

ing to the songs they were singing. I was happy with all of us singing together. It was fun, but they all whipped out the iPods and started listening to music. I sat back, closed my eyes and just listened to the sounds of the cafeteria. I just… listened. The noise grew louder and louder and it was like when the boy in American Beauty said he was going to burst. The noise kept getting louder when all of a sudden I hear a voice ask me "Are you sleeping?"
                                      -Brittany

৵৹

Today I found out that food tastes much better when you are not watching TV.
                                      -John

৵৹

During lunch, instead of hanging out and texting some friends, we all engaged in many interesting conversations at our table.
                                      -Zak

Aware of homework:

It is now 9:45 and I think I am going to bed early. I've done all my homework (surprisingly.)
                                      -Phil

৵৹

I have been getting my homework done more quickly, giving me more time to think.
                                      -Zak

৵৹

I actually looked up a word in a book dictionary instead

of asking my sister to look it up for me online.

-Skylar, who will be attending
Ithaca College

Of sleep:

I have been having trouble getting right to sleep with no music, so I have been reflecting on the days before. I have been staying up thinking about how much more efficient I am with no technology, and that I have more time with my family.

-Zak

❧

My dreams have been extreme lately and although I cannot remember them I wake up sweating every time. I pretty much slept for the rest of the day lost in my own thoughts.

-Chris

❧

I went to bed at 10:40 last night instead of my usual 2 or 3.

-Lesley

❧

I have found myself thinking so much that I am not really able to go to sleep easily. I just keep thinking.

-John

❧

Of television:

When I came home my little sister was glued to the TV as usual. When I was a little kid did everyone ignore me?

Did they let me sit there for hours by myself? Now that I think about it I feel they did.

-Shannon

꧁꧂

TV, video games, computers, we are striving for instant gratification. We want to be entar... entre... entertained (look! I can't even spell entertained without looking it up on Google!) entertained anyway and anyhow and the quicker the better. The constant want to be entertained every five seconds results in nothing but lazy unrewarding false satisfaction.

-Devon, who will be attending Penn State

Of dads and moms:

My dad is a workaholic and I never spend a lot of time with him. Going on a college visit today with him meant that we would have to spend the entire day together. At first it started off a little awkward and I was tempted to put my iPod on and zone out, but because of the project I resisted. Instead of listening to it, I randomly started talking to my dad about random things like the weather, sports, and the economy. Although I have little or no interest in these things, it was refreshing to have a conversation with him without interruption. If I had listened to my iPod the entire visit I feel like an opportunity to save our relationship would have been lost and we would have ended up like Lester and Jane from American Beauty.

-Shannon

꧁꧂

It was time to go out to dinner with my family to cele-

brate my mom's birthday. Normally I would waste time on my cell phone while waiting in the restaurant but instead I talked to my mom. We discussed my interest in entrepreneurship and developing businesses, which I had never shared with her before. I explained the science behind gaining and losing weight. I dispelled quite a few common myths that she believed. We discussed the technology behind HDTVs. Definitely a random group of topics but never in a million years would I have guessed that I would talk to my mom about these things. I got home feeling happy.

-Richard

I practiced the piano and enjoyed it for the first time ever, then I had lunch with my mom.

-Lesley

I'm sitting in the car in front of my house; it's the first time I haven't rushed my mom to give me the keys to get in the house because I have no urge to get in because I have nothing to do. She's already in the house. I'm still writing in the car, this is weird.

-Mollyanne

Stress:

Distracting ourselves with technology is a release for stress as it brings us into yet another fantasy world where everything is totally peaceful because there is no emotion and no feeling.

-Richard

It's weird; the technology built for convenience and for actuality makes us so much more stressful, while the simplest things that nature provides can make us so joyful.

-Jiwoo

❦

Ironically technology is supposed to make our lives easier and more efficient but in reality in only adds chaos.

-Shannon

❦

I noticed a sensation of light-weightedness every time I left my house without my cell phone.

-Jenna

Creativity:

I've come to realize I've gotten my creative juices flowing ever since this technology project started. I've had time to think of things to do. I've decided to take my boyfriend out for his birthday and try and add some surprises. I like the freedom this project has given me. Along with the dinner I decided to surprise him with making fondue and have wine and candles out. I wouldn't have done it if I didn't have all this time on my hands to think. I've also been going to sleep so freaking early because I've had no random conversations or internet hopping, so I just go to sleep. I'm much less angry in the morning.

-Lesley

❦

The most interesting moment of my day was figuring out what to do with myself. I decided to throw a ball against a wall in my room. It wasn't a specific game or anything I had ever done before. For forty-five minutes I was mesmer-ized by this simple repetitive action. I didn't really think about it. I just did it and I was entertained. I created my own patterns and techniques of how to do it and I changed walls. I probably haven't had an experience like that since 3rd grade, the time I built a fort.

-Jeremy

❧

I dragged my brother from the TV where he was playing Xbox and made him practice the wind ensemble pieces. This was the first time I have played the flute at my house in several years.

-Olivia

Sisters and brothers:

I never thought my sister and I would be able to talk alone with each other for a half hour walk, but we did, and even though she didn't say it, I could tell she was happy.

-Nicola

❧

From 7:50—8:40 I was with my youngest sister, she wanted ice-cream, usually I would give it to her and I would be go back to whatever I was doing. But this time I stayed and talked to her, then we started to play around and I fed her ice cream. I would pretend it was going in her mouth and she would laugh which caused me to laugh. I haven't laughed as much as I did in a long time. Maybe because it was genuine and her happiness did not come from eating ice-cream but because of me. After this I got her ready for bed with changing and brushing her teeth then I even read to her. Usually I rush this moment but seeing her laugh and smile just made me love it more.

-Jackie

❧

I went downstairs and saw my brother watching TV. It was so subconscious, but I sat there and watched it with him. During the commercial, he asked me if the no technology project was over, and I screamed. I hadn't realized what I was doing. I ran upstairs to my room while I heard him laughing his butt off. A couple of minutes later he came in feeling bad. He told me he had something to tell me. He told me how he really liked this girl and wasn't sure what to do. He was coming to me for help. I put my work aside and actually talked to him, giving him pointers. We have never had a conversation like that. It was amazing. That's all I can really say.

-Aisha

❧

When I got home I was really bored. I was going to take a nap but then I saw my little sister sitting on the couch watching some mindless cartoon show. I was not going to let technology control her too, so I asked if she wanted to play a game. Most afternoons I would spend hours on my laptop. She said she wanted to play store... to my surprise I had an amazing time, and noticed new phrases, movements and facial expressions. Before she was a little baby and now she was a little person.

-Shannon

❧

The second day of the project it snowed beautifully. The snow wafted down in big feathery flakes. It began in the morning shortly after we arrived in school and continued heavily, causing the kids to grumble about why they couldn't have a snow day. A controversy erupted over why the superintendent hadn't heeded the weather report and closed the schools. Parents were texting, concerned for their kids' safety. It was all quite sad. A snowstorm, to me anyway, is such a wonderfully elemental thing, a gift. So I decided to create a controversy of my own. I cancelled all my classes and took the seniors outside to play. We had a giant snowball fight, which is strictly against the rules.

We went outside to play with snow. I don't remember the last time I played with snow. I don't remember the last time I made a snowman, and I don't remember the time when playing with snow was more fun than sitting in front of a computer. It was cold and yet it was warm and inviting. The football field and the track had been transformed into a virtual playground, which seemed so white and pure. It was like an ocean telling me to jump in and go back to my child self. This completely changed my state from being gloomy to being joyful.

-Jiwoo

◈

Today we went outside to play in the snow. This will go down as one of the highlights of my high school years. I have not gone in the snow to play the way we did today in many years and I must say, it brought spiritual moments. Seeing everyone have a great time made my happy because it showed me that they all have that touch of mirth to their soul, that they still have a sense of what living life is all about.

-Matt

◈

Everyone's personality really came out in the way we played in the snow much more than what we would see on Facebook.

-Phil

❧

Playing in the snow today was one of the greatest things I've ever done during school. I feel like a lot of people don't realize things like that which is unfortunate and one of the main reasons why we spend so much time social networking,

-Melissa

❧

So my English class went outside to play. Just like we were five years old we ran out, threw snowballs and made snow angels. We played. For some reason, it was this un-conventional happiness where you could not stop smiling and laughing. We made a snowman and even though it toppled over as we left it was just so much fun. It has been a good day. This no technology thing is getting easier.

-Lilly

❧

Today I had the best English class of my life. Not only did we do no work, we got to go outside and play in the snow.

-Jack

❧

You take us outside to play in the snow. I will have you know I loathe the snow. I hate all things cold and wet. Even as a child I don't remember ever playing in the snow. But when I came home I put a jacket on my dog and took her

> *out into the yard and sat with her for a while outside. It was peaceful. I don't spend that much time with my dog. I never really thought about it. I was peaceful.*
>
> *-Mollyanne*

Something as simple as playing in the snow is foreign to them because of what we've done to them, because of how their technology and we have isolated them.

> *When the project was done, I went home and straight to my room and grabbed my laptop. I thought there would be so much for me to do. After all, 5 days without the Internet means a whole lot of Facebook notifications to catch up on. I was right. A lot had built up while I was gone, but I just didn't care. What I really wanted to do was go outside and have fun in the real world. Sometimes I mistook the Internet for the universe. I have discovered just how fun it can be to live without relying so much on technology in my daily life. There is this whole world out there, waiting to be explored.*
>
> *-Aisha*

When the project was over, Jake's mom emailed me the following:

> *Thank you for the wonderful assignment of no TV, computer, cell phones, etc. this week. How nice it was for Jake to have enough free time in his day to accompany me to the vet with our dog, go food shopping with me, play gin rummy (nice to be able to beat him in something), watch him read for pleasure, and have conversations with him without being interrupted by ring tones. He learned that there is life without electronics, and by the way my 87-year old father thinks you are the best for teaching him this lesson!*

25
COUNTERFEIT KIDS

IT IS ALMOST AS if they aren't really eighteen-year-olds. From their own words, you'd think they are more like alien robots who, when suddenly unplugged, are utterly unfamiliar with what it means to be living here on Earth as a human being. They behave exactly the way the prisoners do in Plato's cave:

> At first, when any of them is liberated and compelled suddenly to stand up and turn his neck round and walk and look towards the light, he will suffer sharp pains; the glare will distress him, and he will be unable to see the realities of which in his former state he had seen the shadows; and then conceive someone saying to him, that what he saw before was an illusion, but that now, when he is approaching nearer to being and his eye is turned towards more real existence, he has a clearer vision,—what will be his reply? And you may further imagine that his instructor is pointing to the objects as they pass and requiring him to name them,—will he not be perplexed? Will he not fancy that the shadows, which he formerly saw are truer than the objects, which are now shown to him? And suppose once

more, that he is reluctantly dragged up a steep and rugged ascent, and held fast until he's forced into the presence of the sun himself, is he not likely to be pained and irritated? When he approaches the light his eyes will be dazzled, and he will not be able to see anything at all of what are now called realities.

Similar to Mollyanne so many of my students seem to find their minds, when exposed to the light, "a scary place," and the reason, I'm afraid, is because their minds are desolate, uninhabited, bleak places, like the barren cold country road that sets the scene in *Waiting for Godot*, made all the more frightening because these young people are so unfamiliar with them, unused to this strange territory. Prompting them to think is like dropping them into an absurdist landscape. Worse, they choose not to think, preferring instead to recline complacently in Plato's shadows. Allan Bloom tells us in his book *The Closing of the American Mind* that, "men cannot remain content with what is given them by their culture if they are to be fully human. That is what Plato meant to show by the image of the cave in the *Republic* and by representing us as prisoners in it. A culture is a cave." Because their minds are untrained, vacant, uncultivated, my young students quickly become bored with them. When they can't dream, imagine, fabricate, envision, analyze, and be curious, when their mindlessness forces them instead to forever wait, they become impatient, desperate for stimulation, any stimulation, even shadows. When people can't think, they come to rely on the drugging effect of their gadgetry. When it comes to the truth, they seek to verify themselves in their technology. They can no longer self-verify. Like the alcohol addict, all that happens is a numbing, not a solution or discovery. Ironically, their fancy technology has made them misfits. Mark Bauerlein warns us that:

It isn't enough to say that these young people are uninterested in world realities. They are actively cut off from

*them. Or a better way to put it is to say that they are en-
cased in more immediate realities that shut out conditions
beyond—friends, work, clothes, cars, pop music, sitcoms,
Facebook. Each day, the information they receive and the
interactions they have must be so local or superficial that
the facts of government, foreign and domestic affairs, the
historical past, and the fine arts never slip through.*

The latest statistics indicate that only about 2 percent of young
adults between the ages of sixteen and twenty-four have attended
a live classical music performance, a play, or visited a museum in
the last year. It appears that for today's parents in the post grown-
up culture, it is far more valuable for their children to be tutored
in SAT prep at $120 per hour than attend a Saturday matinee at
Carnegie Hall.

Not wanting my students to embark on life post high school
without at least a glimpse of high culture, I take a group of twenty or
so seniors each year to see an opera at the Met. (I invite all of them,
of course, but out of a hundred only these few decide to go.) Even
though they live only twenty miles from Lincoln Center and can
certainly afford the price, none have ever been before.

That first time, six or so years ago, was a bit of an adventure,
because, naively, I presumed they would know how to behave. I
gave instructions that I believed were clear, such as dress appropriately. I would be taking them to dinner at The New York Athletic Club before the performance. But some showed up in jeans.
Others wore sandals. The boys apparently had never tied a tie before. The girls' dresses weren't appropriate. A few had attempted
heels and could barely walk in them. Their make-up was exaggerated. They looked like little kids playing dress-up. I asked one
boy in sneakers why he didn't wear his good shoes. "I don't think
I have any," he said. Of course he does; it's just that he had never
had to wear them. The club has a strict dress code. I had to beg to
get them in.

Strangely, one of the more talkative girls who hardly spoke during dinner kept disappearing to the ladies room.

"What's going on?" I asked one of her friends.

She giggled. Then I smelled it. Pot.

We were sitting at three elegant tables overlooking Central Park. Other members dined nearby, Wall Street types, attorneys, young executives dressed in stylish business apparel, and it occurred to me that here was the lifestyle these kids aspired to, but they had no idea how it worked or what it required. They didn't even recognize it for what it was. They and their parents had contrived and conspired since kindergarten to achieve this, and, while they were all set to go off to "good" colleges, they weren't even remotely prepared socially.

"Okay," I said, gathering everyone over to me. "Listen, you know me. I'm not going to bust you, but I need to know right now before we go any further how many of you have been smoking."

Five hands went up.

"Drinking?" I asked.

Everyone else.

"But we're okay, really, Mr. B. No one's wasted."

"Where?" I asked.

"We smoked before we got on the bus."

"We snuck some Grey Goose on the bus in water bottles."

Grey Goose. Whatever happened to Absolut? "Why did you feel the need to do this? We are going to the Met, for God's sake. You don't need to be high!"

"We're sorry."

"Where is it now?"

"Gone."

"We feel terrible."

"Get her cleaned up," I said about the silent girl as she finally returned to the table. "She is going to the performance. You're all going. You are going to sit there for four hours and not move. We'll see how funny this is then."

I was angry at them (and at me for not knowing any better) but more than that I felt sorry for them. I liked them. They were my students, Nikki and Gulia and Jon and Jan and all of the rest of them. It was March and we had been through a lot during our class together. I was saddened that this is how they approached life, how little these otherwise privileged young people know about how to behave in the larger, higher world outside the confinement of their contrived culture, allowed, even created, by their parents. And where were their parents? How could they have let them go out like this? These kids and their parents know how to finagle a five on an AP exam but don't know how to attend the theater? Quintessentially they are cultural and intellectual counterfeits.

But of course once they beheld the magnificent winding Met staircase, the plush red velvet, the ornate crystal chandeliers rising like miniature galaxies and the orchestra playing the stirring overture to *The Magic Flute*, they sat transfixed for the entire performance. Mr. Mozart cast a spell of his own on them that night and they will never forget it. We go each year, and there have been no more misadventures. Word has spread about what is expected of them. Even the parents are now into the act, encouraging me, thanking me, asking if they can help. *Carmen, La Boehme, The Marriage of Figaro.* Each year I'm delighted by their reaction and reminded all over again that these seniors are still kids. They need to be shown. They need to be taught. They can learn.

"Mr. B! Did you see? Did you see that man in front of us texting during the performance," one of them said to me after this year's visit to see *Rigoletto*. "How could he do that? Doesn't he know any better?"

26
Something Out of Nothing

DURING HER FIRST YEAR at college where she was studying art Sam sent me this email:

> I've been thinking about stuff, mainly about love because I've been in it now for two weeks. It didn't scare me until tonight when he kissed me. I feel like I went eighteen years without it. It hit me like a freight train, and even though I never felt it before I knew what it was because my heart swelled and I felt my eyes tear and then I felt so light, like a hot air balloon, full of hot glow, but floating. I had always wondered if love was something that didn't happened to someone like me. After he said goodnight I wanted to curl up inside myself and bathe in his words. I feel so different now. Half a year after I tried to kill myself, I'm in love, thinking about my future and smiling because I like living. I like thinking about today and tomorrow and twenty years from now and I appreciate this feeling so much. I feel like I was born tonight. Hate almost killed me last April, but love gave birth to me. I'm going to send you a poem I wrote, probably later today, but I want to show it to him first.

I like living. I like thinking about today and tomorrow and twenty years from now and I appreciate this feeling so much. Yes, Samantha. Me too. Living is so much better than dying, thinking so much better than not thinking, and maybe love is the light that Plato ultimately urges us toward.

I save the teaching of *Waiting for Godot,* my favorite text, until after I have spent many months with my students and therefore feel I have the best chance of conveying its mysteries. We spend a lot of time debating who or what Godot is. Of course Beckett would probably laugh at our efforts. Any attempt to interpret absurdity is absurd, he might say. But our very human need for explanations and reasons compels us. Is Godot happiness? Is Godot meaning? Safety? Certainty? Success? All theories my students have posited over the years. Beckett himself said he didn't know who Godot was. When asked if Godot was God he famously said, if I mean Godot to be God I would have said so.

One day, poking through some of my old books, I happened to come across the edition of the play I had read in high school when I was a 12th grader and scribbled in the margin I found this: Godot = Death. It's as good a guess as any. And it fits. The problem is the concept of death is irrelevant, nearly inaccessible to eighteen-year-olds, so using it as a launching point for a conversation is difficult. I try anyway. Death, I tell them, if we truly acknowledge its inevitability, can define us. I ask them the following question: if you learned that due to some genetic mutation you would live forever, how would that change your day to day behavior right now? The question intrigues them and they immediately get the point, that time is the great determiner. Most say they would stop coming to school. The pressure and urgency to get into good college would be gone. And of course we follow up by probing what we would do differently if we learned we only had a little time left. Death, we then decide, is the one thing we know for certain will happen to us during our life, so it most certainly defines it. And if we think carefully the play can teach us how to live while we are waiting for it. For example, there is

Pozzo gazing at the sky, pontificating metaphorically about human-kind and our essential sad predicament:

> *An hour ago, having poured forth ever since say ten o'clock in the morning tireless torrents of red and white light it begins to lose its effulgence, to grow pale, pale, ever a little paler, a little paler until pppffff! Finished! It comes to rest. But—but behind this veil of gentleness and peace night is charging and will bust upon us pop! Like that! Just when we least expect it. That's how it is on this bitch of an earth.*

Certainly he is right about the undeniability of our doom, bound to come sooner or later, and I have always believed we need to be mindful of that, because a sense of how temporary and impermanent we are can focus us. It is existential. But Pozzo is wrong when he says that's how life is on this bitch of an earth. Although life is usually difficult and indecipherable, like Beckett's plays, it also offers so much more than bitchiness. Take Vladimir and Estragon themselves, those adorable vagabonds who just can't seem to get along without each other. They are cosmically, eternally inseparable. Although they are quite different, they finish each other's sentences, think each other's thoughts. There's nothing bitchy about that; on the contrary, their relationship is beautiful. Take the way they react to Pozzo's whiny lamentation, unfazed, no big deal:

> **Estragon:** *So long as one knows.*
> **Vladimir:** *One can bide one's time.*
> **Estragon:** *One knows what to expect.*
> **Vladimir:** *No further need to worry.*
> **Estragon:** *Simply wait.*
> **Vladimir:** *We're used to that.*

You've got to love these guys, and of course they represent us, the human race, our grit and determination, our muted dignity and reluctant courage that reside somewhere within each of us, if only we know how to summon them more often.

Later the two have another comic exchange as they wait, passing the time, distracting themselves again from their bleak situation through trivial pursuits.

> **Estragon:** *I tell you I wasn't doing anything.*
> **Vladimir:** *Perhaps you weren't. But it's the way of doing it that counts, the way of doing it, if you want to go on living.*

Yes, while waiting for Godot it is the way of doing things that matters. Hemingway said that too. They play off each other like vaudeville clowns; together, collectively, they are very wise.

It is the banter between Vladimir and Estragon that draws me in; when we stop and linger over what appears to be nonsensical discourse, often disjointed and unintelligible, we hear how connected they are, as if they are one, and when their words run together they become subtle poems. While they are just as likely not to have a clue what each other is talking about, theirs is like any wonderful long-term relationship. They deeply care for each other; and this old crony affection and agitated dependence are all they have to protect themselves from the bleak emptiness of an indifferent universe. But it is all they need. It is all any of us need. They are like an old married couple, so much beauty and tenderness and commiseration and compassion amidst the incessant nagging, the bulwark against the descending night.

There is a moment in the play when their absurd and hilarious rants and raves coalesce into what I think is one of the most profound and beautiful moments in all literature:

> **Estragon:** *All the dead voices.*
> **Vladimir:** *They make a noise like wings.*
> **Estragon:** *Like leaves.*
> **Vladimir:** *Like sand.*
> **Estragon:** *Like leaves.*
> **Vladimir:** *They all speak at once.*

> *Estragon: Each one to itself.*
> *Vladimir: Rather they whisper.*
> *Estragon: They rustle.*
> *Vladimir: They murmur.*
> *Estragon: They rustle.*
> *Vladimir: What do they say?*
> *Estragon: They talk about their lives.*
> *Vladimir: To have lived is not enough for them.*
> *Estragon: They have to talk about it.*
> *Vladimir: To be dead is not enough for them.*
> *Estragon: It is not sufficient.*
> *Vladimir: They make a noise like feathers.*
> *Estragon: Like leaves.*
> *Vladimir: Like ashes.*
> *Estragon: Like leaves.*

To have lived is not enough for them. The dead have to talk about it. This is how precious and wonderful life is. Let's make sure the counterfeit kids learn this before it is too late, so that when they are gone from this earth they too will be able to make a noise like feathers, like leaves, rejoicing in what they had.

And let's also make sure they heed Vladimir's call to action, after Pozzo and Lucky reappear. Pozzo is now blind. He falls and cannot get up and cries out for help. Vladimir and Estragon don't know what to do so they play around foolishly with the possibilities of the situation until something stirs within Vladimir, my unlikely hero, and he launches his own immortal soliloquy, pleading with his friend Estragon to join him, trumping Hamlet, I believe, and setting up for us something as hilariously simple as helping Pozzo and Lucky, a code of conduct suffused with perfect meaning and hope in an otherwise meaningless and hopeless landscape:

> *Let us not waste our time in idle discourse! Let us do*
> *something, while we have the chance. It is not every day*

that we are needed. Not indeed that we are personally need-
ed. Others would meet the case equally well, if not better.
To all mankind they were addressed, those cries for help
still ringing in our ears! But at this place, at this moment of
time, all mankind is us, whether we like or not. Let us make
the most of it, before it is too late. Let us represent worthily
for once the foul brood to which a cruel fate consigned us!

Unfortunately most of my students hate the play and that is a shame. They moan and groan and complain that it's about nothing, that nothing happens, wondering why anyone would pay to see a play about nothing. It doesn't make any sense, has no beginning, middle or end. I persevere anyway. It wasn't always the case. Ten years ago I was able to interest most of them. Only four years ago, when it played on Broadway with John Goodman as Pozzo, I took more than thirty of them into the city to see it. But since then, there has been an undeniable trend downward, a slow slide toward un-consciousness, a giving in by too many of my students to the lure of *The Matrix*. As we read the play in class, Jenna, typical, who will be attending Washington University in St. Louis because of her stellar GPA, distractedly writes something on a piece of paper. I ask her what: "I am so bored that I am writing down numbers." I could say of her and many like her what Vladimir says of Estragon… *He is sleeping, he knows nothing, let him sleep on.*

But then there are still the pleasant surprises like Mitch who was a cynical and shrewd student like Jenna, "learning" just enough to get good grades, but treating *Hamlet* and Hemingway's grace un-der pressure with easy scorn, laughing at Gregor's plight, treating these philosophies as mere annoyances on his way to a career in sports management, the kind of kid who would rather have another quiz he could ace than a class discussion. Why should he worry about matters of the soul? He achieved his life goal, acceptance to Northwestern University. But in the end he found a way to write the following in his final reflection essay:

There were many moments where I sat there and wondered what the hell was going on. I just wanted to leave for lunch, but there were also moments where I felt like your class was another world—a world my mind was getting lost in. Not only did the literature we read have an impact but also the conversations that pervaded through the classroom made their mark. Your perspective on many issues involving our generation was eye opening. I truly did admire your "off the path" methods.

We as students have gone through the past four years entering and exiting classrooms with only grades in mind—with college at the end of the tunnel. We have spent the past four years listening to teachers teach the same way—teaching exactly to the curriculum, piling review sheets on our desks, and giving us more homework than we could possibly handle. I feel that if we were given the opportunity to teach ourselves more, we would have been able to do more true learning—discovering the meaning of life.

I can point to one exact day over the course of the year where my attitude towards your class changed for the better. It was the day I asked for the grade back on my "no technology" journal. You gave me a D. Now, I will admit that I did not complete the project to the point where it should've. I attempted to use no technology for a day or two and then came to the revelation that technology is no longer a privilege but a necessity to our generation. However, my journal was certainly an afterthought and it was completed with a lackluster effort. As I received that grade, I was compelled to come and talk to you about it after school—not to change the grade, simply to explain my revelation. We ended up talking for the duration of 9th period and I can say that I walked out of your room with a changed perspective. You said that I was a very intelligent kid but that I need to open my mind to more and not close it off. From that point on, I truly did attempt to give each issue in class more of a chance to affect me.

I will remember the oddities of Waiting for Godot *for many years to come. I find myself on certain occasions reciting lines from Beckett's play. The reason however that I enjoyed* Waiting for Godot *is that for the first time, I actually understood the point of something. When the end of* Waiting for Godot *came along, I understood the point of it. It was the first time for me that something had come out of nothing.*

-Mitch

We do not have to steer our children toward getting into a good college so they can get a good job at the expense of their real education. Getting good jobs is the easy part of life, and doing a good job and being paid well is even easier, especially when you are a cut above the crowd. And by that I don't mean what college you graduated from. I mean when you know and have genuine thoughts about Mozart and Matisse and Beckett and what they and others like them desperately try to teach us. If we must push, let's push our children toward being worldly, interesting, interested, thoughtful, and yes knowledgeable, not about some vocation, but knowledgeable so that they might one day become what Aristotle called the "great-souled man." Let's push them to be as fully alive as they can possibly be, as opposed to dead inside. Instead of turning them from the delightful something of youthful creativity and curiosity into the dreary nothingness of jaded ambition, let us educate them into being human beings, so that they too will be able to create something out nothing.

I see signs of hope. After much debate, my school district, much to its credit, did away with the weighting of grades. And even more positively, sensing a need for change, my school approved a radically different course from Cambridge University that I am now teaching with my social studies colleague, Jason, which allows students to choose topics of global perspective and spend extended time researching and writing on them in the form of sustained arguments, resulting in pure independent critical thinking.

But then I read the other day of a Pennsylvania mother who hacked into her daughter's school's website in order to bump her grade from a 98 to a 99.

After my reunion lunch that day, Brian went back to his office to write reports and I boarded the uptown subway, floating in thought. I had hired this man straight out of college, given him his first job, and now he was running an entire magazine group. I thought about the path I had taken, veering to become a teacher, and a new and profound sense of appreciation and satisfaction washed through me. I felt strangely relieved, as if after all of life's tumbles and turns and twists I had somehow gotten through to the other side in one piece, like I'd survived some impassable test or achieved an impossible feat, and realized in no uncertain terms what a good life I had led and how deeply joyful I was and thankful for it and to all the people who had contributed. I was sixty years old and had not one single regret, other than I would only get to spend one lifetime with my wife.

Climbing the stairs out of the subway station I heard my name called.

"Mr. Baird! Mr. Baird!"

I stopped and looked back. There in at the ticket window, deep in the steamy bowels of New York were two of my former students, waving up, smiling. I went back down, hoping I would remember their names.

"Hey!" I said.

Yes. One was that cheerleader. Cory! I remembered! But I couldn't recall her friend's name, although I remember her being a quiet student, studious. I didn't want to hurt her feelings so I pretended to know her as well.

They told me they had just graduated from college. Cory had studied communications and was interning at television network and wanted to be an anchorwoman. "And you?" I asked the quiet one.

"I am starting at Teacher's College in September."

"You're going to be a teacher!" I said enthusiastically. "What subject?"

"English."

"English! What level?"

"High school," she said. "Like you."

"No, seriously," Cory laughed. "She wants to be you. No, like she wants to be YOU."

I laughed and rolled my eyes.

Cory went on. "She wants your life. I can't tell you how much she talks about all those books we read. 'We're waiting for Godot.' 'Don't be a bug like Gregor.' She says that all the time."

The quiet one smiled and nodded.

The quiet one.

"Well, good luck," I said. "And when you're ready for your student teaching, email me. Maybe we can work together," I offered.

"I would like that," she said.

"We can be colleagues," I said.

They laughed. I said good-by and climbed out of the subway station, finally remembering her name, but it was too late. They were gone.

Crossing the miraculous concourse echoing with the frantic business day's activities, I did what I always do whenever I walk through Grand Central Terminal. I stopped and glanced up at the twinkling constellations embedded in the vast ceiling. Throngs of commuters hurried past. Announcements blared from the PA. While I still recognized some of this place I had once inhabited I was no longer a part of it, and soon I would no longer belong to my classroom either. I wouldn't be able to understand my students and they would no longer be able to understand me. Time was quickly rendering me irrelevant, relegated to the back bench. Writing this book, I suppose, is another way for me to heed Vladimir's warning: *Let us do something, while we have the chance!* It is my way of remaining involved at least for another moment or two in this marvelous event called human existence. I do not want to go gentle into that good night. I want to rage against the dying of the light.

I waited behind a couple of young executives at the bar on the platform and bought a Foster's "Oil Can" for old time sake. The familiar grimy Metro North train hissed, smelling of stale electricity. I stepped on board, popped opened my beer, made a quiet toast to nothing in particular, took a deep, nostalgic swig and began the short, jerky journey back home.

BIBLIOGRAPHY

Baker, Vicky and Baldwin, Roger. "The Case of the Disappearing Liberal Arts College." *Inside Higher Ed.* July, 2009. http://www.insidehighered.com/views/2009/07/09/baldwin

Bauerlein, Mark. *The Dumbest Generation: How the Digital Age Stupefies Young Americans and Jeopardizes Our Future.* New York: Jeremy P. Tarcher/Penguin, 2009.

Bloom, Allan. *The Closing of the American Mind: How Higher Eductation Has Failed Democracy and Impoverished the Souls of Today's Students.* New York: Simon and Shuster, 1987.

Bloom, Harold. *Shakespeare: The Invention of the Human.* New York: Riverhead Books, 1998.

Brandon, Craig. *The Five-Year Party: How Colleges Have Given Up On Educating Your Child and What You Can Do About It.* Dallas: BenBella Books, 2010.

Brown, Emma. "Debate on playtime's value grows as more states fund preschool." *Washington Post*, November 21, 2009.

Erwin, Tim. *Derailed: Five Lessons Learned from Catastrophic Failures of Leadership.* Nashville: Thomas Nelson. 2009.

Evans, Teri and Merritt, Jennifer. "Employers Favor State Schools for Hire." *Wall Street Journal*, September 13, 2010.

Felton, Eric. "Those Little Lists: What College Rankings Tell Us." *Wall Street Journal,* August 21, 2009.

Finn, Jr., Chester E. "Can Parents Be Trusted?" *Commentary*, September, 1999.

Gibbs, Nancy. "The Case Against Over-Parenting: Why Mom and Dad Need to Cut The Strings." *Time,* November 30, 2009.

Grossman, Lev. "Grow Up? Not so Fast." *Time,* January 16, 2005.

Hacker, Andrew, and Claudia Dreifus. *Higher Education? How Colleges Are Wasting Our Money and Failing Our Kids—And What We Can Do About It.* New York: Times Books/Henry Holt, 2010.

Himmelfarb, Gertrude. *The De-Moralization of Society: From Victorian Virtues to Modern Values.* New York: Alfred A. Knopf, 1994.

Honore, Carl. *Under Pressure: Rescuing Our Children From the Culture of Hyper-Parenting.* New York: Harper Collins, 2008.

Hutchins, Robert Maynard. *Great Books: The Foundation of a Liberal Education.* New York: Simon & Schuster, 1954.

Jan, Tracy. "Worn-Out Students Choose a Timeout." *Boston Globe,* July 19, 2010.

Kolbert, Elisabeth. "XXXL—Why Are We So Fat." *The New Yorker,* July 20, 2009.

Levine, Madeline. *The Price of Privilege: How Parental Pressure and Material Advantage Are Creating a Generation of Disconnected and Unhappy Kids.* New York: Harper Collins, 2006.

Murray, Charles. *Real Education: Four Simple Truths for Bringing America's Schools Back to Reality.* New York: Crown Forum, 2008.

Pope, Loren. *Colleges That Change Lives: 40 Schools That Will Change the Way You Think About Colleges.* New York: Penguin Books: 2000.

Prose, Francine. "I Know Why The Caged Bird Cannot Read: How American High School Students Learn to Loathe Literature." *Harper's Magazine,* September, 1999.

Singer, Mark. "The Domestic Life, Mom Overboard!" *The New Yorker,* February 26, 1996.

Stumpf, Samuel Enoch, and James Fieser. *Socrates to Sartre and Beyond, A History of Philosophy.* New York: McGraw Hill, 2007.

Twenge, Jean M., *Generation Me: Why Today's Young Americans Are More Confident, Assertive, Entitled—and More Miserable Than Ever Before.* New York: Free Press, 2006.

Wilson, Eric G., *Against Happiness*. New York: Sarah Crichton Books, 2008.

West, Diane., *The Death of the Grown-up: How America's Arrested Development is Bringing Down Western Civilization*. New York: St Martins, 2007.

Winerip, Michael. "10 Years of Assessing Students with Scientific Exactitude." *The New York Times,* December 18, 2011.

Wolfe, Tom. "The Me Decade." *New York,* August 26, 1976.

Zakaria, Fareed. "Is America Losing Its Mojo?" *Newsweek,* November 23, 2009.

About the Author

Rod Baird has been a high school English teacher for eleven years. He is a graduate of St. Lawrence University. He earned his MFA degree in Creative Writing from Brooklyn College and attended Teacher's College/Columbia University.

Before teaching, Baird worked for *The New Yorker* for many years, then founded Salesconcepts Associates, Inc., a national firm that develops markets for consumer magazines. Later he started The Natural Athlete LLC, a sports event-marketing group. In 2001, he sold his businesses to become a teacher.

Baird and his wife have three daughters. They live in Westchester County and in Stratton Mountain, Vermont.

CPSIA information can be obtained at www.ICGtesting.com
Printed in the USA
LVOW121005010213

318039LV00002B/239/P

9 780985 660673